SECULARISM AT BAY

Uzbekistan at the Turn of the Century

SECULARISM AT BAY

Uzbekistan at the Turn of the Century

BARUN DE

MANOHAR
2005

First published 2005

ISBN 81-7304-606-9

Published by
Ajay Kumar Jain for
Manohar Publishers & Distributors
4753/23 Ansari Road, Daryaganj
New Delhi 110 002

Distributed in South Asia by
FOUNDATION BOOKS
4381/4, Ansari Road
Daryaganj, New Delhi 110 002
and its branches at Mumbai, Hyderabad,
Bangalore, Chennai, Kolkata

Printed at
Lordson Publishers Pvt Ltd
Delhi 110 007

Contents

Introduction

Central Asia as a geographic entity captured the popular imagination in the 1980s, during the Afghan resistance. In the last years of Brezhnev's thrust between Iran and Pakistan, it became the base from which the Soviet Union tried to swallow Afghanistan. From Uzbekistan, and its south-eastern neighbour, Tajikistan, Soviet armies marched to occupy Kabul, Kandahar, and Herat in 1979-80 in the wake of a bloody transfer of power from the Muhammadzai dynasty to the Khalq and Parcham communist groupings. The USSR controlled part of Eurasia, particularly the southern bulge of the Amu Darya (Oxus) that forms the border of the Uzbek and Tajik Republics, was seen as the 'soft underbelly' of the flabby and overstretched Soviet Union. This was how a CIA chief, William Casey, described it to his Pakistani ISI (Inter Services Intelligence) collaborator, General Akhtar Abdur Rahman, jabbing his finger at the Oxus bend on the map in the days of President Zia-ul-Huq.[1] Gorbachev retreated from Asia south of Siberia, and the spirals of Soviet state collapse began, culminating in the disintegration of the USSR and Russia's jettisoning of the Caucasus and the predominantly Muslim republics of Central Asia.

In 1993, the Governor of West Bengal, Professor S. Nurul Hasan, a historian who had been India's ambassador to the Soviet Union from 1982 to 1986, fulfilled his ambition to set up an Institute of Asian Studies in Calcutta, to focus research on particularly those Islamic countries where the struggle for secularism had not yet been lost to fundamentalist forces backed by the USA. That was how Pakistan, Afghanistan, Saudi Arabia, and the Gulf States had turned out to be. As the first President *ex officio* of the Maulana Abul Kalam Azad Institute's general council, and the first Chairman of its executive body, he saw post-Soviet Central Asia as part of the same geo-cultural, economic, and political strategic perspective as Afghanistan, Iran and Turkey, states which border the old Russian Empire/Soviet Union. Prof. Nurul Hasan had been India's Education and Culture Minister from 1972 to 1977. At that time he had emphasized, in keeping with the ideas of the Nehru–Azad era, that Indian education and culture should comprehend India's composite culture as part of an overlapping network of regional, and not specifically religious, cultures. In the early 1990s, he consistently argued that Calcutta should regain the old historical position in the subcontinent that it had held in the nineteenth century Indian Renaissance of keeping abreast with the radical transformation of Asia. He suggested that we could start by studying the primary sources of the change in secular values that was current in Turco-Iranian civilization all the way from Istanbul and Kabul to southern Kazakhstan and the Caspian Sea.

I was entrusted in 1993 by the Government of India in the Department of Culture with the work of actualizing this idea. It had implications, not just for foreign policy, on which Prof. Nurul Hasan had laid stress before his death in 1993, but also for updating the academic understanding of hinterland Asian geography, cultural history, and current international relations in Calcutta. I thus had the chance to extend my limited knowledge of modern Russian history into an arena that specialists in Russian affairs generally view from the northern perspective, i.e. from Moscow and St. Petersburg, of a subordinated (since the mid-nineteenth century) Turkestan and the Caucasus. American and French contemporary affairs specialists had already begun to realize, through the Brezhnev era, that the different Republics into which Stalin had carved Turkestan in 1924 had very strong local and national traditions of linguistic and tribal dominance, identity, and an overarching consciousness of being secular forces on the north-east frontier of Islam.

In 1998, I was offered a chance to work in Tashkent. It was an opportunity to study endogenous influences and traditions in a once communist region, to live there as a part of its social milieu. At that time I hoped to work on a history of twentieth-century Turkestan between two empires—the Russian in the west and the north, and the Chinese in the east in Xinjiang—with attendant differences of social consequence. Problems of learning the archive languages, in the Arabic script for the Bukhara Emirate period and then in Russian, diverted my attention. More important was the discovery that the modern history of these lands cannot be found in the scanty English library resources of Uzbekistan. These are better for mediaeval and ancient history than for the period of Russian rule. I thus turned my attention to the contemporary milieu in which we lived and mixed socially, and thus to the circumstances of transition within early post-communism.

This publication takes the format of a monograph within the stylistic structure of a memoir. I have adopted the style of reflecting on our experiences, as individuals, and as essentially alien observers from the sidelines, amongst a people and a nation that was remaking itself. This was just after a state that had endured for about three quarters of a century had dissolved. No great generalization is claimed from these plain tales. Yet the end of the twentieth century and the beginning of the present one has been an epoch when state forms are undergoing a process of change, not only in Uzbekistan and Kazakhstan where we went, but also in other parts of Asia—Afghanistan, East Timor, and most recently Iraq; which has been reverted after seventy years to the beaten and defeated condition of a post-Mandated Territory, without even the League of Nations figleaf to legitimate US and British occupation of the land and its oil riches. The Central Asian happenings seem to be have been a pre-visage of the shape of things to come. My ideas may have some relevance for contemporary historical Asian studies, as well as general studies of transition during the first post-communist decade. It is also a contribution to the study of the origins of the new international disorder that a neo-conservative North Atlantic coterie seeks to foist on the world.

The idea of international order has undergone many changes since Woodrow Wilson and his vision of a League of Nations. Its mutation into Mandates by those European Atlantic powers who had won the First World War, backed by the USA, may now be making its phantom presence felt again in Iraq. The League collapsed before a bullying force, as the United Nations is collapsing today. The horror of a unilateral attack on a small Asian nation under the flimsy excuse of enforcing investigation of proliferation of weapons of mass destruction may be shocking. The build up, however, had taken place from the time communism began to collapse. Since the Gulf War, the unilateral use of force by the western side of the NATO alliance has sought to challenge the idea of multipolar authority, be it in the rocket attack on Khost in

Afghanistan, or in the enforcement of no-fly zones in the Middle East, or in Bosnia and Kosovo. The early Yeltsin policies of repressing Islamic nationalism in Chechnya, or Putin's use of an overdose of sleeping gas to overpower terrorist rebels in a Moscow theatre, no matter the consequences to innocent people, also show a callous disregard for human suffering in the interest of 'national security'. As the millennium began we witnessed, from the margins of Eurasian affairs, this mounting trend of authoritarianism, supported by manipulative news management by hard-faced politicians.

At a personal level, as distinct from the international one, this account is one of everyday forms of life in the large Uzbek cities during the transition. Two opposite views are heard.

One view is popular with the lobby for human rights, free market domination of civil society. Anglo-American diplomats, international economic officials, and foreign private businessmen harassed by a corrupt bureaucracy, subscribe and propagate through the press that Uzbekistan in particular was ruled by a dictatorship. Some said Karimov was above all. Others would have it that the entrenched vested interests of the *nouveau riche* worked mafia-like through the organs of administration. Both believe that token opposition was either provoked by shadowy agents or brutally crushed in concentration camps in the western deserts, which are not dissimilar to latter day Gulags, that people were bowed down by a fear of voicing dissent.

The opposite view was common amongst Indian diplomats trained in the logic of the benefits of the public sector and mixed economy in the pre-authoritarian days before Indira Gandhi changed the norms of public service. This view is that Karimov faced the same imperatives of uneven and backward development as did Asian countries under post-colonialism. They seek to justify many compromises with ideas of unalloyed freedom of choice, socio-cultural liberty, and unrestricted public opinion. A generation of socialism which had brought at least literacy and primary education for practically the entire country, as well as the concept of the dignity of labour, subsidized essential services, elementary food products and housing for the masses. The present government could ill afford to give up these in the interests of a raging and tearing free market 'shock therapy' of the sort that experts like

Jeffrey Sachs were advocating. Karimov and his authorities were seen in this view as required to exercise control and regulation for a step-by-step change of the Chinese type. These problems, as they affected our daily life, have been explicated in my narrative.

My own sympathies predisposed me to the second view. Yet the inevitable assault on civil liberties and democratic rights, which the second course entails led to a dead hand on popular consciousness and to its legacy, fear of challenging the political establishment. This does impair the possibilities of social and political transformation. Some instances have been given of how, in this deadening milieu, young people as in the rest of Asia are seeking better life prospects and satisfaction in the West, leaving their own country impoverished of brightness and talent in a drab, globalizing world.

It is customary in a book to gratefully acknowledge stimulation and help. Before my wife and I went to live in Tashkent, M.K. Bhadrakumar previously the Indian Ambassador there, and Aloke Sen, who was first posted in Tashkent Minister-Counsellor and then was Joint Secretary of the Central Asia Division of the Indian Ministry for External Affairs, gave much help to us at the Maulana Azad Institute. Himachal Som, when he became Director General of the Indian Council for Cultural Relations, extended unstinted support during our stay in Uzbekistan. In Tashkent Ashok Sharma, Vinay Kwatra, and Uma Mishra and their families were a source of friendship. One recalls the respect we received from junior members of the Mission staff. Ramakant (now Dr) Dwivedi was a good friend. We made many Uzbek friends: some have been mentioned in the text. In particular we recall with affection Dinora Sadikovna Azimova and all her family, Stanislas Levich Nigai, and the Mirkasimovs. Hari Shankar Vasudevan and Rudrangshu Mukherjee kindly read through a first draft and made useful suggestions. Bhola Nath Varma and Mr Ramesh Jain have made the unfamiliar work of publishing much smoother. Arun Ghosh, Ramkrishna Chatterjee and Gautam Sengupta have given unstinted help. I would like to thank the unknown artist of the painting on the jacket that we found in Sailgokh and also Shri Siharan Nandi of the Archaeology Directorate, Government of West Bengal, who helped in the slide preparation, as well as my friend, the librarian, Shri Arun Ghosh for preparing the index.

Through the years, many people have influenced my outlook about the rational history of Islamic civilization. I recall with affection Irfan Habib and Iqtidar Alam Khan of Aligarh, A.F. Salahuddin Ahmed of Dhaka, and Anouar Abdel Malek of Cairo and Paris. I also gratefully recall my parents Pramila Gupta and Basanta Kumar De, who bred in me a firm faith in the composite culture of India.

No diary or notes were kept during the three years stay in Tashkent. That I could set down my thoughts and memories in the way that I have is thanks to Romabai and the constant partnership through which this book has specifically evolved. This book is a joint effort in ways to which my wife refuses to testify or to allow me to detail. A eulogy to her would only banalize the genuine collectivity of our effort.

BARUN DE

NOTE

1. This is described firsthand in a eulogy of Zia and General Rahman's measures of Islamist espionage against Afghanistan by Brigadier Muhammad Yusuf and Captain Mark Adkin in *The Bear Trap* (Lahore 1991).

1

The Last Days of the Twentieth Century in Tashkent

A STATE IN TRANSITION

Uzbekistan as it exists today is a new country, newer as a nation, and even newer as a state. Part northern plains and steppe, part deserts and mountains in the east, south and west, it comprises territory that in India was called in Urdu, a Doab, 'between the rivers', or in the language of western Turkestan, Mawar-an-Nahr, 'beyond the river' (viz., the Amu Darya to its south). Mawar-an-Nahr, or Soghdiana as the land was called in ancient days, was traditionally the settled and cultivated gateway towards the Chinese dominions, through the Ferghana Valley, and towards the Kara Kum, the Syr Darya and the Aral and Caspian Seas to Tartary and the later Cossack Steppe. The land was settled and cultivated (where there were no deserts such as the Kara Kum in the north and the Kyzil Kum in the south-west), colonized, and then occupied once again, over and over, by warlike tribes from Inner Asia to its east, and from Khurasan in Iran and Afghanistan to its south.

The Uzbeks who gave the land its name (according to Stalin's ethnography in the 1920s) ruled it for 500 years. They had wrested it from Babur Mirza, the last of the Timurid princes of the soil, as late as the beginning of the sixteenth century. The Uzbeks were subjugated and their Emirs drawn into the Russian empire in the late nineteenth century. The present borders of the country were demarcated only in the 1920s. The nation's spirit, as it exists today, developed after that, subordinate to citizenship in the USSR.

Yet elements of Uzbek nationalism go back to pre-Soviet roots in the soil. Most Uzbeks however thought of themselves from the 1920s till the early 1990s as part of the USSR with only subordinate Uzbek nationality. This tension still exists in a daily duality of language and other marks of recent heritage, which are based on the formation of Uzbek nationality by Stalin's Nationality Law for the USSR of 1924.

The state comprises the post-Revolutionary conflation of the three principalities of Bukhara in the south, Khiva (in the western delta where the Amu Darya and the northern Syr Darya fall into the Aral Sea) and Kokand (in the upper reaches of the Syr Darya as it flows through the Ferghana valley between the Tien Shan mountains and the Alai range to its south) and also what was then Russian Turkestan around Tashkent and Samarkand. The state was initially composed of its present territory and the autonomous Republic of Tajikistan around the Pamir Mountains, south of the Alai and north of the British Indian princely state of Jammu and Kashmir. In 1929 the Tajiks were created into a separate republic; and the Kara Kalpak tribal people, west of Khiva proper, were given the status of an autonomous republic—Karakalpakstan—within Uzbekistan. Uzbekistan was allowed independence from the Russians who had dominated the USSR, after Gorbachev fell from power in 1991.

In Calcutta more than a thousand miles from Kashmir and very much further from the mountains of Central Asia, people who have heard that my wife and I spent three years in the Uzbek capital Tashkent, keep asking whether we are going back to Tajikistan or Azerbaijan again. If one says, perhaps with exasperation, that it is Uzbek-istan, they will cheerfully reply, 'Oh, Kyrgyzstan, Kazakhstan, they are all the same thing'. This is not a joke.

The popular perception is of a people far from arid mountains in the heart of Asia. In the mid-1990s, when the Central Asian states had just become independent, Jean Racine, the cultural geographer at the Maison de Sciences de l'Homme, in Paris, wrote the lead article in a journal whose special issue was entitled *La Cercle de Samarcande*. He drew around the fabled city of Samarkand an imaginary circle. On its circumference were north India, Pakistan, Afghanistan, Iran, the Caucasian Republics, the southern part of the Russian Federation, other Central Asian Republics, Turkmenistan, Tajikistan, Kyrgyzstan, Kazakstan and China. He thought they were all concerned with a region to which the Uzbeks are central. Whether this is so or not, is what his interesting book[1] is about. But protract the radius of the circle, and whether your point of observation is in Calcutta or in Shanghai, or westwards in Mombasa, Dakar or London, the view blurs. Uzbek or Kazak, Azerbaijan or Tatar, they all appear to be Russians in popular consciousness.

Names such as Tashkent are jumbled with tales of fantasy. 'Tashkent, isn't that where Lal Bahadur Shastri died?' people asked us, without any notion of where the place was, before last year when the Taliban and Bush briefly brought it back on their mental maps. There was the bemused wonder of the Muslim egg-vendor, who has been coming to our door for more than a decade. We would be going away for quite some time, my wife had told him. He asked where we were going: was it 'Amrika'? No, he was told, 'Tashkent in Uzbekistan'. Since he did not recognize either name, he was told this was near Samarkand and Bukhara Sharif. Much relieved he said, *woh to hamara muluk hai* (that's our patrimonial land). My wife pointed out that it couldn't be his land, it just happened to be a land mostly inhabited by Muslims. He insisted that this was what he meant. But, a year later, when she was returning at the end of summer from visiting our children in Oxford, people in a shop where she was filling in a form for VAT refund at Heathrow airport, were quizzical when she wrote the country of her destination. Surely you mean Pakistan, they corrected her, supremely confident in their knowledge of Asian ethnicity.

We had of course been hearing of the country for many years from our neighbour, Binode Kishor Roy Chowdhuri, who had gone through it to Dushanbe in Tajikistan, way back in 1968 to attend a conference commemorating Kanishka, the great Kushan emperor. Kanishka had ruled the lands from Samarkand to Mathura and Gujarat seventeen hundred years ago. Roy Chowdhuri was full of the music, the green tea and the culture of the land. I had gratefully read his fine collection of books on Islamic culture, and the latest book in the 1980s on modern Uzbek and other Central Asian history, the first that I had read.[2] The Soviet Union had been slowly losing faith in itself in the twenty-five years since I had first visited Moscow in 1973. In those days, the Uzbeks were known as a people who were rather proud—dominating their southern neighbours, the Tajiks of the hills. In 1984, when the Mujahideen resistance in Afghanistan was in full swing, we were flown over Uzbekistan direct to Dushanbe. The Tajiks were extremely friendly and simple, we were told by our guide, Professor G.G. Kotovsky, a Deputy Chief of the Oriental Institute in Moscow (Academician

Primakov, later Prime Minister, was then its Director). This was much in the way Bengalis used to speak patronizingly of the 'simplicity and loyalty' of Nepalis in Darjeeling in the 1970s and early 1980s. And so they were, taking us, as an Indian delegation, to picnics in the foothills below the Hissar highlands, across from where Babur had once hidden barefoot and scratched his name on stones; where bottles of white wine were cooled for us in a rushing mountain stream, while toasts were raised to the memory of Amir Khusrau Dehlavi by Academician Asimov. That Tajikistan is no more, racked as it was by civil war between Muslim fanatics, hooligan mafia, and ex-communist cadres, in which only Russian armed support kept the latter in power. A gangster whom even his followers called 'Hitler' gunned down the learned Asimov.

These contradictions were evident in Uzbekistan in 1997, when I was invited to give lectures in Institutes concerned with Indology and the social sciences. The government hotel in Tashkent's central square was crutty; but the buffet breakfasts lavish. The scholars whom I was programmed to meet morning and evening, were friendly but completely devoid of the sort of information or ideas that agitated historians, archaeologists, or Indologists in Calcutta and Delhi, Paris, or Britain. The March weather was damp and chilly. Ferghana, through which I was driven by car, was barren. Andijan, Babur's first capital, was warmly hospitable with a lavish dinner at the home of a history professor interested in 'Baburology', by which he meant Mughal genealogy, but the town was devoid of anything except square buildings in the city centre, and traditional dagger shops in a little bazaar. Samarkand was a lovely drive three hours away; the snow came down over the hills and blanketed the monuments in soft white. I saw very little of Tashkent on that trip, except spotlessly clean, broad avenues in which practically no one walked. The driver of the Embassy car said they all took the Metro. But even the Alaisky bazaar near the Embassy seemed empty at lunchtime. So, in the winter of 1998, Uzbekistan was in a sense *terra incognita* to us.

It is the change from the familiar that makes its first mark on newcomers. I had been attached as India Chair or visiting professor from the Indian Council of Cultural Relations in the University of World Economy and Diplomacy in Tashkent to the Indian Embassy. Two professors had welcomed us at the airport. The Embassy car brought us to a small but relatively cosy apartment, between the Embassy and the University. The centrally piped heating and the fairly clean bathroom were unexpected, because of previous experiences of fittings in communist style public sanitation in Russia, Tajikistan or Georgia. The furniture was Westernized and comfortable. On the other hand, there were Indians in the Embassy living in 'dachas', sprawling bungalow style houses with plots of land, in which later we would find flowers and fruit trees in profusion, the rooms full of heavy Russian furniture and the inevitable bookshelf of bound volumes in Cyrillic script, which landlords invariably leave behind, perhaps to prove that their home was not *nekulturnii*. By contrast our small, groundfloor flat was uncluttered: it had white walls, and modern Italian furniture, perhaps because the landlord's son had spent some years studying in the USA, where, he later told us, his mind had been changed by looking at the lifestyle of a world utterly new to him. This, we would later find, had its pitfalls. The furniture though modern was flimsy. When a leg, or a backrest of a bed, or a chair would come apart, or a chest of drawers would get totally jammed because of faulty fittings, the landlord, otherwise very amiable, when summoned would throw up his hands and merely grumble 'Italiano, Italiano', as if it was our good fortune to have such foreign furniture.

The second difference was the cultural ambivalence of the people. There are few Russians left in Uzbekistan. The 1980s had been a period of sudden alienation between the Russians, who dominated the communist parties all over the Soviet Union, and the local, indigenous racial groups or 'nationalities' as they are called in the USSR and in the post-Soviet constitutions. Perhaps it was the defeat at the hands of Mujahideen, armed by the CIA in the Afghan war, and a feeling—among Muslims in the USSR—of affinity with the liberation movement of Muslim Afghanistan. Perhaps it was also a new generation, which scholars like George Kennan and Selig Harrison have pointed out, grew in conditions of European style urbanization and movement away from the communes and villages in the post-Stalinist era from 1950 to 1980.[3] Or perhaps it was the sudden collapse of a command economy stretched beyond its capacity to produce cheap food and cheap health and public utility services for the masses, because of escalating investment in armaments for the nuclear race in which the USA went ahead of the Soviet Union during the Second Cold War at the turn of the 1980s. Whatever the complex causation, the Russians had responded to Gorbachev's slogans, the human face of Socialism (so similar to Eurocommunism), the withdrawal of forces from North Asia, arrayed against both Japan and China in the Brezhnev era, and 'Europe is our common home', with its memories of old Europhile policies of the Tsarist periods of capitalist industrialization. They had pulled away from Central Asia after abandoning the Afghan extremities to the Mujahideen and its Pakistani backers. The Uzbeks were left high and dry. They gave up Russian military support and had to upgrade their army. The social economy of the non-Russian Republics from the Black Sea to Lake Baikal had been heavily subsidized by the allocative system of Soviet planning. When the Russians began to look west for their models of comfort, the non-Russians, largely Muslim, had to devise their own models of political economy and cultural development.

Already the Muslim Republics were split, as indeed were the Russians themselves. An educated elite was allocated dachas in the towns and sometimes additionally in the countryside, and had graded access to better amenities, such as private cars, more equipped hospitals, sanatoria for the mandatory holidays, and restaurants. On the other hand the masses had basic comforts, if they were urban workers. But they had much less in the rural backwoods. The Muslim elites followed the Russian nomenklatura or hierarchy of Party functionaries in Westernized aspirations—trips to Europe, or even some education in the USA after 1989—and emulation of at least a Central European, or secularist Turkish, lifestyle. But the rest had no such access. This led to either envy or anger about lifestyles and particularly dress and the freedom of morality, which went with dress, in the permissive 1970s.

This social rift was culturally over-determined in the Muslim Republics as well as in the Baltic by various forms of religious fundamentalism, which appealed particularly to those who had a sense of either deprivation or outraged morality. In Latvia, Estonia, and Lithuania, the rift took even the masses of the CIS on a pro-Western tide. A Catholic resurgence in Lithuania evoked memories of independence from the Greek Orthodoxy of the Tsarist period and from the Communist regimes imposed in 1940, after the Molotov-Ribbentrop Pact that had carved up Poland in 1939. In

Azerbaijan, west of the Caspian Sea, and certainly in Central Asia, however, the drift was south and east.

An Islamic resurgence, symbolized by Ayatollah Khomeini's Shia radicalism in Iran and by the Wahhabi-financed, local Sunni and often Sufi Pir-dominated orders in Afghanistan and Pakistan, resonated in Central Asian religion, particularly in Tajikistan and north of it, in the Ferghana Valley of the upper reaches of the Syr Darya, which was shared by the Tajiks in the south-east, the Uzbeks in its fertile plains and the Kyrgyz in the mountainous north, further east.[4] Scattered revolts against Westernized modernity accentuated tensions between the political class in power and the underclasses, ethnic, linguistic or religious, that felt deprived, frustrated, or enraged by the way the world was going. All this culminated in racial anger against Gorbachev's regime, as it prepared to pull out of Inner Asia and collapsed in the process, carrying communism with it.

SETTLING IN AT UWED

When we arrived in Tashkent these events were already eight or nine years old. The echoes could still be heard, as the twentieth century limped to its close and people began to talk vaguely of a new millennium. Ambassador Bhadrakumar, with whom I had interacted on my previous visit, worked through his contacts and sympathies with the old guard post-communist scholars in academia, largely pro-Soviet and wary of change from old values, had, unfortunately for me, left two days earlier to take up a new embassy in Iraq. The officer he had deputed to handle my assignment to the University of World Economy and Diplomacy (acronymically UWED, or in Russian, UMED, for Universitet Mezhdunarodnaya Ekonomia I Diplomatiya) briefed me in terms reflecting diplomatic caution.

The University to which I would be attached had been, until the early 1990s, the old Party School of all the Muslim republics of Central Asia. I later heard that Presidents of several of them today, like Geidar Aliev of Azarbaijan, or Nazarbaev of Kazakhstan, were trained there, perhaps in short courses on party management. It had been given university status with B.A. degree granting authority (called the Baccalaureat in the Russian language which every educated person spoke in these countries). Perhaps this was because the President of Uzbekistan had sent his daughters to study there, and not to Tashkent State University, located in the sprawling Universitet Gorodok (University Town) to the north-west of the old city (Stary Gorod), that had become notorious for student unrest just before independence. It was renamed University of World Economy and Diplomacy, with three faculties of International Relations, International Law, and Economics. The institution had a superb campus, palatial administrative blocks, and apparently beautiful hostels along two inner rows of tree-lined avenues in a park-like expanse, parallel to two boulevards, which met just past it. It was interesting that these were the only two avenues whose Russian names remain, Pushkin in front and Maxim Gorky at the back.

The officer from the Embassy informed me as, underpassing the main railway line from Tashkent towards the north and Russia, we neared the University, that teachers and students knew very little about world affairs. Also, he said, they were dubious about any scholar who sought to learn about current affairs from members of the diplomatic community other than his or her own. In fact, there had been an occasion when it had been suspected that a scholar attending the German Ambassador's party on a personal invitation might belong to his country's intelligence service. Keep your eyes and ears open, and your mouth shut, seemed to be the message: but of course this was left to be inferred, nothing was put as a norm, even in words. One supposes this was the way Russian diplomats themselves thought and Indians had learnt to respond. This was the atmosphere that pervaded official life in the next years; an ambiguity leading to a series of misunderstandings that I never got used to.

The first meeting with a Pro-Vice-Chancellor, and also the Dean of International Relations and the Head of Department of Politology (Russian for Political Science)—the last two had met us at the airport—was not very different from the briefing. Everyone was formally polite, smiled but gave no information unless specifically asked—very much like every formal meeting I had had with petty Soviet dignitaries since 1973. I was told that I would sign a contract to teach courses during term time, and could do whatever I pleased during the long vacation in summer. Everything else in service conditions, including pay and accommodation, was the Embassy's business. Taken to the Political Science Department, where I found the names in Russian in Cyrillic script as well as in Uzbek in Roman script (the latter said 'Siyasatshunoslik'—Statology it would be in English), I was told I could teach whatever I pleased for the rest of the winter semester, which would end three weeks thence before New Year, in place of the last Russian scholar who had worked at the University, someone called Etnyukov. He used to teach area studies and had died the previous day. No one had a clue what I was meant to do, though there had been a long correspondence about my clearance, presumably with state security, since September when the first semester began. A youngish Korean teacher introduced himself to me as the only person who knew English in the Department. He said he looked forward to 'my co-operation' in his endeavour to make English the medium of instruction in all the faculties. This was to be one of my few but lasting and consistent routes of entry into the academic mind of Uzbeks outside the Tashkent Indologists in the Oriental Institute with whom I was already in touch.

The first month of classes were, in retrospect, weird. I had been clear in every discussion with the Indian Council of Cultural Relations and the Ministry of External Affairs that I knew no Russian; and that, like my predecessor, a scholar of diplomacy, would lecture on International Relations. In my case this would mean the history of International Relations in Asia since 1945 when the Second World War ended with the nuclear bombing of Japan. The late Etnyukov's students were being taught about political systems in the contemporary world. He had just disposed of France! I gathered that it would be good if I dealt with the Indian Constitution! The head of political science, Professor Farmanov, who spoke to me in French and also through interpretation, one of the nicest colleagues I have worked with, assured me that this was all that was necessary for the students to know about the Indian political system before the semester ended, the following month.

Trying to talk about Indian politics and the differences between aspirations in the early years, later realities, and current practice, was indeed useful to me as a refreshing learning process, even at my age. The students may well have been quite baffled. One of them, who became quite attached to me when he later went up to the Third Year (and after that when he applied for scholarships to Germany and finally got there) asked me after a whole hour of explanation about the principles of secularism in India, whether I believed in God or not: and also what I, as a Hindu, called God. At that juncture I did not ask whether the rest of the class shared his declaration of devotion to Allah. Nor did I probe what they thought when I said that I was not a Hindu, but my parents had been members of the Brahmo Samaj and that I supposed I was an agnostic.

The semester examination, which I had to take, was instructive. Written answers were brief and strictly factual. Analytical interpretations were totally missing. Where dates were relevant, they were correct. Answers did not go into more than one and a half pages demi. This was just as well. Those were the limits of the English that was mandatory for them. They had obviously heard my facts and me. Their training, since childhood, to scan out only factual information had erased my interpretations and analysis. On the other hand, the oral tests that I insisted upon (and for which a good English-speaking Uzbek research scholar, a girl, just back from Indiana, with a US accent, was told to assist me), at least one-fourth of the students, who spoke good English were thoughtful and interesting when I probed their knowledge. Many who could not were equally good. At least 5 per cent of the class could have been graded as excellent, which was no worse than what I had been used to in the M.A. classes of Calcutta University. I had heard stories that the students often did not pay attention or even amused themselves reading magazines or otherwise, at the back of the class. There was a bit of this in December 1998. I put it down to the incapacity of some of the students to understand my English, or their unfamiliarity with my ways of thought. That there was another reason and a local social one, that these were the *bagatey* or 'rich' scions of nomenklatura or mafia, who feared no disciplinary action, I was told later. At that time a tongue lashing in simple terms or telling the ruder ones to go out of class brought to heel the young blood at the back of the class, who included quite a few young girls in fur coats. By and large, Uzbek students respond to firm discipline.

These first classroom experiences reminded me of the early days of the post-graduate programme at the Indian Institute of Management, Calcutta from 1964. Management had then been an academic discipline, unfamiliar to Indian students. Even commerce graduates hardly went beyond the accountancy or a bit of commercial geography that business economics used to offer. The multi-disciplinary and social science approaches, plural, diversified, and open-ended with regard to answers to questions raised, permitting a variety of choices with no necessary certitude, and grading or evaluation according to the consistency of the logic used to formulate the answer, was something that was not generally common in our country in the 1960s. The engineers and arts and science graduates who came to the IIMs in the early 1960s had been as unprepared for open-ended teaching as my UWED students in the 1990s were in Uzbekistan. Trained in the Soviet command system of education where questions could be raised about information, but hardly about arguments, only the too few were marked for the KGB and the guarding of 'national security' and encouraged to be free. And yet the Party School outlook dominated. The brightest were as intelligent as any bright Indian student from a *mufassil* town. However, the social continuities of cadre-based state power ensured that the nomenklatura's children or relatives would land the top jobs in the foreign service or in banks or in the marketing systems that UWED was now meant to serve.

RURAL OPINION AND LIFE IN THE HIGHLANDS

Winter arrived in Tashkent. The trees, in serried ranks on either side of our apartment buildings, lost their leaves and stood bare. We had made a few new friends and I contacted some old ones. One of the latter, Professor Azad Nasridin Shamatov of the Tashkent Institute of Oriental Studies, suggested to our new acquaintance, Ramakant Dwivedi, Nehru Scholar from the School of International Studies, Jawaharlal Nehru University, who had just come to research on fundamentalism in Central Asia, that both might come with us in the car for an idea of village life in the mountains just to the north of Tashkent.

Tashkent had become the capital of Uzbekistan after 1929. The Stone City, which is what Tashkent means, lies just below where the Tian Shan range, supposed to mean 'heavenly mountains' in Chinese, tapers down to snowcapped foothills. From it streams, like the Chirchik River, bring their cold waters through a network of channels, which run through the city, down to the Syr Darya, as it bends northwards towards the deserts of the Aral. This was the point where, legend has it, Sikandar (Alexander) halted and then turned south towards the Hydaspes or Jhelum River in Punjab. To the north of the mountains in Kazakhstan is Taras, where in the eighth century the Chinese fended off the Arabs who had just conquered Turkestan. Close to that is a town where Amir Timur, who had repeated the Kushan ruler Kanishka's feat of imperium from Turkestan to Delhi, died on his way to attack China.

In many ways Tashkent has the same geopolitical location of bridge and buffer that Delhi has *vis-à-vis* the Punjab and the Gangetic Plains. It was the first Russian bridgehead into Mawar-an-Nahr, in 1863, when General Cherniaev, followed by a Russian Orthodox priest holding aloft a cross, stormed the Samarkand Darwaza of what had till then been a small city state, for almost a century, stretching for a few kilometres from the mountains along the irrigation canals of the Chirchik River to the Syr Darya. The Russians made it their capital, much as the British made its Bengal bridgehead at Calcutta, the capital of British India till 1911. Russian Governors-General, like their British counterparts, hankered for the cool breeze, heather, and snow-covered slopes, to recuperate from the summer heat of their fertile, subject plains. Like Ootacamund, Darjeeling, and then Simla, the Russians built summer stations for their senior officers in the mountains south of Samarkand, and at Chimgan to the north of Tashkent.

These residences had fallen to pieces in the civil wars of the 1920s. When Tashkent was restored to the position of capital, after a gap in the 1920s Chimgan was slowly restored as a hill resort for the masses and for Soviet youth groups (known as Pioneer campers) from all over the USSR or for sanatoria residents. Elementary facilities were developed for a ski-lift in summer to the highest range, the Bolshoi, Chimgan, for sledding down the snow slope, and for various other diversions. A little village with dachas was built above a sylvan stream that came down through its street from a lower range, the Mala Chimgan. Smaller resorts grew up in the other valleys. There was a flourishing hill tourist economy until the last years of the Soviet regime with several sanatoria and tourist camp facilities. But the bottom fell out of this with the collapse of Russian subsidies. The crisis in the market abroad for Uzbek cotton, and the state of heavy industry, forced after Russian decolonization in 1991 to compete in far more modernized world markets, made the situation worse. The Uzbek state was unable to compensate, starved for funds as it was. The easy consumer lifestyle of workers and professionals alike was destroyed by economic crisis, job restrictions, and downsizing. One of the casualties was the occupation of the poor people in the hills, who found tourism drying up, pioneer camps empty, and the dachas again falling into ruin.

On the last day of 1998, we drove with our friends not to Chimgan but to a small village in the adjacent valley of Humsan, Prof. Shamatov's ancestral home. The professor's father had lived there and indeed died in a car crash on a bend of the road we travelled. He pointed out places with names like Gazalkent (Guzal in Turki means the same as in Persian, beautiful) and told us that '*-kent*', a common suffix in Central Asia, means the same as *khanda* or territorial place in Sanskrit. We were beginning to learn about the Central Asian pleasure in pointing out affinities between Turki and Urdu vocabulary. Many liked to believe that these languages had been influenced by mediaeval conquests, much as the Normans had influenced the Saxon by an overlay of French in English. We were often told that *bazaar* was the same as *bozor*, *dukan* was the same as *dokon*, *aina* was the same as *oina* or *darwaza* the same as *darwoza*. And even more complex words had Turki roots: linguists had counted about three thousand such roots.

Humsan when we reached it was snowbound under a gray sky with a promise of snow and rain. Professionals use Humsan as a summer resort. Their houses are dilapidated; kitchens exiguous, and the toilet facilities are outside latrines, practically bogs, of a sort that went out of fashion in English slums by the late 1950s. The external polish of Westernization in urban Uzbekistan is sadly smeared by its primitive toilet facilities, whether in the ladies' chambers of the magnificent opera houses, in lower middle class homes, or along the highways. This is probably true of the entire Commonwealth of Independent States. Country loos resemble the filthy holes in the ground that still exist in the Himalayan hill resorts in India and Nepal. Azad Shamatov had few facilities in his villa and was sad about the fact that local villagers were stripping his apple trees, then in deep snow, and even his gate off its hinges. These were people to whom he was related, who had not risen in the world like his late father. He took us to one of their homes. The path was down a fairly steep slope, frozen like glass, down which my wife trod lightly with him. As she walked gingerly in her squelching shoes, women and children flocked out of their homes to gaze curiously at an obvious foreigner: recognition of her Indian nationality brought smiles to their faces with which we would become familiar in the years to come. My flounders led to my being driven in the car by a circuitous route to the valley bottom, and then trudging up. The village was a mess of mud and slush. Water coursed down the middle of the lanes. Far outside it on the way to the main road, the Professor would later stop the car, to collect cool, clean and fresh water from a spring, which was much prized by Tashkent people. The river that ran through Humsan was red, and presumably full of iron.

The mediaeval atmosphere in this village was even more marked when we entered through the usual big *darwaza* (portal). We found a simple dwelling place, or rather a long shed partitioned into living areas, with a fairly large plot of ground, fruit trees then bare, and the mandatory *aiwan* or kiosk of open wrought-iron, on which the residents sit in summer under the shade of trees to drink their *choi* or tea in a ceremonial way. The rooms were carpeted, with a low *dastarkhwan* or eating table, and narrow mattresses around it to recline upon. Fitted into one of the walls was an iron stove fed by wood. Against another wall was a long sofa. Uzbeks interact with their guests only around the eating table, partaking of light snacks and tea, or fruit juice, all home made. Spirits are taken at home on rare occasions. In fact there is an Uzbek popular perception that the Russians are a drunken lot.

It was the Ramzan season. Everyone in the house was on fast. We had arrived soaking wet. We took off our shoes, the rule in every Uzbek home, and were given warm slippers to tread the carpet. Shamatov Saheb, a sound, old-fashioned non-believer in religious observances, had apologetically warned us to take tea in his own home before we went. We were moved by the warm way in which the elderly women in the house welcomed us with whatever there was in the larder. Indeed, as we sat down, two or three older women, invariably with traditionally sober headscarves around their foreheads, appeared from neighbouring houses. In their memories of the fading Communist past, *Induskii Mir,* India, land of peace, meant people for whom their warmth is greater than even their curiosity.

We listened to their simple responses to questions about daily life and ideas, which were initiated by Ramakant. The family, distantly related to Azad Saheb, had only one earning member.

This young man worked as a guard in a Pioneer holiday camp along the riverbank. Outside the season, his wages went down to a bare minimum. Life was hard. Asked about religious practices and matters of personal faith, they said, of course they were Muslims. What else could they be? At that point of time we were not clear whether the scarves round the ladies' heads were part of a religious or a customary rural practice. Questions of a general nature about politics, Party, and economic conditions were deflected by wary silence. Or, it could simply have been incomprehension. As they became more familiar, we learned that conditions had been much more stable and better even in wintertime in Soviet days. Life was easier, was the refrain. Freedom was something they found difficult to comprehend, given the economic misery that accompanied it. These were the annals of the poor.

Children played in the room while the talk went on, watching TV in the room itself. The film was neither Russian, nor dubbed European as is more common in Tashkent. It was a truly Bombay brand, blood and gore shocker, in Hindi, dubbed in Uzbek, in which trucks went up in gouts of flame, and villains with red eyes grimaced like Ravana. The main point we were told by the children was that Shah Rukh Khan was the hero. Raj Kapoor was no more the focus of this village, even if we were to find him still reigning over bazaar sentiments in Tashkent, and there were many people in the village nearing middle age who were called Raj or Nargiza. We left these good people; saddened and perhaps shamed by the thought that all that India was today contributing to the popular culture that Raj Kapoor had once stood for was the brutal violence and sleazy rape scenes of contemporary Mumbai. It was on the last day of 1998 that we realized India had really lost in the 1990s the decisive edge in cultural fellowship that the generation of Nehru and Abul Kalam Azad had gained for us after Independence.

The next morning, to our joy, we woke up to a white new year. Thick snow lay over Tashkent. The trees on either side of our flat were broad glittering cones of fluff while water had turned into icicles as they dripped off the branches. The ensemble looked like one of the memorable scenes in David Lean's *Dr. Zhivago*. The city would remain like this for the next ten days or so. This was the closest that we got to the stereotypical northern winter that the USSR evokes, and indeed identifies with Russia, in the Indian imagination. One day we joined an Embassy picnic journey by bus to Chimgan itself. My wife joined others on the ski-lift, a most precarious looking couple of metal half-bucket chairs without any footrest in which you have to cling to a rusty, metal rod which hangs from the pulley. I suffer from fear of heights, and stood frightened as she travelled up the ropeway to Bolshoi Chimgan, crossing a deep ravine. Then the peak reared up. Suspended over it, she said, was heart stopping. The pull of the ground far below enticed one to letting the rod go. The silence all around seemed to have a voice of its own. On her way down, my own heart stopped, when I saw her clicking pictures with one hand while holding the rod with the other.

The views were lovely from above. On the summit, strips of cloth of many colours fluttered from bushes and iron rails, tied by visitors calling for fulfilment of their vows. This was a practice, frowned upon by the Communist orthodoxy, that we would see later also in the mountains of Kazakhstan. It is a remnant of pagan naturalism. It has parallels in Buddhist folk practice on hilltops in Darjeeling or Sikkim in India, where prayer flags, nothing but regular cloth rectangles, flutter around the gompas. Neither Islam nor Communism have made dents deep enough in Central Asian Islam to eradicate popular communion with Buddhist or earlier roots. It is this that adds moderation to Central Asian Islam, helping to keep *jihadi* violence at Bay.

Buddhism is a social product of the relative solitude of the mountains. Gautama came from Kapilavastu, commonly supposed to be in the Nepal foothills. Though it extended over the north Indian plains, and from there south, west and east by land and sea, its most sacred caves, rock-cut temples and *stupas* (Tepe or mounds of ruins in Muslim Turki) will be found on the slopes of mountain ranges, along trade routes linking hills with plains and the sea, or crossing them along river beds or passes from one side to another. The Udayagiri hills north of Bhubaneshwar where Asoka left his famous Dhauli Edict on non-violence, Karle, Ajanta, Ellora, north of Mumbai, Elephanta or even Anakapalle, south of Waltair, are all fastnesses where the monastic retreat was practised, with a mixture of art and asceticism. These aesthetic values inform the cultural diffusion that has linked India with Central Asia and Tibet, Central Asia with the Gobi Desert, and the latter with China and Japan, all the way from Bukhara to Dunhuang to Korea and thence to Nara and Kyoto. There has been much research on this diffusion from the days of Aurel Stein, Pelliot, Grunwedel, and Tucci to those of Prabodh Bagchi.[5] The followers of the Buddhist Sangha had their most sacred places in the valleys and on the summits of mountains. Their *stupas* resembled holy mounds, whether at Sanchi in Central India or in Borobudur, Prambanan and Angkor Thom in South-East Asia.

In Central Asia the earliest cave temples were along the Oxus. But the famous sites around Termez, excavated by Russian (and now French and Uzbek) archaeologists, are to be found in chronological order pushing northward along rivers descending the hills of western Tajikistan and southern Uzbekistan. Termez as the Bactrian focal point of the spread of Buddhist culture from the mountains of Afghanistan (such as the monumental Buddhas of Bamiyan) was the node for monastic communities in the find spots in the Kashka Darya and Surkhan Darya valleys (the latter leading up to Timur's fort of Shahr-i-Sabz and thus to Samarkand). According to the great Khurasani historian and administrator for the Mongols Ata Malik Juvaini, author of *The Tarikh-i-Jahankusha*, Bukhara in the western desert had indeed once been a Bihara (monastery) of Buddhism, where the Zarafshan range came down to the plains, and the river of that name lost itself in the sand. The real movement of Buddhism was north along the mountain ranges past Ferghana into the Tian Shan and thus towards China. Its sites were generally between hills and plains.

Many of these sites fell victim to the Arab conquest and the first idol breakers. *But* became the Arabic spelling for Buddha and *butparasti* the name for idol worship by Central, Inner or South Asians, Buddhist or Hindu, as distinct from non-idolatrous Muslims. In many of the sites mentioned above, reclining images of the Buddha are to be found resembling the Ananthasayanam Vishnu of Thiruvananthapuram (Trivandrum). Many are smashed, but still discernible. The Taliban in 2001 were desperately seeking to push history backwards to the first millennium, instead of living in the present. Such fantasy about the Muslim past was not possible beyond the Amu Darya, where the Arabs had been resisted by local forces, as well as by the desert nomad nature worshippers. This is not the place to describe the revolt of the idol-worshipping princelings of Mawar-un-Nahr soon after the entry of the Arabs. The furies of idol breaking in revenge against political subaltern revolts increased the enmity of Muslim fanatics against first Buddhism and then Hinduism: This pattern would be repeated in India. Nor is this the place to go into the waves of shamanist nomadic thrusts against the Muslim towns of the plains, from Mongolia and Kazakhstan. The best known of these was Chingiz Khan's irruption in the thirteenth century. Even the Muslim chronicles of those times, for instance by Ata Malik Juvaini, record the arrogance of the Muslim rulers of the plains (such as Alauddin Muhammad Shah of Khwarizm) in rejecting Chingiz's overtures for peaceful trade and perhaps tribute. This led to the latter's sack of the northern route from Tashkent to Samarkand and Bukhara. Christians and pagans worked and gathered in the Mongol camps. The syncretism, however brutal, of the Mongols was to find its way into the low-key moderation of subsequent Central Asian Islam.

Even before the thirteenth-century devastation of the Turkistan plains and its old cultures, the religious life of the common people had been influenced by this moderation. It amounted to the quietism of the *pirs,* local holy men who spoke in their *khanqas* (hospices) about spiritual matters and Islamic practice. Some like Bahauddin Naqshbandi and others in different towns, were to be venerated as founders of *silsilahs,* traditions carried on from preceptor to disciple, and taken by other disciples to the frontiers of what Marshall Hodgson in *The Venture of Islam*, called the Islamicate. The Mongol invasions of Turan, Iran, Afghanistan and the Indus basin of Punjab and Sind scattered fugitives and the Sufi principles of the *pirs* in a crescent from the northern borders of Iran to the southern shores of the Gangetic delta in Bengal.[6] Ottoman Turks took these ideas into Turkey and the Balkans. A spirit of mixture and accretion, though not necessarily of tolerance, was bred of earlier faiths—and Islamic dominant groups, camp followers and converts co-existed with this through the mediaeval period of Asian history.[7] The syncretism that resulted was not necessarily amicable. Nor was it devoid of struggles for power and for resistance among the elements of the composite culture, produced in different layers.

Pluralism is not necessarily non-violent. Nor is it always co-operative. But it can be found deep down in the structure of traditions of culture, so to speak deconstructed from the pathetic little coloured strips of cloth, fluttering in the breeze on a Chimgan range, or floating above a narrow stream that we were to see two years later, coming down from the snows above the Kazakh cultural metropolis of Almaty.

BILINGUALISM AND THE MULTICULTURAL SECTOR

In the first month we spent in Tashkent, we tried to familiarize ourselves with the only path of access to a new culture, learning the language. Here we faced the issue of access to bi-lingualism. Practically every Uzbek we met, elite or plebeian, speaks two languages—the Uzbek form of Turki of his or her ancestors, and the Russian of the dominant elite from the 1860s to the 1980s.

The Uzbek language, which goes back to the fine flush of Turki writing by fifteenth-century poets and writers of prose like Ali Shir Nawai and Zahiruddin Muhammad Babur, does not lack tradition or grace. Many loan words from it, we were later to find, have travelled to north Indian languages such as Hindustani or Bengali, in whose territories Uzbek migrants settled in the period of the Sultanates and the Mughals. By the nineteenth century, Uzbeki had lost its vitality, something that had happened to the north Indian languages a century before, when the British began to conquer India piecemeal. Where the ground springs of Bengali, Hindi, Urdu, Marathi, or Telegu and Tamil at the grassroots could successfully learn from, as well as contest, the dominance of Macaulay's Minute and Victorian English, Uzbek literature buckled, first under Tsarist and then under Bolshevik dominance. The *maktabs* (primary and secondary schools) and *madrasas* (institutions of higher learning) with their outmoded syllabus, in which the scientific and technological discoveries of the West had no place, could do no more than prop up the brutal, social repression of the nineteenth-century Amirs, subservient to the Tsars.

The new learning, or, as it came to be called in modern Islamic renaissance, Jadidism, emphasized methods of teaching a modicum of modernity (along with the Koran and indigenous knowledge). This became associated with protest against the ramshackle twentieth-century Tsarist-Amiri feudal establishment.[8] Jadid ideas had originated in Tatar Crimea from a teacher, Ismail Bey Gasprolu. They spread to Kazan and Bashkiria in the north and Turkistan as well as Afghanistan in the south. They were as severely repressed by the Bukhari nobility in the early twentieth century, as were the Bolsheviks and Social Revolutionaries in Russia and Siberia. Hence grew a certain common front among their young politicians in Bukhara, like Faizullah Khodjaev and Sadruddin Aini with the new Communist revolutionaries sent by Moscow to take over governance after the Bolshevik uprising in Tashkent in 1917.

Young Bukhara participated in the overthrow of the last Bukhara Amir by the Bolshevik general Mikhail Frunze in 1922. In that moment of the collapse all over Central and Inner Asia, Jadid affinity for the Russian revolution has a parallel in more modern Asian history with the place of Nepal in South Asia after 1947. Nepal Congressmen, educated in Indian cities like Benares, Calcutta, and Patna, worked during the Second War with socialists like Ram Manohar Lohia, or Jayaprakash Narayan for political freedom from Rana rule. In the new Uzbekistan, Faizulla was given charge. When Tajikistan was carved out of the eastern part of the Bukhara Emirate, Aini was sent with advisers from Samarkand University to develop modern culture in Dushanbe, its new capital. Here he lies buried in glory on a hilltop with an Orientalist Tajik politician, Bobojan Gafurov.

After the Jadids-turned-Communists like Faizullah or the equally famous Abdur Rauf Fitrat, who looked to India for models, had been purged or liquidated by 1938, Stalin halted the Uzbek enlightenment, and began to Russianize the elite and the masses in the 1940s. Where the Uzbek language had flourished under the Jadids, the mother tongue was now meant to be only for domestic use. Russian became the international language of Uzbekistan, and the medium of public affairs. The people had little choice but to accept or be repressed.

We were to come to the stories of repression by Communists in the inter World War years, much later; as people began to talk more easily with us in their homes. I am not still sure that they know, or are prepared to talk about, the details of how Uzbek nationalist communists were wiped out in the 1930s. What was clear was that a change came in the pattern of repression in the 1940s. The next rank after the Jadids—careerists, who had grown up under Stalinism—gave loyal service to him after Hitler attacked the USSR in 1941. The flower of Uzbek and Kazakh youth was raised in the Panfilovsky Battalions, which held the Panzer attack just ahead of Moscow. A memorial between Sheremetyevo Airport and the city commemorates the spot where the Soviet Army dug in. Even in 2000, most old men in Tashkent were to be found with a row of war medals displayed on their chests on the day of national rejoicing. Till 1999, 8 March, the Day of Victory over Germany, was observed with great éclat all over the country. We heard that younger relatives would on this day visit war veterans with flowers to congratulate them. The reward for the sacrifice that the Uzbeks undertook to save Stalingrad and then join in the push westwards from 1944 was a certain relaxation of social control. Uzbeks were permitted a slight relief from official atheism but only to the extent of the opening of a few closed mosques, and permission for the study of Arabic and theology in two *madrasas*, the sixteenth-century Barak Khan in the old city in Tashkent, where the Religious Board for Central Asia was located, and the Mir Arab in Bukhara.

A permissive attitude now prevailed about the private use of Uzbek language. After Stalin died, the Khruschev and Brezhnev regimes gave latitude to cultural endogeneity. During the War, many industries had been shifted from the line of German advance into Russia, to the region north and east of Tashkent around Chirchik, Kokand, and further south-west up to the Tajik border of Khojent (then called Leninabad). This development of machine building and the aeronautical industry, as well as the location of a major Soviet base at Chirchik and an army training college near the place where I was to teach all made Tashkent the fourth city of the Soviet Union—after Moscow, Leningrad, and Kiev (in the Ukraine). As a result in the second half of the twentieth century, the Uzbek language came back to cultural view, but now in a subaltern form.

In the bazaars, the peasant working women, wearing their traditional padded warm clothes and head covers, spoke Uzbek, but would respond in Russian whenever necessary. In the theatres and concert halls, which were aplenty in the heart of Tashkent, some Uzbek plays, generally deeply pedagogical in their social reform messages, were watched by less well-to-do people. The better off went to the concerts and the theatre in Russian. An eminent mediaevalist, Dr. Sulaimanov, who had built up a superb collection of very rare Arabic, Persian and Turki manuscripts, was encouraged to build the Alberuni Institute, commemorating the eleventh-century Khiva scholar carried into captivity by Sultan Mahmud to Ghazni, who had, among many books on science and geodesy, written a famous one on the Arabic knowledge of 'Al Hind'. Indeed this was the age when from the complete works of Al Beruni to translations of Rabindranath Tagore, Uzbek scholars carried on the study of Indian, Persian, and Turkish, as well as Chinese and Japanese language materials, with a strong modernist and vernacular bias.

Cultural idealism was explicit here. At the practical level, Russian remained the language of international access. I got a clear picture of this from the lady at the reception counter of the Indian Embassy, Gul Bahor. Uzbek to the core, living in an Uzbek *mahalla* in the new city she told me that her daughters were reading Russian in school. How else could they get good jobs with the multinationals? And what was more, how could they read world classics from Europe, which had been translated into Russian, but of which there were very few still in the Uzbek language? So, the Uzbek people we met had a veneer of Russian that they generally displayed, but deep down there were layers of Uzbek consciousness. Initially the tension did not appear very marked to us.

Before I left India, the Joint Secretary in charge of the Central Asia desk in the Ministry of External Affairs, had advised me to learn Uzbek if I was thinking of future research on the country. But in the capital itself, people were gloomier about prospects of getting easy access to anything but the Uzbek State Archives and their records of administration. People advised us that Russian was still the common language in the shops, on the metro and public transport, and with one's colleagues. Uzbek, the expatriates said, was still not the language of polite conversation. A young lady from West Bengal, wife of a multinational executive, said she was learning Russian to read Turgenev and Dosteyevski. It was only much later that we realized that practically no Tashkent expat had Uzbek friends or knew a single Uzbek word.

Before we came, I had heard of the first Indian Ambassador to Tashkent from 1992 till 1995, Dalip Mehta who was much liked by every Uzbek I had dealt with. Significantly, they spoke of his wife, Mrs. Nandini Mehta, once a journalist, who spoke fluent Uzbek and invited Uzbek ladies to tea. My wife recalls that the only foreigner she met in Tashkent who not only knew Uzbek but spoke it fluently, was Felicity Timcke, the wife of a South African well known in Consular circles. This lady had made her mark not only as teacher of the International School of Tashkent, but also as the editorial adviser of Uzbekistan Airways' seasonal journal, the only publication we saw in the country which was published in passable English.

Unfortunately, we accepted the current expatriate elite advice and began to learn, not Uzbek, but Russian from a lady who knew no English and brought along her young daughter of 13 years, who did, since the latter had began to learn English at school. The experience, which lasted for three months, was disastrous. My wife picked up the Russian alphabet in Cyrillic script very fast. I did not pick it up at all, as I am exceptionally bad at languages and new scripts. The teacher rushed ahead at my wife's pace. She learnt quite a bit of Russian to ultimately cope with the maid and the bazaar, though falteringly. She would have learnt more, had my slowness not held her up. If we had been able to talk to each other in the language, we might have gone faster. As I could not, I lost patience. I asked the teacher to give me some sense of Uzbek in the Latin script. This was then beginning to be introduced by the government in place of the Cyrillic script imposed on it during the purges of the 1930s, when the Latin script brought in place of Arabic, to follow the Kemalist experiment in Turkey, was scrapped. I got some idea of Uzbek words. By dint of regularly asking our driver what the Uzbek words were for familiar objects, I began to understand some simple conversations. Fairly soon we gave up the teacher. More diligent and consistent interaction with the people would have given us closer touch with Uzbek realities in those days of rapid transition towards Westernization, social and economic decline and the US embrace.

One aspect of middle-class culture in the CIS we did get used to. This was the concerts and ballets, all mostly in the Russian version of European classical music and dance, in which Tashkent still remained excellent. I had gone to the mandatory ballet performances of delegations to Moscow in the previous twenty years and had seen Brecht's *Caucasian Chalk Circle* performed in the gorgeous Tbilisi Opera Theatre with the Georgian audience and their President, Shevardnadze, singing along with the actors in the tense, post-civil war, murderous days of 1995. The theatres of Tashkent were still a revelation. The Turkestan Palace, at the base of a series of squares and gardens, where the old Governor-General's house had once stood between the old and the new cities, was splendid: long murals decorated various floors of an atrium entrance and foyer. The chandeliers, however common this form of lighting was in the city homes, were superb. So was the banked auditorium.

We would later find a smaller version in the main Opera House, a grim piece of late Stalinist architecture, rather like the Georgian one, built by the forced labour of Japanese soldiers taken prisoner in Manchuria when the Soviets decided to declare war on Japan as it tottered to defeat, just before Hiroshima and Nagasaki in 1945. The theatres reminded us of the nineteenth-century halls in Paris but were remarkably cheap when we started going in 1998. Concerts were more costly. Uzbek families we found would more often go to the Conservatoire or a Lycee called after Ouspenskaya where the best teaching was offered in classical music. Our apartment block was very close to both.

Western classical music is very much part of the heritage of the Uzbek middle-class intelligentsia. It gives them the same sense of equality with the Russian cultured classes, which Anglicized Bengali gentry affected through the British Indian music schools, just before the British quit India in 1947. My Chairperson in the University from 1999 began to invite us to concerts whenever she heard of one. She would always take along her youngest son, aged eight, who would join his father, an engineer and architect with a passion for music, in the front rows, and would discuss the performance with sundry older people. Young performers were encouraged on the piano by the entire orchestra and audience with loud and repeated encores. One of them, who once failed to keep pace with the score and fainted at the keyboard, was recalled with great sympathy for weeks after. This easy acquaintance with the classics was, however, at a point of transition. We were to see the cost of entrance go up in the years we were there. The middle classes became more constrained in their choice of entertainment. Paradoxically, a vast new Conservatoria was coming up in one of the avenues of the centre of the city near the President's city palace. It was to open soon after we left.

We did not get to see Uzbek cinema. The Soviet film medium, including Gorbachev's introduction of Glasnost through the liberalization of film messages, which I had heard so much of, were not in evidence. Cinema halls generally showed European or American films dubbed in Russian or Uzbek. The same was true of television. Tashkent had once been famous for its film festivals. These appeared to have become a financial casualty of Soviet dissolution. Most people remembered Raj Kapoor and Nargis and Raj's songs like '*lal topi Roosi, par dil hai Hindustani*' or '*ichak dana bighak dana*' which a bazaari treated us to while selling potatoes. Mr. Ziadullah who taught in the Conservatoria had a wonderful singing voice and still sang the songs familiar to the generation of Muhammad Rafi. Hindi heroes who were shown on television were, however, Shah Rukh Khan or Mithun Chakrabarty. Amitabh Bachchan was not as popular.

The great exception to this popularization of contemporaneity was the Uzbek-dubbed *Mahabharata*. Many families scrupulously waited for its weekly performances. The gentleman who had translated the script from Hindi to Uzbek used to attend the Indian Cultural Centre functions. He was then translating the *Ramayana* for television. Young people attending the functions would fall over each other to be introduced to him. My students of the fourth year, once they became more familiar with me, would stop me after class to enlighten themselves about particular mythological characters. This was pure secular pleasure at the tawdry costumes and ranting oratory of the various characters, and at best a taste for the mythical. It struck a chord among Uzbeks without reference to the religious flavour, that I earlier used to think Indians had endowed on the epics in the 1980s. Perhaps it was the same situation in India at that time. Through the three years we were in Uzbekistan, it was the human agency, whether in dance, drama, or films that we watched. A performance of *Swan Lake* or *Giselle* at the Opera was as good as any I had seen in Moscow. What will happen to it in the CIS under market competition or ethnic nationalism in different Republics is anybody's guess.

BRIC-A-BRAC AND THE BAZAAR

Tashkent as a city is a set of unequal concentric circles, overlapping each other. Downtown today, the Russian headquarters of Tsarist days has been rebuilt as monumental government blocks and open spaces or grassy squares. Among the remnants are a little palatial villa built for a disgraced Romanov cadet, sent to live in exile with his morganatic wife. After her death the villa was meant for ceremonial use by the new rulers. Leading from it along new gardens was a little street closed to cars called Sailgokh (strollers' path or promenade) known nowadays as Broadway. This street has become like the cobbled lanes and square by the side of the Cathedral of Sacre-Coeur in Paris on the heights of Montmartre.

Food stalls line either side, open to the air in summer, with canvas covers in the winter, where meals are available. Vendors sell a variety of stuff on the road. The most striking are paintings by Uzbek artists, generally of landscapes in Turkestan but also oriental portraits or reproductions of Russian pictures. These are kept on the ground in serried ranks or along the walls. In the middle of the road, with low folding chairs, sit pavement artists, offering to do your portrait as you pose. On one side are vendors of curios, old crimson medals of Lenin or the Red Star, little icons in various shapes, and other bric-a-brac. Here the road opens out to the great park, shaded by trees, with a massive statue in the middle. Once, the statue was of General Kaufman, the Russian conqueror of Turkestan. The Revolution replaced him with a colossal head of Karl Marx. Independence replaced Karl Marx Square with Amir Timur Square. The Samarkand ruler now rides high on his horse above where Marx once ruminated. A blue domed memorial next to the square now houses pictures of Amir Timur.

In summer the Broadway region comes alive. The gardens by its side have an open-air dance plaza. Young people gather by early evening to dance into the late night. There was a melee of Russian and Uzbek popular tunes, some of the Uzbek ones to the beat of Hindi film songs. We would hear Hindi songs such as *choli ke peechey kya hai*, *choli ke peechey*. The light smoke and the pungent smell of barbecued shashlik wafts across as the crowd passes up and down from the Park to the area at the base of Broadway. Here there is a huddle of costlier restaurants and striptease joints, dignified by the name of night clubs as well as a rather old fashioned music hall, where one of the numbers we once were taken to watch was a version of Indian dance, perhaps several removes from the classes in the Indian Cultural Centre. The entire area lights up at night and conveys an air of gaiety, which even the biting cold of winter nights is unable to dispel. We would go back again and again to Broadway, even more so in the evenings of years to come, either to seek bargain paintings or have hot shashlik and tea, but mainly to pass time in a generally somnolent city.

Another place we used to go to in the first year on Sunday mornings was Tizikovka. We never found out the meaning of this word. It was an open-air market, on the pavements of a small road, parallel to the one from the airport from the main Nukus avenue to the railway line, as it came east out of the Severny

Vokzal or main north station. When we had come to Tashkent, Embassy wives were talking of the good crystal wares, which were being sold by people of once affluent families, as inflation battered their domestic economy. We would go in the company of officers' families in the Mission. The fairly long street would be packed each weekend with all and sundry, from townsfolk looking for spare parts for household machinery to Ambassadors and their ladies, appraising old Dresden China. The variety on offer included old encyclopaedias, books on materialist philosophy, atlases, and the collected works of Arab scientists in Russian; brass and copper massive tea urns, called samovars, often marked with the date they were made in the days of Tsar Nikolai II (before 1917), or straightforward junk, such as second hand fur caps or medals. Of course, there was crystal in many shapes and sizes. Some of this was Uzbek, of a sort we saw in the great departmental stores. More was either Russian or the superior quality of Czech cut glass. Till the 1980s Czech crystal had been among the most prized possessions of a Soviet home. I can recall ladies ferociously elbowing each other out of the way to get to a Czech glass store counter in central Moscow in 1987, where word had spread that a new consignment had arrived. In these hard times, Czech crystal had become as much a counter of exchange as gold is for the Indian housewife. We heard that in the same way as bellmetal or silver utensils were presented in a bride's trousseau in Indian weddings, crystal came to an Uzbek bride as financial security for the future.

Along the railway line ran a row of tumbledown dachas, in one of which we were invited to view the antiques. The family selling them were obviously professional, with catalogues of old Russian and Uzbek household stuff, and with ornate objects at prices considerably higher than the pavement commodities. Many of the pavement vendors were not common hawkers. Some looked like Russian working class people, dressed in a more northern way, not in the flowing costumes and robes of Central Asia. They may have fallen on hard days and taken to this business as part-time self-employment. There were also the usual tinkers, like the one reeking of cheap vodka who offered a large rustic samovar to my wife for merely 800 *soum* (about a dollar then), and when she hesitated, said, 'take it away, I need the money for a drink'. Two years later when we were preparing to leave the country we learned about the date on the samovar, which classified it on the list of antiques that the Uzbek Ministry of Culture would arbitrarily promulgate from time to time—a list meant to restrict exports of cultural heritage.

We started going to Tizikovka out of curiosity. It also became a diversion, a sort of Sunday morning club for expeditions with acquaintances. Not everyone thought so. A correct and serious officer, whose wife had persuaded him to accompany her, was exasperated by a colleague getting himself some secondhand spiralled shashlik skewers. '*Kya kurhey dekh rahey hain, Sir*' (why must you look at this trash, Sir) he admonished, trying to chivvy him away to more salubrious surroundings. Over the years, the raffish charm of the place, somewhat like the jumble sales of pre-War, or the car boot sales on open meadows in present-day England, began to pall. As the stock of genuine crystal diminished and new crockery sets began to be dumped on the road, the crowd too became less friendly. Purse cutting or bag snatching made its appearance. There was talk of Pakistani petty thieves who had taken up abode in the locality, where police found bomb-manufacturing outfits, linked with *jihadis*.

By spring we began to discover the network of formal markets and the top echelon of departmental stores so marked in old Soviet society. The idea of a huge building catering to every need of every class, and that too cheaply, was a prized notion of the Soviet Union from at least the 1930s. The two co-operatives, GUM and TSUM, palatial buildings close to the Kremlin and Red Square, were replicated in cities of the Republics. They formed the main access to consumer goods in the high tide of Communism till the 1970s. Foreign products and a limited degree of choice were available only in the old Beriozhka shops, which were attached to the principal Intourist hotel in large cities. Access to dollars was then limited to the top rungs of the regime. Public flashing of dollars was quite unthinkable. Uzbeks remembered days before Independence when consignments of goods would suddenly be available, even in the great departmental stores and in smaller locality shops or marketplaces. A rush to buy up before stocks were exhausted would ensue. In 1989 to 1991, as the USSR began to crack at the peripheries, faulty distribution scheduling by the regime led to the breakdown of availability of most things, and not just bread and vodka. Below the central stores (indeed TS in TSUM stands for 'Tsentralnyi' or central) was a network of markets.

In Tashkent, the big wholesale markets had stalls stretching in clean arenas. The biggest was the Hippodrome on the southern outskirts of the city on the Samarkand Road, for distribution of internationally procured household nêcessities such as textiles, furs, electrical assortments, carpets, etc. The Chorsu bazaar in the old city was remarkable for its separate markets of similar products and a great dome for vegetables and dried fruits. All of it was not too unclean, but in the cloth market where stationery goods, drapery, shoes, etc., were also sold, the crowd in the narrow alleyways pushed each other cheerfully to get a move on. There was also the Alaisky or superior market, where vegetables, fruits, eggs, meat, fish, and other perishable commodities were available in neat rows of low stone platforms in a covered market, sold by women wearing traditional peasant costumes with headscarves, who were uniformly courteous and friendly. One alleyway had Korean descendants of migrants, ladies in smocks, who sold the sour salads and pickles, so dear to Uzbeks. On the peripheries of the city were other markets, with covered areas as well as open spaces, never dirty, serving the need of *mahallas* and specializing in a variety of commodities.

This market grid spreads out from Tashkent or Almaty to other places in their countries. It belies the old picture of an austere Soviet command economy. The feel of Middle Eastern souks had been greatly enhanced by Turkish influence in the later days of the Soviet Union. In the Soviet period there had of course been open markets for the villagers to bring in their produce.

What developed like mushrooms in the last decade of twentieth century were super markets, replacing the old concept of the beriozhka for foreign goods bought by dollars. One of the first had come up in the late Soviet period. Known as Ganga Shop or Ganga Magazini, because high above the corner block, which housed it, was written, and still exists, the letters Ganga in Devanagari script, it is said to have been a place where a range of Indian goods were sold. Local people spoke wistfully about its collapse, along with the Soviet Union and of the preferential trade agreements and exchange programmes for people from India as well as the weakening of Indo-Soviet relations, as Uzbekistan began to be pulled into the Turco-US orbit. After a brief phase of being taken over by Pakistanis, who sold cheap leather goods, the Ganga Shop ended up as a grocery store. It was on the verge of closing down when we left at the end of 2001—a sad example of the fate of Hindi-Uzbek *bhai-bhai*. Independence brought new attempts to replicate GUM and TSUM (the former opposite Chorsu, itself in a state of crisis), but as private enterprise.

We never ceased to wonder how such crony capitalist ventures continued to keep alive. One, next to the University where I taught, was perpetually empty. Others like the one close to our apartments, a franchise of an English company, was small but patronized mainly by affluent Uzbeks and foreigners, except for the bread, snapped up by all and sundry. Yet others seemed to stock up with certain perishable or tinned goods, for which there would be a rush to buy because periods of scarcity of particular items would follow. Sometimes there were problems of the availability of sugar, or fine quality rice, or even milk in polypacks, a recent innovation which could hardly compete with the old fashioned milk, cream, and curd vending women who would hawk fresh milk, curds or yoghurts, early in the morning from door to door even in winter, rousing the late sleepers with their cries of '*malako*, *kisli malako*'. The milk vendors were invariably people of integrity. We never were given short weight or milk adulterated with water, the common dodge of their Indian counterparts. The woman who sold vegetables from a lean-to, where our little street came out on Pushkin Boulevard, was the same. She never ever forgot to greet us with *salaam aleikum* when we passed.

NOTES

1. Jean-Luc Racine, 'Le cercle de Samarcande: geopolitique de l'Asie centrale', in *Le Cercle de Samarcande*, 2e trimestre, 1997, *Herodote*, Revue de geographie et de geopolitique, No. 84 (Paris), particularly the schematic maps on pp. 11, 14-15, 18, 22-3, 33.
2. Edward Allworth (ed.) with Helene Carrere d'Encausse, Ian Murray Matley, Karl H. Menges, Johanna Spector, Arthur Sprague, *Central Asia: A Century of Russian Rule* (Columbia University Press, N.Y. and London, 1967), which despite a generation of US and French research on Central Asian nationalities, is still the best general reference on the subject.
3. 'Kennan has declared that the general affect of Cold War extremism was to delay rather than hasten the great change that overtook the Soviet Union at the end of 1920s. . . . The ailing Yuri Andropov, during his brief tenure, failed to consolidate his control, but was sensitive to the turbulence beneath the surface and consequently paved

the way for Gorbachev . . . a product of the surging growth in Soviet education . . . new professions and the social mix that resulted . . . of booming blackmarkets, changing lifestyle, new class divisions and new expectations.' Diego Cordovez, Selig S. Harrison, *Out of Afghanistan. The Inside Story of the Soviet Withdrawal* (New York, Oxford University Press, 1995).

4. A clear account of changes in state power during the collapse of Soviet Union in this region will be found in Dilip Hiro, *Between Marx and Muhammad: The Changing Face of Central Asia* (Harper Collins, London, 1994).
5. The European information, which was gathered from these researches, has been distilled in the British Raj-obsessed books by Peter Hopkirk, about the linkages of European scholarly research with espionage. Three of them specifically deal with European travellers in Central and Inner Asia: *Foreign Devils on the Silk Road* (1980), *Setting the East Ablaze* (1984), *The Great Game* (1990). A summary will be found in his wife, Kathleen Hopkirk's *Central Asia, A Traveller's Companion* (John Murray, London, 1993). A guide to early Indian antiquarian research on Sino-Indian culture contact in the region will be found in Dilip Kumar Biswas, 'Acharya Prabodh Chandra Bagchi: Shatabarsher Shraddhanjali' (in Bengali), in *Bangadarshan*, New Series, No. 3, November 2001, Bankim Bhavan Gaveshana Kendra, Kantalpara, Naihati, West Bengal.
6. Marshall Hodgson, *The Venture of Islam: Conscience and History in a World of Civilisation*, 3 vols. (Chicago University Press, 1974) and Richard M. Eaton, *The Rise of Islam and the Bengal Frontier*, 1204-1760 (New Delhi, Oxford University Press, 1994).
7. The best secular account of the incorporative and assimilative dominance of mediaeval political Islam is by Muhammad Habib, 'Life and Thought of Ziyauddin Barani', particularly Section 5 'The Governing Class', in *Politics and Society during the Early Mediaeval Period: Collected Works of Professor Muhammad Habib* (ed. by K.A. Nizami, New Delhi, People's Publishing House, Vol. 2, 1981).
8. A dated account, still useful for reference will be found in Edward Allworth (ed.) et al., *Central Asia: A Century of Russian Rule* (Columbia University Press, New York and London, 1967). Many subsequent historians have described the Jadid Enlightenment in the early twentieth century and after 1999, there has been Uzbek official licence for recognizing the work of many leaders, most of whom, builders of Soviet Uzbekistan, were liquidated by Stalin in purges of the 1930s. But there is still no substantial research on the content of the Turki, Tajik, or Arabic and Persian texts of the reformers themselves.

2

Omens and Portents

TERRORISM AND COUNTER-TERROR COME TO TASHKENT

When classes resumed in January 1999, my status in UWED was clarified. A new Head of Department of International Relations had joined after a stint at Stanford University. She made a point to come to meet me in the Political Science Department and ask for my help in teaching post-Second World War International Relations in the East, which I was happy to shift to. This was closer to my interests and more significant for Uzbek students than the exegesis of the Indian Constitution. Two one and half hour periods per week till the end of the semester in May were allocated to me. I began to get into the swing of the lectures and was just beginning to realize that there were practically no books in the library, except for encyclopaedias and some multi-national corporate gifts on marketing and management literature, when an unexpected event on 16 February jolted the Sleepy Hollow of Uzbekistan's capital.

I had dropped in, after a morning class in the University, to chat with friends in the Embassy. The First Secretary who looked after political affairs and the media would go on working, while I sat on his sofa reading the English summaries of the daily press in Uzbek and Russian, impeccably drafted by a Tatar lady translator, Shembiye Seitadjieva, but giving next to no news beyond which delegation the President had met the day before, which bureaucrat he had sacked; or whom he had transferred from one part of the country to another, in an attempt to maintain production schedules of cotton, the 'golden' (*zoloti*) crop on which Uzbek national pride had flourished after 1950. I was speaking facing the window, with the back to which the officer sat, when there was an almighty bang, somewhere beyond the trees at the back of the Embassy. Then there was another, somewhat less loud: I must have looked curious. He said, 'Oh, probably repairs in the Metro.' He was referring to the large junction, Amir Timur Khieboni, that passed directly under our Embassy. The faint rumble of a passing train would sometimes be thrown up from it. But within two or three minutes, there were more bangs. The Counsellor put his head round the door and said 'my windows have cracked: were those bombs?'

I describe this in detail because in 1942 and 1943, at the height of the August Uprising, when acid bulbs were hurled at people who travelled in Calcutta's trams, then run by a British company, and again in the mid-1970s when the London Underground was thick with notices warning people about suitcases being left in it by IRA bombers, I use to fantasize about whether I would run for cover or just freeze and gape if an explosion took place in my presence. In the event, the two of us in the room did neither; the initial reaction being to think that it might not have happened. My next reaction was to make tracks for home where my wife was. The driver, despite a couple of years of national service driving trucks for the Soviet Army in Hungary on the borders of Austria, could apparently not recognize bombs when he heard them: or perhaps he had learned to mask his feelings, when he did. I took him inside the flat and asked him to listen to the local Uzbek news. Five blasts had taken place, half an hour before, around the city centre and several people were dead. One had been on the road entering the principal Government Offices (south of the Turkestan Palace theatre), which President Karimov was scheduled to enter two minutes later. This was obviously an attempt on his life. What was striking was the speed and total brevity with which the news was managed.

On returning to the Embassy after lunch, I saw no signs of panic on the road. It was remarkable that detailed information about where the blasts had taken place was not available or at least not shared. Several months later I heard that the dacha in which the bombs were manufactured, on Abdullah Kakhor Street near Tizikovka, was identified by the evening. It was very close to the UN offices and the airport. Rumours were being exchanged by the Indian wives. For the next few days, the tobacco multinational, UzBAT, a subsidiary of British American Tobacco, which had been permitted by President Karimov to monopolize the tobacco industry, would brief its expatriate wives regularly about flying them out of the country at half a day's notice, the minute the situation was deemed unstable.

Then I visited the residence of an Uzbek colleague. I asked what they thought about the events. They spoke in lowered voices and I realized that secrecy had been ingrained into the public tradition when two people privately and frankly discussed political matters. Whether the product of Bukharan despotism or Communist rigidity, the end product led to the muffling of protest or dissent. Several people had been rounded up by the security forces, their pictures were being shown on television, and they must have been Tajiks of southern Uzbekistan. How did they know, I asked, that the culprits were Tajiks? Look at the faces on the television, it was pointed out. Indeed those shown had narrower features and darker hues than the more fair and burly Uzbeks.

I was to notice this tendency to impute ethnic labels over and over again. People of all classes nowadays in India find it easy to ascribe criminality to archetypal 'Muslims' or to 'one community found in every terrorist act' instead of arguing that poverty, and unemployment, or the malaise of the 'Lonely Crowd' even among well to do people, might lead individuals of any class or community, Christian, Hindu, Buddhist, or Muslims, to criminality. Affluent as well as more indigent Uzbeks make nonsense of theories of class structure: they ascribe 'terrorism' to 'Tajik fundamentalists'. The repression of the ethnically stereotyped Other is now a global phenomenon. In the case of my Uzbek friends, who were culturally Muslims, as much as they were ex-communists, a strong anti-Jewish sentiment was also marked. Jews were not liked, though their professional efficiency was acknowledged. There was little regret that the Jewish doctors of Bukhara had scattered out westwards. Kazakhs were rustic, Kyrgyz were brigands, Turkmen were braggarts, and of course the Tajiks must be terrorist crooks. This was not said openly, but certainly it was the first reaction.

As the facts emerged, it appeared that the plot had been hatched by a religious fundamentalist group of devout Muslims holed up in northern Tajikistan to prepare bombs inside Tashkent, pack them into cars, and drive them to important places to be set off. The plot had misfired when people in one of the cars meant to assassinate the President, who was supposed to attend a cabinet meeting in the government offices, had driven in a few minutes before his convoy arrived. The Captain of the Presidential guard in a pilot vehicle, was able to alert the drivers of the convoy of three black cars that drove abreast, one carrying Karimov, to halt close to the President's official residence, the Ak Sarai or 'White House' nearby.[1]

Most of the windows of the massive glass Cabinet Secretariat were blown in. The terrorists escaped. The same happened in the futuristic tower block of the National Bank of Uzbekistan, where the cash counter area to which I used to go was also blown up. It had to be shrouded in great plastic sheets for months, while banking for me and our neighbourhood shifted to another building on Pushkin Boulevard. The presidential reaction was swift. He announced to the High Assembly of notables, the Oli Majlis or Parliament, that he had identified the religious sectarians responsible for the act, whom he dubbed as Hizb-ut-Tahrir and other miscreants, and that he would break the arms and the legs of the evil doers. Various bodies of notables responded with loyal addresses, affirming the same sentiments.

One such space of authoritarianism turned out to be my University. Word had it that several students in the hostels had been told to pack their bags and go. They were the poorer ones—or those who came from small towns in the country areas. They have been given no more than twelve hours to go. It was said that the charge made against them by one of the Pro-Vice-Chancellors, a notorious Party hack, was that pamphlets of commentaries of the Koran had been found in their rooms. A Dean of one of the faculties, no better scholar himself than such functionaries, according to common opinion, had ventured to point out that some of the students were among the best in the faculty. He had been asked whether he knew what his job was. Yes, he had said, to be concerned with the affairs of the faculty. Then just do your job and don't question my doing mine, had been the P-V-C's reply. Teachers bemoaned the loss of good students. But they had no more say about this than Jawaharlal Nehru University authorities had, when their students were picked up and taken away during the Indian Emergency in 1976. What was different in post-Soviet Uzbekistan was that authoritarianism had gained almost total hegemony over the public mind of the political classes. In India, such a culture, whenever and by whomever it is attempted, is contested by a variety of democratic institutions of civil society.

The number of arrests grew, as did the numbers of the dead. Rumours spread that Karimov's cronies had staged the events to increase the repression of militant Islam. It was also said by the authorities that the stories were being put out by critics of the Karimov regime such as Muhammad Salih, the Khwarizmian, who had run against him for President in 1992, and had gained many votes in his own region but nowhere else. Or else the rumours were ascribed to Abdurahman Pulatov, a human rights activist and liberal of the 1980s, who had taken shelter in the USA. There were suspicions that the regime was staging a drama to gain popularity by spinning a tale of national crisis. This was repeated in the Russian and English language press, the latter published freely in neighbouring Bishkek (once Frunze), the capital of Kyrgyzstan. It was coolly passed from mouth to mouth in the cocktail parties of the Western diplomatic missions and through their conduits. However, Indian and Bangladesh diplomats whom I met did not indulge in such rumours. They reacted much as supporters of the contemporary state system in South Asia have always done—there was, they would say, no alternative to firm government, if stability had to be gained.

It was generally accepted that the Hizb-ut-Tahrir was creating instability. This was an obscure coterie of Islamic fanatics, who had broken away from the Muslim Brotherhood of Egypt, on the ground that it was not theologically radical or extremist enough, and that it was necessary to abolish the modern state and declare a universal Caliphate of all true believers in *jihad*. They were believed to be socially influential in the economically run-down region of Ferghana and the backward valleys on both sides of the Kyrgyz-Tajik border, north of Termez and Afghanistan. This was then in turmoil under the Taliban. The actual bombings, however, were the work of religious terrorists of the Islamic Movement of Uzbekistan from a hideout across the Kyrgyz border in Tajikistan. As the trials continued in a non-descript building across the canals from the Turkestan Palace, and were televized, a senior US diplomat told one of my acquaintances that Karimov's kangaroo trials were a travesty of justice. This diplomat was very much in service when Donald Rumsfeld, two years later, turned Islam Karimov round into an ally of the USA.

The bomb blasts and their fallout got no more than one little sound byte from the BBC and perhaps from the CNN. In Oxford during the summer vacation of 1999, no one really bothered about turmoil in Tashkent. At a seminar organized by an ex-British Ambassador to Uzbekistan and his wife, with South Korean business support in St. Antony's College in June, eminent scholars inveighed against the lack of a free market in Uzbekistan, insufficient infrastructure for economic development and Karimov's excessive authoritarianism. Except for an young Indian scholar, Bhavna Dave, trained in the USA, who spoke about traditional clan or *juz* kinship-structure politics in Kazakhstan, the rest of the liberal dons were no more specific about the problems of Central Asia than those of the London School of Economics or Oxbridge had been about India under the Emergency. If people in Calcutta thought of Tashkent as just another Russian city where Lal Bahadur Shastri had died, the British and the French still saw Central Asia as an exotic part of the back of beyond a destination for inexpensive tourist excursions or of hardship postings, with inflated pay. Already events were maturing with growing economic distress and political disturbance. A lid had to be firmly put on it.

A PICNIC IN FERGHANA

While I was reading secondary sources on mediaeval Turkestan history in the Bodleian Library in Oxford in summer, the gunmen began to take extremist measures in the hill fastnesses north and south of Ferghana. We had taken a guided tour of the north-eastern valley some months before it came back to world news. This was in the spring with TWIG, the Tashkent Women's International Group, by chartered plane to the town of Marghilan and the archaeological site of Kuwwa in Central Ferghana. The Marghilan journey, organized by enterprising women of the expatriate communities, in a group of which my wife was a member, gave insight into a region whose local dynamics are often ignored by social scientists and journalists, who are content to merely lump it among the trouble spots of the world after 1989.

Recent US material put out by the 'national security state' lobbies, both Democrat and Republican, have completely ignored the fact that the *wadi* (valley) used to be a prosperous, though antiquated, area before the end of the Afghan war turned it into a nightmare construct of Western strategists. Hence, one media standby of such groups, the competent specialist Ahmed Rashid, approvingly quotes the study of Anthony Lake, 'the former national security advisor to President Clinton' . . . 'in which he labelled the Ferghana region one of the world's three "hottest danger zones" for the future'.[2]

Jawaharlal Nehru in *Glimpses of World History* and *The Discovery of India* expressed the early twentieth-century Indian fascination with Babur's nostalgia for his roots in the far northern towns and villages of the valley between Osh and Tashkent. Driven out of his father's principality at the end of the fifteenth century by struggles of Mughals from the east and Uzbeks from the north of Turkestan, this Timurid with a Mughal mother (whose father, Yunus Khan's mausoleum still exists in Tashkent near the procurator's court which we have just mentioned) wrote in the *Baburnama*, from first Afghanistan and then Hindostan, with longing for the melons, the peaches and the other fruits of Ferghana. The valley receded from popular memory after the Uzbek conquest. Towns like Khokhand, Marghilan, Nomonghan and Andijan were noted only in the nineteenth century as being on the route from the Chinese outpost of Kashgar in south-west Xinjiang to Osh and Tashkent in Russian Turkestan. This was the route taken by Indian merchants and British spies until 1917 from Srinagar, Leh, Yarkand and Kashgar into Russian domains. At the same time, Muslim preachers from north India were making their way into the area. A scholar from an Indian *madrasa* nicknamed Mullah Hindustani is heard of, preaching in the Syr Darya valley just before the Russian revolution.

The Bolsheviks closed the southern borders of Central Asia after they suppressed the Basmachi revolts in the 1920s. Ferghana became a backwater till it gained modern relevance during the troubles of 1989 and 1990 between Uzbeks and Kyrgyz for control of land and housing, when there were Uzbek riots against migrants from the Caucasus and Crimea (Meskhetian Turks and Chechens) who had been deported there by Stalin for alleged pro-German sympathies before 1945. Instead of recognizing the tensions over nationality, Gorbachev had chosen to propagate that these riots were instigated by fundamentalism from the south (Afghanistan, or Arabia). Hints were rife that Wahhabi preachers and money from Saudi Arabia, as well as Turkish Right wing funding for Korans was available for the renaissance of orthodox Islam. Islam Karimov visited the orthodox town of Nomongan on the northern side of the Syr Darya as it comes out of the mountains, to admonish fundamentalists. He was shouldered aside in a public meeting by a young Islamic radical, Tohir Abduhalilovitch Yuldashev, then a twenty-four year old mullah, in what was in 1992 'the Islamic underground' trying to establish an Islamic state in Central Asia. The latter grabbed the microphone and demanded that the communist remnants in the new regime should declare themselves Islamists then and there. Karimov was said to have muttered *kharasho* (which means good, but in this case obviously, a dismissive 'all right then') and walked off the platform, never to publicly venture back into the town. In 1992 itself Ahmed Rashid was told by an Imam of a mosque in Nomongan that 'they had no time for constitutional games'. They wanted Karimov to proclaim an Islamic state then and there; . . . visiting the Mosque was to become compulsory for all Muslims, including leaders of the state who must pray together with the people; Friday (to) be announced as a day off, and religious schools to open immediately'.

The troubles of this time came from a group called Adolat (Justice), which broke away from the Erk party, which in its turn had broken away from the larger Birlik party of liberals, who were against communism in the period of Glasnost. These rifts on the basis of increasingly fanatical principles were typical of a period of dissolution in the Caucasus and Central Asia. Its appropriation by religious fundamentalists supplied ammunition for conservatives, who had earlier supported Gorbachev to recapture power on the southern periphery of the CIS. The group in Nomongan had formed the Adolat Party for social and community self-determination. The Khwarezm poet, Salih Madaminov, better known by his pseudonym Muhammad Salih, led Erk, while the Pulatov brothers were leaders of the more urban Birlik party. All of them were lumped together by the new regime as dissidents. As it happened, Islamic groups had also sprung up, such as Tovba (Repentance), Islam Lashkarlari (Fighters for Islam) and Hizb-i-Islami (Islamic Party). The situation was not very different from that in Kashmir at the same time.

Geo-political issues of autonomy for small nationalities were hijacked by fundamentalism, emboldened by its victory against communism and by US backing for the Afghan struggle. Authoritarian governments in Central Asia sought to resist this fundamentalism by chauvinism. The same thing was going on in Kashmir during the Narasimha Rao government in the early 1990s. When that government lost its legitimacy and the BJP took power through the National Democratic Alliance in 1998, this chauvinism turned to militarism counter-dependant on Pakistani militarism.

The President of Uzbekistan could hardly be blamed for lumping the small factions in Ferghana together as threats to national security. He appeared to triumph in the 1990s when the small parties were marginalized, and, according to them beaten up or cowed down. But the situation changed when Yuldashev, accompanied by a younger friend, Juma Khojiev, who had fought in the Soviet Army in Afghanistan, been impressed by the Mujahids, and called himself Nomongani, travelled for help to Turkey and Pakistan, and ultimately found support from Islamic rebels in Tajikistan, as well as from the Taliban. Nomongani set up a guerilla training camp in a farm called Hoit, near Garm, in an inaccessible valley of the Karategin region, just south of the Kyrgyz border overlooking Ferghana, with consequences that led to the bomb blasts of 16 February.

I had visited Ferghana on my first trip to Uzbekistan in 1997, to lecture in the universities of Andijan and Nomongan. On the way there my very hospitable guide, Professor Rustombek Samsiddinov, had shown us some *madrasas* by the road that had been newly opened, but he was typically cautious when my companion from our Embassy and I asked for details about whether they were teaching new and radical ideas. He was more interested in the prospects of new wealth in Ferghana from the Asaka factory where Daewoo were mass-producing cars for the Uzbeks. There was nothing remarkable, even among the students, who seemed to be the average that I had found in Georgia or in Tashkent. So in 1999 we enthusiastically seized the TWIG opportunity to take a new look at Ferghana.

It was of course only a day's excursion, organized by the wife of an Ambassador from the Baltic States, in which we would be flown in and out, shown a traditional silk factory in Marghilan and also archaeological excavation near by. The flight out was breath taking, between two snow ranges, much as tourists are taken from Kathmandu to Pokhra in Nepal with peaks rising on either side. As we touched down, there were girls dressed in traditional Uzbek costume blowing on the long Alpine-style horn called Tarnai, similar to the ones in Tibetan monasteries and dancing with hand movements, common in Uzbek rituals. Driven in a bus, we were piloted and followed by police cars flashing red lights on top and stopping traffic wherever we went from morning to evening. Whether this was to keep us away from the people, or whether more probably it was merely the ceremonial practice of a bureaucratic regime, we could not say. Perhaps it was the presence of an Ambassador himself and several diplomats' wives, which was sufficient to keep us under ministering care and surveillance.

The silk factory was an old fashioned one. It sprawled over several sheds with pink-blossomed trees in bloom in between them, as it was early Bahor, which is what they call spring (*bahar* is the same word in Urdu). The processes of turning the mulberry into yarn, dyeing it, and then weaving the complicated colours, which run in the traditional stripes of red, yellow, and green and other combinations, known as Khan Atlas, were being carried out by men as well as women. The processes were carefully explained to the women who were interested. As important for the hosts was the welcoming traditional round, raised-edge *lipioshki* or bread, somewhat like north Indian *nan*, offered to each guest along with ceremonial green tea. We were taken to lunch, organized by the businesswomen's association of Marghilan, in a big park where a large Catherine wheel with bucket chairs was being spruced up for children in the spring. On the way the guide on the bus gave us a local version of the name of the town. Alexander, he said, on his sweep north from Samarkand had reached the place more than two millennia before. The inhabitants timidly came out to meet him and asked for mercy. They bore platters of murgh-i-nan, cocks meat and the local bread for his troops. Alexander was pleased and called the town Marghinan, and so it has remained with 'u' elided into 'a'. Apocryphal this may be, but it is a fact that many towns in the region claim the presence of the hero whom the Russians call Aleksandr Makedonski. Indeed, central Tashkent has an old tomb from which a tree has grown, supposedly out of a cut in the earth made by the latter's sword.

The lunch was notable for the pile of food that was becoming common in all such gatherings—a spread on the table of *kalbasa* or cold cuts of all varieties, beef, lamb, tongue, chicken, pork, duck, and that great Uzbek delicacy (which my wife passed on with a shudder), horse meat, along with delicious cold salads, Russian and Korean, and then *lagma* or soup of noodles, meat, and vegetables, then *somsa* (meat patties), then finally, *plov*, somewhat like Indian *biriyani* but far more oily and sweet, the sign among the Uzbek that the repast was over. Vodka and wine were plied in abundance. With a few variations in this sequence, this was the standard menu at every invitation. At family gatherings the all-popular *shashlik* or skewered barbecued meat might also be served, as well as *manti*, a version of the Tibetan *momo*.

Dances of Ferghana were put on for the diners through the lunch. These were accompaniments to Uzbek songs and music, the core of such entertainments: the dances were more in the nature of improving the level of festivities. In India, the dance form has a separate dignity of its own, it origins devotional in character. This is not to be found in Central Asia, where dancing comes naturally with food, drink, song and jollity. Also there were from the head of the table, presided over by the ubiquitous *tamaga* or master of ceremony, the interminable toasts by notables accompanied with florid speeches eulogizing guests, hosts, and *tout le compagnie*.

Fortified and elevated with so much sustenance, we made our way out, passing a monumental new statue of Ahmed al-Farghani, an early mediaeval mathematician, whom the Uzbek government, then intent on devising new Muslim heroes in place of their old Russian Communist ones, had just commemorated. There, my wife was waylaid by a group of buxom, middle aged, matrons who asked where she came from, *Induskii ili Pakistanskii*? Being told she was Indian, they clasped her to their bosoms and bussed her firmly on both cheeks. It was the standard one she received from many ladies in the country, who would compliment her for being *guzol* and *chiroili* (Uzbek words for good looks) and for coming from a great country, friendly to the Uzbeks. The compliments were genuine. Many times she was asked to pose for pictures. Expressing themselves in these personal ways, they unfortunately found no reciprocal concomitant in Indians themselves, who were condescending about having to live among 'Musalmans'.

From Marghilan, we drove along tree-lined roads, but a relatively bare countryside. There was only the hint of hills on the southern horizon. Passing orchards of apple trees, about to bloom, we came to a late ancient, fortified settlement, known in the old texts as al-Quwwa or the refuge. This had been a staging point of the Silk Road, before it reached the Chinese deserts. A small new town had grown up around the diggings. On the way, the guide spoke of the digging in the 1920s of the Great Ferghana Canal, which we were following. This had, he said, been so welcomed by the masses for the fertility it would bring to the previously arid foothills, that the women had turned out from the villages to dig out the earth and welcome water with their bare hands. Later we met an

American historian, researching the KGB archives in the Ferghana towns, which the Uzbeks had opened to him. He had come to interview Dinora Azimova's mother, Rakhima Aminova, who had written the first thesis on agrarian development in the region under communism. His version had less euphoria. The conscription of the masses for labour service was certainly not entirely voluntary. As time passed, I was to note the general tone of self-congratulation in the popular Uzbek versions of their recent past, their capacity to romanticize and to construct a rosy picture of whatever any of their 'glorious forebears', whom they called *Bobomiz*, Our Forefathers, however ferocious they may have been. This showed through in the new school textbooks, in which Russian initiatives were quietly forgotten, and Uzbek actors replaced for them. Kuwwa was certainly dressed up, with fake ramparts and dancers on stilts and bread breaking laid on for us, as usual. The welcome seems to have been the standard Soviet one, continuing in post-Soviet times. I had come across an exactly similar ceremonial in a UNESCO conference in Georgia in 1995, when we were taken to visit a very old, mediaeval Orthodox Christian Cathedral in the hills above Tbilisi.

We had no expertise to judge the value of the antiquities and excavated artefacts we were shown in Kuwwa, but the entire village seemed to have turned out to gape at the foreign visitors. This was the only place where people were far more interested in the European or American guests, and merely curious about us. There were droves of police keeping the crowds at a distance.

The entire road and area seemed to be made of the hardest earth. The coming of water through the canal must have changed the traditional life of the people from arid steppe to fertile fruit groves and vineyards, as the blossoming trees bore witness. We would have liked to know what the people were feeling, now that independence had come back to them. These certainly were the people among whom fundamentalism tried to rear its head that summer.

THE ROAD SOUTH TO SAMARKAND

Another trip we made was our first among many to Samarkand. The heart of Uzbekistan lies on a road running south to the Zarafshan ranges, and then down through the Iron Gates, to

Termez, Afghanistan and the Khyber Pass and thence South Asia. The road itself marks the great change that has come over the land since the Middle Ages or even since Tsarism. Of one part of it, after the Syr Darya has been crossed, Babur wrote in his memoirs that it was called 'Ha-Darwesh'—after the desolate wind which howled through its wastes, screaming 'alas, Dervish'. Of the reaches after that, George Nathaniel Curzon, later Viceroy of India, wrote in his travel account of the 1890s that it was so rough and uncultivated, that his horse-carriage took several days to traverse it. Tsarists officially called it the Golodnaya or Hungry Steppe; and Soviet agriculture brought water piped from long distances to it, leading degradation of the water resources of the Syr Darya and pollution of the Aral Sea.

The land was under cotton cultivation, until the hills were reached. The road had been improved when Brezhnev's tanks rolled into Afghanistan after 1980. At one point, the dividers had been removed. It was possible to block off the entire level road so that armoured planes could land on it during emergencies. When it entered the hills, it did so by an easy gradient and came down into a little valley known as Timur's Gates, which the ferocious Amir used to pass, on his northern expeditions. Here, a wayside village close to a brawling stream called Bahmalsoy, boasted a small bazaar. Along the road, vendors sold fresh apples and oranges, as well as jars of local honey of many varieties at the cheapest prices. Then one passed through one upland village after another until the point where one looked at the ancient ramparts of the earliest Soghdian settlement, which later became Samarkand.

Samarkand and Bukhara are names that conjure up an exotic image. Their histories are different. Samarkand had been a principality noted for its heroes battling with the ancient Iranian rulers, long before Alexander met Roxane (presumably Rukhsana) in its fortress, which he had captured. The city is surrounded by hills over which ruins lie scattered. Archaeologists still come across artefacts of the most ancient periods, for which there is an excellent museum: as well as a good archaeological institute. One of these ruins, beside what is known as the old bus stand, a cemented area gone wild, is the two-thousand-year old remnant of a Soghdian wall. Packed earth rises like a bastion with thin bricks which would crumble if they were pulled out. Next to it is a scarped drop to the road, below which post-Soviet patriotic enthusiasm has placed a rank of tawdry life-size statues of warriors, meant to look like Soghdians. This is the usual case of the old Soviet mentality of prettying up the past by cloaking the actual ruins. The view from the scarp is worth coming to see. Samarkand monuments lie spread over the horizon, like a cabinet photograph.

After the Greeks left, the old fortress' fortune declined. It was reduced to the status of other cities like Bukhara, the ancient Buddhist *vihara*, ruled by pre-Islamic *khudats*. When the Arabs stormed across the Oxus, these were swept aside. Legend had it that one of the companions of the Prophet himself, a good looking youth, had earlier come to the city on a mission to convert the kafirs. Entranced by his looks rather than his holy message, the girls of Samarkand pursued him, offering him their favours. The virginal missionary, loth to succumb, ultimately cut-off his own head and bearing it in his hand, walked into a well on one of the hills close by. He became known as Shah-i-Zinda, the living holy ruler. When Samarkand turned to Islam, its oldest shrine was built over the well. This still exists, with a series of intricate chambers, up and down steps, through arched doors with ancient pre-Islamic designs on them, in patches covered by the classic blue tiles of Samarkand's mediaeval age. The chambers below are smaller, while the ones above the slope of the hill are larger and chronologically of a later period. The tops of later shrines are built around it. Their ornate arched gateways are covered with designs of the same blue and other coloured tile work.

The city was, like others, part of the region sacked by Chingiz in 1217-18 rose a new capital on its ruins, at the end of the fourteenth century, built by the son of an indigent chief of a mountain village (not far south, Shahr-i-Sabz, the green city). Timur was a local Turk of the Barlas tribe, who organized mercenary bands to gain power over the countryside. After a career of ups and downs, he subjugated rulers from Tashkent to Bukhara. Then began a stupendous career of sack and rapine, extending from Delhi in India to Damascus in Syria, the borders of Egypt, and of the Byzantine rulers, of what had still not wholly become Ottoman Turkey. Amir Timur, as he remained known till the end of his years, though I have been told by the eminent mediaeval historian, Satish Chandra that in official documents he has been referred to as Aanh Hazrat, the 'Highest Himself', has been much reviled in world history.

His massacres, and the abusive term in hostile histories, of Timur-i-Lang (Timur the Lame from a wound received in his youth) led to his attaining among Europeans almost mythical status as 'the oriental despot' of all times. Marlowe's Elizabethan drama about him has him cry out to subject princes, yoked to his chariot, as he lashes them, 'Hola, ye pampered jades of Asia! What, can ye not ride ten thousand leagues a day?' And, in India, historians from centuries before the years of rule by his descendant Babur, noted the hundred thousand people slaughtered in Delhi in the last decade of the fourteenth century. Mughal historians, however, showed awestruck respect, particularly those who accepted Shah Jahan's revival of the Timur myth in the sixteenth century, at the very time Marlowe wrote his play. The British historians showed sanctimonious distaste, forgetting their own systematic drain of wealth from India and their own excesses in Delhi and Lucknow during uprising of 1857. Like any European or Russian monarch of the Middle Ages and the Renaissance, Timur's personality has run into aesthetic dialectics.

The plunder of West Asia and north India ended up in the beautification of Timur's capital. Again, the rustic legends so plentiful among Uzbek guides, have it that casting about for a capital to beautify, he looked for lands with fresh air. For this, joints of meat were hung up at certain points. One that was hung up at Samarkand on one of the promontories did not putrefy for several days, while those hung up in well-known old cities such as Bukhara had turned rancid. So he chose this area as the headquarters of his establishment. The fact is that Samarkand has the greatest space for city building close to Timur's mountain fastness in Shahr-i-Sabz. Also it was a nodal point for expeditions to all sides of the compass.

The Uzbeks, who conquered the region more than a century after Timur's death, were in a such a state of tribal fission without any roots other than the bigotry of their mosques and madrasas in Bukhara, that the people of Turkestan lost their feel for state history. When the Russians took over, it was folk myth, which remained in the popular consciousness. Not all the rigorous research of Russian mediaeval historians, led by V.V. Barthold, could turn these myths into a rational popular history. This still eludes Central Asia. It was to the advantage of modern imperialism to keep these fantasies alive. Only the elite intelligentsia, with their version of rationality, could manipulate the popular mind. Uzbeks, in any case, are eager to appropriate any martial traditions that glorify the territorial expansion in their past.

Timur flourished in days when the rulers of the Christian frontier in the Iberian Peninsula still lived in interaction and struggle with the Moorish rulers of Spain. One of them sent an Ambassador to his court, Ruy Gonzalez de Clavijo. His account of the emperor is as resplendent about an age of courtly chivalry as any of the accounts of Froissart in the age of the Hundred Years War between France and England or of the Portuguese Ambassador Paes to the court of Vijayanagara some time later. Clavijo came to gardens on the hills, stately buildings, and finally courtyards, surrounding a royal palace, the Kok Sarai, where the king sat, surrounded by officials on all four quarters. This description could be the conceptual core of variations on a theme, which would be repeated by travellers to the Mughal Empire of India like Roe, Bernier, and Tavernier. Many of these buildings of Timur's age had crumbled, many of the gardens and shrines had gone into disrepair, when, in the early sixteenth century, a most improbable traveller, Sidi Ali Rais, a Ottoman Turk admiral (whose navy had been routed by the Portuguese off Diu in Gujarat) had to flee back to Istanbul via Delhi and Samarkand. His journal reads like a guidebook of pilgrimages to broken palaces and ruined shrines, without much maintenance by the Uzbeks, who had just conquered the land from Babur and the Safavid invaders from Iran.

One of the finest accounts of the city, available for the general reader, about a period slightly before Sidi Ali, is in the *Baburnama*. Before talking of the three occasions in his youth when he raised his standard and claimed to rule the city (only to be driven out by the older Uzbek prince and adventurer, Muhamad Shaibani Khan, who on the third occasion also carried off Babur's elder sister, Khanzada Begum) Babur describes the delectable air, pleasant gardens, and general ease of the cultured population of Late Timurid Samarkand.[3] He delves into the etymology of the name and speculates whether it should be read as 'Simiz Kint' or Fat City, in the sense of a prosperous place.

This culture was expressed in the richly ornamented and gold encrusted decorations inside the tomb of Timur, the Gur-Emir and in the tile work on the portals of the line of tombs of Timurid princesses, which cluster down the slope of the narrow lane that comes down from the Shah-i-Zinda, and ends in a steep flight of stairs. Another symbol of the time is the great madrasa built by the Amir's grandson, Ulugh Beg, one of the many that he raised in the towns from here to Bukhara, next to the Registan or dusty ground, the main marketplace. Babur writes about setting up camp on its roof and firing arrows into the besieging Shaibanid troops.[4] A half-century later, an Uzbek prince, Yelenktash Bahadur, who then held the city, constructed a magnificent frame for the Registan, with the Shir-Dor Madrasa on its left, a replica more or less of the Ulugh Beg Madrasa facing it, in the style of twinning. This style was then being practised in Bukhara. Twenty years later, the same prince built a broader *madrasa*, with a superb mosque on its right flank, seeming to join the two in a backdrop, looking down a terrace leading to the Registan. This was the Tillah Kari, the gold-work dome, set between the two domes on either side, with flanking wall frontages, boldly designed in transverse striped colours, rather like a great hanging of Atlas cloth. The same blue of Samarkand predominates. It was in this city that we heard of the blue pottery workers who had later migrated to satisfy the demand for tiles in the cities of the Indian Doab. Perhaps it was one such family that settled in the wayside town of Khurja between Aligarh and Delhi, where blue pottery is still sold by the road.

Another monument of the pre-Uzbek era lies in the underground remains, dug out at the end of the nineteenth century by a Russian devoted to archaeology. The Observatory from where the scholarly Ulugh Beg constructed his astronomical tables were the model for Sawai Jai Singh's efforts at the Jantar Mantar in Delhi, and at Mathura and Jaipur in the eighteenth century. Ulugh Beg, like his grandfather, took the title of 'Kuragan' or son-in-law, since his grandmother too was descended from the Mughal imperial lineage. The tables are famous to astronomers as the 'Zij-i-Kuragani'. Contemporaries described the Observatory as a three-storied building on a hill outside the city, with a huge curving sextant for measuring the position of astral bodies. Ulugh Beg was so immersed in science, away from the tasks of kingship, that the fanatical mullah priesthood is reputed to have incited one of his sons to murder him and aspire for the throne of Samarkand. After the deed was done, the culprit too was stoned to death. (Even today, if the latter's name comes to the lips of a Samarkandi, he is supposed to cast a stone in execration of his memory.) This building also was pulled down and the sextant lay buried in rubble. A dome now covers it. A modern kiosk-like structure houses a Central Asian scientific history museum. Ulugh Beg's decapitated body was found, by a mid-twentieth century Russian archaeologist, at the feet of his grandfather's grave in the Gur-Emir, when the scientist defying Islamic sentiment dug into Timur's grave in 1940 to verify that this was actually the grim conqueror.

A visit to the remains of Samarkand is a trip into fantasy rather than a journey into carefully documented vestiges of the past: as would be the case if one visited cities of the Western end of the Silk Route like Bruges or Ghent in Belgium. The buildings are certainly there. But they are mixed up with restored facades and childish legends creating the ambience of a Never-Never Land. Nowhere is this more obvious than what I consider to be the most magnificent remnant of Timur's imperial vision.

Looking down from the Soghdian Wall, the perspective is straddled by a great hall with symmetrical structures on either side, domed and resplendent with coloured tiles and bold slashes of Kufic lettering, blazoning the Holy Koran at sky level. This is known as the Bibi Khanum; it is next to the quaint bazaar complex and close by Shah-i-Zinda, and meant to be in honour of Timur's principal queen, otherwise known as Saray Malik Khanum (the lady proprietor of the palace). The stories go that having seen the dimensions of the old Jama Masjid in the south of Delhi, Timur planned an even more magnificent version for his capital. Captured elephants brought materials from South Asia, and skilled artisans were forcibly brought to embellish the complex. But the ruler died before the massive portal in front of the courtyard, with its great inner arch, was completed. The portal soon began to collapse, and became what it is now, a remarkable ruin.

This is an occasion for another piece of patter from the guides whom you can hire for a few dollars. The Amir, busy on his expeditions, left his Begum to supervise the architect's labours. But the latter delayed. Taken to task, as the ruler was due to return soon, the architect importuned the queen for a kiss without which he would commit suicide. Fearful of delay, she consented. Such was the architect's passion that a red mark appeared on the queen's cheek. When her husband arrived, this aroused his suspicion. The architect was summoned. To avoid punishment he fled up to one of the towers of the portal and jumped off it. Becoming an angel, he was transported into the firmament and the gate that he was building was not completed. Anthropologists may draw their own conclusions about the fidelity of nomadic warriors' brides, and the way architects were punished for unreliable work. Actually, a beautiful tomb in front of the *madrasa* is supposed to be the tomb of the queen. It is possible that Shah Jahan, who is known to have been an admirer of Timur, drew the conception of the Taj Mahal from this ensemble of buildings, though in his own original way.

What never ceased to thrill me in many visits past the high walls of the complex into the courtyard, particularly in bright sunlight when the structures seem to glitter, is the semiotics of its architecture. The great curve of the central arch soars above one's strenuously craned neck as one looks up at it, even more than the Buland Darwaza of Fatehpur Sikri. Set in the middle of this perspective, in the centre of the courtyard, is an immense stone lectern, with eight squat pillars as a stand. An open book was meant to be placed on the top, a particularly holy copy of the Koran that Timur is supposed to have looted from Damascus. The book had been taken there, after it was stained with the blood of the third Just Caliph of Islam, Osman, stabbed as he read it. It no longer lies on its lectern on great occasions. Looted in turn by a Russian Governor General, it went as treasure to St. Petersburg. Khruschev had it sent back to the Central Asian Islamic Board at Tashkent. It is kept with great reverence in a quaint old library opposite the madrasa. If the librarian is not away for four leisurely hours of lunch, one may be lucky enough to see the leather bound parchment, or its more accessible copy.

Standing under the arch of Bibi Khanum and looking out to the lectern, one can imagine the conjuncture of the sword and the book, which militant Islam did represent 500 years ago. Fanatics unfortunately try to return to this, even in these troubled days. The present in Bibi Khanum is desolate. Tribal practices have taken over. The low pillars of the lectern are reputed to be used by peasant women, desirous of fertility, to crawl snakelike through its apertures, as a primitive charm. Many of the tiles as they crumble down are replaced by ersatz ones. They are being manufactured with intricate accuracy, but with no semblance to antiquity, in a workshop that is snuggled into one of the walls. Old photographs show that the Bibi Khanum was in total ruins before restoration of the heritage character of the building began. It is this which leads people without any knowledge of the history or the legends to wonder if the Disneyland character of such ensembles is not being overdone. My wife was able to ask for one of these tiles from the workshop. Fifty years later, similar tiles on the great arch will be mistaken for the real thing. In Uzbekistan 'the making of history' can be seen in practice. Mediaeval history is being produced in the workshop.

This visit was memorable for the snow that covered the city, giving the place a distinctly northern flavour. There is a distinctly Russian look about the houses in what had been the foreign rulers' quarters, with its rectangular grid roads, spotlessly clean, and embellished by a little cathedral. The line of separation from the old ruins is a striking avenue with a double line of trees where the first Governor-General's house, a small building, still stands. The rest of the buildings are the location of Samarkand University. On either side are monumental seated statues of Timur and Ulugh Beg. It is easy to look only at the principal historical remains and come back the same day to Tashkent, as we found many acquaintances were doing. This gave them no idea of the differences between the two cities in terms of social ambience. It was only after a year, when we returned for a seminar to commemorate Babur, that the far more rustic simplicity of the social milieu became evident.

At the foot of the hill below the Observatory, just before the road turns into the Tashkent Highway, is a throng of small shops, which sell the harder, more substantial *lipioshki* of Samarkand. This is much prized. It can keep for a long time and Rustom would buy several rounds for his relatives back home. He had the usual fable with which Uzbeks make any point. Soldiers going to a war hang a round loaf from the door for luck. It stayed fresh for them to take the first welcome bite from, when they came back from war. Much later I saw a painting of Uzbek soldiers going to the Polish front in 1914, with mothers hanging up their loaves. Rustom remembered taking a loaf with him on his military service in Hungary in 1982, and eating from it for three months. In any case the scene, as we stopped to buy the bread, could have taken place in any country village in Asia. Mainly women and some men and boys rushed to surround the car to thrust their wares and demand that we buy only theirs.

There were very few women we saw in Samarkand who wore

the modern costumes affected by the more Westernized Tashkent ladies. Apart from a few students, whom we saw the next year, all wore gowns to their ankles, covering the arms as well, in various vivid colours. In winter, they had long, cotton, *salwar*-type *pyjamas*. Most women had scarves covering their heads. This was the general dress to be seen in the older and more popular bazaars in Tashkent, as well as in Bukhara or Andijan. It marked out the Uzbek masses from the small upper crust of elites in northern Tashkent. The men of Samarkand too were more sober in their dress, more of them with the round skullcap or *tubiteika*—a word similar to the Hindustani *topi*—than would be occasionally found in Tashkent streets.

CULTURAL REVIVALISM

In early 1999, I heard talk, muted but critical, about Karimov's notification of a 'secular' dress code. Ostentation of religious costume, and signs of religious orthodoxy in dress had been made punishable offences. This was obviously directed against Islamic puritan dress codes, such as compulsory veiling and *hijabs* for women, or long facial hair for men, as the Taliban were then enforcing in neighbouring Afghanistan. People asked why exact signs of orthodoxy in dress had not been specified. It was also said that such victimization of taste would only lead to distinctive emphasis on manifestations of orthodoxy, and push people of simple faith into shows of defiance. The bomb blast added fuel to this speculation. There were signs of a private increase of celebration of religious symbols.

The Haj pilgrimage that year had attracted more than a thousand people. The aunt of one of our acquaintances had been one of them and he showed me a little chain of beads she had brought for him, like for other relatives, from Mecca. In those days he had no objection to eating pork. It was still sold, along with other meat, in the main bazaar of the Alaiski market, the most modern of Tashkent's many markets. A separate area would be demarcated by 2001. By that time our acquaintance had given up eating pork.

In March, Nauroz, an ancient Iranian festival, which some Turanians used to celebrate in central and parts of South Asia, was observed. Accounts of it being celebrated in Akbar's courts are well known. This was the old new year or spring festival when a gruel called *sumolak*, made of young wheat sprouts, is prepared overnight by women in each *mahalla*, sitting up through the night to stir the pot. Apart from the family eating this preparation, whose sweetness had come from seedlings, and not from any sugar or added flavour, it would be carried in jars by some people and offered to wayfarers as a mark of fellowship. Our Russian teacher told us that the practice had been discouraged in Soviet days as an example of what was seen as feudal, religious superstition. So, people would make the gruel in secrecy and were liable to punishment or reprimand if spies reported them. The prohibition was presumably to eradicate what Marxists considered pre-scientific superstition. It ignored the fact that such suppression of communal fellowship would only lead to religion reviving itself in the guise of private morality, all the more so as they failed to build a public morality, or to eradicate bureaucratic whims and corruption which were the reason for private distress and increased frustration.

Nauroz was a pleasant social practice marking the joy that came with new leaves and buds, which sprouted in profusion. The occasion brought the crowds out to impromptu shashlik stalls, massed bands and Uzbek dances and songs, in temporarily set up arenas in the central parks. The state encouraged it as a secular example of tradition from what it chose to believe were pre-Islamic times. The revival of the Haj, though it was intrinsically a community activity for individual piety meant the spread of Islamic faith along the margins of a society, cut-off from the subsidies of the Soviet era and looking for spiritual sustenance, as an alternative to materialism. It was in this overdetermined mood of doubt and transition that the bomb blasts heralded a Muslim call to martyrdom, from the dissident groups in Ferghana. A new phase began before our eyes in the transition of Uzbekistan.

NOTES

1. After this book had been drafted, my attention was drawn to the neoliberal and modernizing view, popular in the USA till August 2001, about the despotic tendencies of Karimov, a view which has been put out by the Islamist opposition to him in Uzbekistan. This view is to be found in Ahmed Rashid, *Jihad: The Rise of Militant Islam in Central Asia* (Yale University Press and Orient Longman, India, 2002). The role of the Islamic opposition has been much exaggerated by Rashid

in his exceptionally lucid text, though Islamic opposition and morality certainly exists along the Tajik and Kyrgyz borders of Ferghana and Surkhan Darya, and also among some of the urban underemployed. Rashid's description of the 16 February bombings will be found on pp. 149-50. The version that I give is my memory of the events, as I heard, or later heard about, them.

2. Ibid., p. 230. Rashid's endnote clarifies the US national security establishment source of his opinions, specifically the Council for Foreign Relations, Ferghana Valley Working Report, *Calming the Ferghana Valley: Development and Dialogue in the Heart of Central Asia* (New York, Century Foundation Press, 1999) and Anthony Lake, *Six Nightmares: Real Threats in a Dangerous World and How America Meets Them* (Boston, Little, Brown, 2000).
3. Annette Susannah Beveridge, translated from the original Turki text of Zahiru'd-din-Muhammad Babur Padshah Ghazi, *Baburnama* (*Memoirs of Babur*) (Low Price Publishers reprint edition, Delhi, 1997), pp. 74-86.
4. Ibid., p. 142 about the final siege of him in Samarkand by the Uzbeks: 'For convenience (to make the fort fast) . . . I took up quarters in the middle of the town in tents pitched on the roof of Aulugh Beg Mirza's College': on p. 147, he writes about his flight, leaving his supporters, the people of Samarkand, to starve, after Shaibani had defeated him and then 'interjected talk of peace . . . I took my mother Khanim, with me . . . other women folk went too . . . at this exodus, my elder sister, Khan-Zada Begum fell into Shaibaq Khan's hand'. In footnote 2, Mrs. Beveridge writes 'Babur's brevity is misleading: his sister was not captured, but married with her own and her mother's consent before attempt to leave the town was made', cf. Gulbadan Begum's *Humayun Namah*, f. 3b.

3

Social Ethnicity and Uzbek Islam

SOCIO-ECONOMIC TRANSITION

The next two years until September 2001 saw three tendencies. The economic crisis intensified. Marginalized orthodox groups such as the Hizb-ut-Tahrir were alienated from an elitist polity, and terrorism grew in Ferghana. Moves also began to stake out Uzbekistan's position in Asian relations.

The economy was still sheltered from the full impact of globalization. The misery of the common people was cloaked by an artificially low rate of exchange of Uzbek currency with regard to the dollar. The greenback had already become all-powerful in the CIS macro-region. The mental horizons of average people were, however, still dominated by Soviet practices. Yet new forces were making them increasingly aware of trends in the growth of conservatism in West and South Asia, as well as in Europe and the USA. The Uzbek state was ready to challenge the position of 'big brotherhood', which Yeltsin in his last days in power seemed to take.

Economically, Uzbekistan had been one of the better off Central Asian Republics of the USSR. Its plains agriculture, its foothill vineyards, its plentiful fruit farming, and its major share in USSR cotton production, as well as its gold mining, all had made it as prosperous as the far more vast span of Kazakhstan (which indeed is almost as big as India), a country devastated often by famine and the forced settlement of nomad pastoralists in the 1930s, and internally colonized in the north by Russian migration. Kazakhstan has very large segments of desert, one of which hides the top secret Baikonur cosmodrome, which even today is held on lease by the Russians. Kazakh mining and heavy industry, as much as the Uzbek economy was obsolescent. Stories of considerable oil reserves along the north and north-east bank of the Caspian in Atyrau and other areas of Kazakhstan were beginning to arouse the cupidity of the Bushes of Texas and Florida, represented in Central Asia among others by the Secretary of State in the time of the senior President Bush's dealings with Gorbachev, James Baker III and also by Condoleezza Rice who was to become Bush junior's National Security Adviser. Interest was shown also by the World Bank, which had begun a mission for reorganization of management and governance in Kazakhstan and in the Caucasian Republics. In the more populated, and still politically dominant Kazakh regions in the south, the population had been less thrusting than the Uzbeks.

The cotton boom of the Khruschev-Brezhnev period saw a remarkable development of prosperity for Uzbek entrepreneurial engagement in public marketing and industrial production in the countryside as well as in the towns. It was led by the First Secretary of the Republic till the 1980s, Sharaf Rashidov, whose name has now replaced Lenin in the main avenue, along which the government buildings lie, in place of the Governor-General's palace and gardens of the olden days. Rashidov, like Brezhnev with whom he was closely associated, was interested in friendship with the East. He visited India and wrote a poem sentimentally expressing affinity with Kashmir. He was a conservative, from a small country town (Dzizzak, between Tashkent and Samarkand). He banked on ethnic and racial identity as a source of political support to proliferate a network of favours for his cadres. In Brezhnev's last years, patronage and corruption flourished in the deals by which cotton was exchanged for other commodities in the fiscal barter arrangements that propped up Uzbekistan's prosperity. These too were the years of the Afghan War, in which Uzbekistan was the headquarters and military base, as well as one of the frontlines of the Soviet thrust south in the 1980s.

With Andropov, Chernenko, and Gorbachev, new brooms began to assert their dominance over the old bosses. In Uzbekistan, older elites were investigated by brutal procuratorial enquiries, such as the commission of the Armenian Gdlyan and his officials—to which even Karimov in his speech in 1999 referred as 'the activities of the Gdlyan gang'. Rashidov had died in disgrace; several functionaries went into penury, or died, falling ill in the harsh atmosphere of the times. For instance, the nuclear physicist Sadik Azimov, after whom a major Tashkent street is named today, died of a heart attack some time after his elder son-in-law, another physicist' father (a very prominent bureaucrat of the Rashidov regime) was thrown into prison and threats were put about that the women of his family would be sent to the police barracks for the guards. Sadik Azimov's family lost privileges for some time, though his wife retained her professional eminence as a historian. Her children date the palsy and general debility from which she was to pass away in 2001, to what they see as the repressive years of Gorbachev's 'human face of socialism'. The elder son migrated to Moscow. The younger one, Rustom Azimov, a trained economist, had married the daughter of one of the junior top Secretaries of the Rashidov regime (who had handled the political management of Afghanistan after its occupation). When this official too was broken, Rustom Azimov earned money in Moscow doing odd jobs in the perestroika years. When Karimov established himself as President, Rustom Azimov rose to Chairmanship of the Bank of Uzbekistan, responsible for much real estate expansion, then Minister for Finance, and at the turn of the century, as Vice-Premier was Uzbekistan's principal negotiator with US, European and world financial agencies. He is said to have recently risen to the rank of Prime Minister.

This bit of prosopography illustrates the informal clan and family structures of the CIS. Among other things, these structures appear to have been based on marriage relationships, carefully nurtured. They did restrict mass access to economic benefits and obviated many costs in the negotiation of networking and patronage utilization. They also made it difficult for outsiders to get a share in the circulation of elites without brutally smashing the structure from time to time. This was what Stalin did in 1937 to the Jadid communists who had controlled the state till then. What 'actually existing socialism' as distinct from its ideals meant for the Uzbek masses, i.e. what has happened to the 'circulation of elites' as a result of the 'purges' deserves research in the KGB archives in Tashkent and other cities. The Ancien Regime of Late Soviet practice grew within its own ruins to co-exist with the Thermidorian reaction in the USSR from 1989 to 1991. 'Old forms of a new state' represented continuities within internal flux.

This continuity could not control the change that came in economic circumstances. Russian foreign policy and increasingly its investment pattern turned to the NATO powers. Relations with the Muslim dependencies, which Yeltsin's cronies had seemed to so decisively cast off in 1991, began to be calculated in market economy terms by the crony capitalism of the Russian Federation. The bottom of the world cotton markets was depressed when cotton prices collapsed. This meant that Uzbekistan, which before the 1990s had made the USSR the third largest cotton producer in the world, lost its advantage. Matters worsened when new mixed crop breeds for more cotton production showed signs of deterioration in quality. It was difficult to face competition from synthetic products. Uzbekistan's barter trade had to be re-negotiated within the CIS. For instance, the Ukraine was now a principal purchaser, and so were the Caucasian Republics of Georgia and Azerbaijan.

This realignment on the southern periphery, based on economic hardships created by Yeltsin's decolonization policy, led to the formation of a new regional grouping within the CIS. It was distinct from the Russians and other northern Republics. This centred on TRACECA—the Trans-Caucasian and Central Asian Association—meant to be a transport corridor, seeking to revive the Silk Road concept between south-east Europe, Turkestan, and China. TRACECA was in vogue in US hopes of a sort of northern tier above and not within the Middle East, in which Turkey was expected to join along with Pakistan for stabilizing energy reserves and prices. The idea of the 'northern tier' is an old NATO-type geopolitical idea of the mid-twentieth century, based on the Baghdad Pact. The Iraqi popular uprising of 1958 against its Hashemite rulers who had been stooges of the British and the USA had disrupted this, leading to Iraqi rivalry with the Shah of Iran, another client of the USA. The difficulties of the USA as well as the Soviet Union in Iran and Afghanistan, and then the Gulf Wars, had led to the development of the newer geopolitical idea of an 'arc of instability', north of Saudi Arabia, the USA's 'faithful ally', which tallied with the Arab and Iranian-Iraqi competition for oil price hike. The latter threatened US super power pre-eminence. The collapse of the Soviet Union weakened Saddam Hussein's plans for Iraqi sub-imperialism. It also left Iran in a situation where two super powers could not be played off against each other. And it brought Muslim fundamentalists to power east of Iran as well. All these factors became elements in the North Atlantic think-tank calculations to form a bloc north of Iraq, which would significantly lower the capacity of competitors to resist US control of oil prices.

The strategic counterpart of this was the GUUAM forum—

comprising Georgia, Ukraine, Uzbekistan, Azerbaijan and Moldavia (the little republic on the north-west edge of the Black Sea in Europe)—which came together for security affinities as well as economic necessity. All members were interested in joining the Partnership for Peace, promoted by NATO, as candidates for junior apprenticeship of the bloc of Atlantic economies. The ground was being prepared for Karimov and the Uzbeks to talk of becoming European. There were shades visible in this of Gorbachev's idea of 'Europe, our common home', but the Uzbeks were being lured to the idea by direct US interest through cultural mechanisms such as the Soros Foundation, or plans for US-Central Asian trade—mooted by the Republican Senator Brownback and his assistant, Christine Rocca, for a Silk Road Bill to facilitate this. The interests of oil price control and 'state security' were coming together.

In this rapidly changing system of new relationships, unlike the other Republics, which accepted multinational domination, Uzbekistan at first sought to strike a middle path, emphasizing sovereignty and self-sufficiency (in the latter case, to the extent possible, and for the interest of local elites rather than plebeian people). It took the old Mexican, Kemalist Turkish, early Indian path of setting up official controls on all conceivable economic activity, so that palm-greasing activities of the past continued at every stage. Certain large foreign corporations were allowed in. Daewoo from Korea had its own concession of several hectares in Asaka, between Marghilan and Andijan. It had its own factories and even laws, and a bank of its own, in a lovely redbrick heritage building (one of the few remaining) opposite the Uzbekistan Hotel in Tashkent's Amir Timur Square. Other entrants included the Newmont Mining Corporation, prospecting for gold, which is reputed to be plentiful on the borders of Kazakhstan and Uzbekistan just to the west of Tashkent, and UzBAT. BAT, we gathered, had paid a great deal to hold cigarette sales for the whole of the country, largly because its American rival Philip Morris had done the same with Nazarbaev in Kazakhstan. Checkmate the conditions of market entry for competitors was the name of the new version of the hackneyed 'Great Game', now, between the North Atlantic rimland powers on the one hand, led by the USA, and a now unconfident Russian Federation on the other in a shrinking heartland, fissured by the collapse of communist power.

What happened in Uzbekistan was that the consumer suffered.

A few became rich: multinationals budgeted for market reservation of the conditions of entry. A few supermarkets were opened in the more affluent parts of Tashkent, and in other cities. Some were the usual holdings by local mafia bosses. For instance, Ardus stood for the initials of the members of a family whose leader had been a cook in Soviet days. He had become a restaurant chain owner and property promoter in the I'm-all-right-Jack phase of new crony capitalism. He had two supermarkets in central Tashkent, where the prices were fairly steep. Close by, he had a building which housed nightclubs from the staid review variety to the really sleazy ones. Two other supermarkets, one very close to our apartment, called 'Anglesey Foods', and the other 'Mir Market' (this one opposite to Ardus, owned by Demir, a Turkish company with its own vegetable farms outside Tashkent) stocked reasonably priced day-to-day household necessities, fresh meat, and fish. This was reasonable for those few who earned in dollars. In 1997, the bazaar rate had been 168 soum (the Uzbek currency) to a dollar, while the official rate had been about 65 soum or so. When we went in 1998, it was about 350 soum bazaar and about 160 official. Rates fluctuated between winter when there were very few vegetables and fruits in the markets and summer when this was in profusion. Or, for instance, when Haj passengers needed dollars for their Arab trip, there would be a flurry in the exchange rackets to make profits out of the sudden increase and demand. An Indian we knew, with business dealings, told us that his private dealer kept stacked between his bed, and the floor carpet, wads of soum for such dealings. Within a year, all rates were to jump sharply, as dollars went into short supply, making all products costlier.

At that point of time, people were beginning to complain of the rising cost of food and services. Central heating and gas was heavily subsidized, with landlords paying not more than the equivalent of few dollars a year as rates. Electricity cost only a little more. The maintenance of installations had been neglected since the 1980s, as the depression of the national economy began to hit the pockets of all but the rich. The *mahalla* system and the presence of local functionaries galore did provide for quick repairs, at very low cost, by mechanics who could be prevailed to come even at midnight. It was food and consumer durables that suddenly became very costly.

We once calculated how much my Uzbek colleagues earned in

terms of their availability of monthly provisions. A simple weekly supply of fresh foodstuffs, excluding protein material, drinks and luxuries cost us about four to five thousand soums. The monthly salary of an Assistant Professor in the University scales in Tashkent amounted to about twelve thousand soums at that time. Professors received between eighteen and twenty-seven thousand soums. Most Uzbeks marry by the time they are twenty, and have children soon after. Thus families were generally not less than three or four. The impact of this on food consumption left us wondering. Uzbek primary diet staples are wheat, meat and milk products. How they could afford this, as regularly as they appeared to, was something we never could understand. Cafeterias in public institutions like my University appeared to be heavily subsidized and wholesome. People in the highest professions were taking more than one job, and seeking consultancies with foreign agencies. This gave them access to dollars, or preferably jobs abroad, starting with Russia, and Germany (where Uzbeks mingled with Turks in places like Hamburg or Hanover) and ideally to the USA, as far west, for instance, as Oregon, where one of our young friends was later invited to help with Uzbek and English linguistic teaching. Without this extra income, something that Indian economists like K.N. Raj and Amit Bhaduri, who had been in Eastern Europe during the 1980s, had been describing as 'moonlighting', it would have been impossible for the professional classes to maintain a decent standard of living. How the working people coped, we did not find out: our informants were extremely chary of talking about income. Definitely, taxpayer numbers were extremely small. In general, only the informal sector, and the mafia, seemed to be thriving.

The fall out for culture was grim. In our *mahalla*, traditionally residences of the professional elite, young people were taking to drugs. In one of our adjacent blocks, police had broken into a flat to find a young foreigner dead on the sofa; some said from drugs, others said murdered. Those with money were investing in pulling down the charming old dachas: and building large and garish villas, sometimes with swimming pools on the first floor. Theft increased. So did beggars at the door asking for food. When we asked about such children who rang the bell, people would summarily dismiss them as Tajik refugees from the civil wars across the southern borders, or as Romany gypsies, who were seen around the markets, squabbling, sometimes with babies in their arms or others with prominent albino features, who thrust their faces into the windows of cars stopped at traffic lights at major junctions. In India, where this was not uncommon, we had grown up thinking it could not happen in the lands of Communism, any more than it could in advanced capitalist countries. Uzbeks were emphatic. Beggary would have been impossible before 1990. We were told that among the citizens of the country—as distinct from refugees—old people who were indigent each received a small pension of about three thousand soum per month and were provided roofs over their heads, one or two rooms in a block, and could at least eat *lipioshki* dipped in tea: they did not starve.

When the contemporary sociology of Uzbekistan is written, it will be worth generating figures about the percentage of employment, disguised unemployment, and the refugee population in the country. One will have to go to the United Nations Development Programme (UNDP) or United Nations High Commission for Refugees (UNHCR) offices in Tashkent for this purpose. But even without statistics, it is clear that the chauvinistic Uzbek explanations that sheer poverty was only a refugee export, was itself an attempt to sweep the growing dust under the carpet.

Women often face a double fall-out from immiserization, i.e. from the decline of exchange entitlements in one class of population, as a direct result of the growth of affluence of the other. They suffer from the usual results of poverty. They also suffer from the neglect of their menfolk. We heard of bigamy being on the increase as the men took advantage of old Muslim tribal practices without being devoutly Muslim. Such men often neglected their first families, driving children to work when they should have been continuing their professional education after school. In the Soviet period, social regimes had been more publicly puritanical. It was not as if marriages did not break up, but divorce was then mandatory. The maintenance of the deserted family had also been more common. A girl who was a student of Kathak at the Indian Cultural Centre in the city, as well as of Urdu in the Institute of Oriental Studies, contributed to her mother and younger siblings' keep by dancing in a cabaret at night. It was very common to see young girls of the middle class earning by dancing in the nightclubs, which proliferated in this decade in Tashkent. Wages were high and the dividing line between so called respectability and the life of the demi-monde blurred.

The economy seemed to be fraying at the edges. People were talking, though in the most hushed drawing rooms, or in foreign academic studies about the regime's graft, gross new styles of building rococo residences, the coarseness of the new people in power, and the possibilities of some sort of violence born out of frustration. The state preferred to manage conflict by turning attention towards national chauvinism. This was the time when the President was making noises about eradicating Russian influence from Uzbek economic and cultural life. The scandals of new industrial barons in the Russian Federation were thrown in bold relief, without heed that the Uzbek elite also lived in glass houses. The latter was engaged in building relations with the Caucasian states and the Ukraine for new barter arrangements. Senator Brownback's Bill in the USA to facilitate world trade along the Silk Route was talked about. Trends seemed to be maturing for the USA to move closer to Uzbekistan and other Central Asian states, closer than even the Russians with their traditional commitment to protection of the Pamir frontier with Afghanistan. Uzbek diplomats appeared to be trying to arrange with Pakistan for some sort of security against infiltration of Islamic propaganda from the Tajik mountains. Uzbekistan seemed on the verge of striking out on a path independent from its northern neighbours.

This fragile autonomous direction did not last long. Terrorism appeared in summer on Ferghana's borders. The Uzbek economy began its sharp downward turn. Yeltsin's last measures of setting aside the claims of aging veterans of the KGB and the army, such as Premier Yevgeny Primakov and General Anatoli Lebed and ultimately bringing in the young and unknown KGB operative, Putin, started a new trend of CIS consolidation. This would improve Russia's position and lead to a further downturn in that of the Uzbeks, pushing the country paradoxically towards first the NATO, and then, after 2000, towards the Texas oil interests of the Bushes.

Before the summer vacation, another event had reinforced my sense that Uzbekistan was becoming a backwater. The Indian Embassy, and the Confederation of Indian Industry (CII) Office, which worked *in tandem* with it through the Commerce and Industry Ministry of the Government of India, had been agog that the Foreign Minister would pay a visit to Karimov in the summer of 1999. This he did, accompanied by a delegation of officials and press. The discussions were not remarkably specific, beyond expression of interest in furthering business links and an invitation to the President to meet India's new rulers—his earliest visit had been way back in 1993.

All Embassy officials were invited for lunch that day, including, for some odd reason, myself, though the India Chair had been ignored in official protocol since my arrival. The Secretary (East) in charge of the Central Asian Division, Nareshwar Dayal, who accompanied the Minister sought to inform himself about my evaluation of the country at large and the development of GUUAM. He was interested in my very emphatic statement that the days were over for Hindi as linguistic base for mutual understanding between Uzbeks and Indians. I had suggested earlier to Navrekha Sharma, Joint Secratary for International and Technical Economic Co-operation in his ministry, who had visited Tashkent in spring, that with the growth of globalization, English was the Asian *lingua franca*. North Americans spoke it and Japan had adopted it for world communication. French, once popular, was being down-played. There were no jobs for Hindi graduates, once in demand in Soviet public sector plants in India. If we wished to offer a economically viable cultural package to any Central Asian country, excluding the Kathak-Tabla training in Tashkent and Almaty, the ICCR should provide quality competition to the US Educational Foundation and the British Council training courses in English, spoken and written, for which there was already roaring demand in Tashkent. India was obviously the best qualified in the Commonwealth, outside the white settler colonies, to set this competition with its solid resources for teaching English, for instance in the Central Institute of English at Hyderabad.

There was nothing original in this proposal and Mrs. Sharma seemed to agree. Its premise was the need for economic viability of India's cultural investment in her foreign policy. I had already communicated to our new Ambassador, that UWED, designated by ICCR as India's link institution with Uzbek academics, had indicated, through one of its Pro-Vice-Chancellors to my Chair-person, that Indian studies would not be fruitful since there was no job market left for Uzbek-Hindi speakers, and they did not visualize research work on South Asia. English studies seemed a more efficient alternative.

The Secretary asked me to convey this at the lunch to Jaswant Singh, the Foreign Minister. The latter responded that he had earlier that year heard the same evaluation, and asked the Ambassador to let him have a proposal for four language instructors, with language lab facilities, which he was willing to provide. He turned aside Ambassador Mitra's point that Hindi was the state language and the only language ICCR could sponsor. English was also an official language, he said. If there was a market for it, there was no harm in presenting it as best we could. The entourage left the next day and there the matter ended. I learned later that in internal discussion, it had been said again that Hindiwallas might raise a hue and cry at such a major patronage shift. It was after all, safer to take one's salary home and not rock any boats.

Another straw in the wind was the Minister's response to a journalist in his party who enquired whether he would join them in a scheduled visit to the Amir Timur Museum, next door. The simple Uzbeks expected the memory of the sacker of Delhi to be venerated by the Indian delegation. The minister said he needed a brief rest before subsequent appointments. Only a very few people went on their own. The Minister was extremely interested in the desert remains of Khiva and the way that old city had been recrafted as a museum piece. He told me he had asked for a seminar to be organized on the pre-Islamic aspects of culture contact between India and Central Asia. 1999 was the peak period when the Islamic period of Turko-Afghan invasions, which culminated in the Mughal Empire, was being sidelined in the official historical consciousness of Hindutva in India. From Bamiyan to Borobudur was the ancient span of Hindu cultural expansion, Murli Manohar Joshi, the BJP Minister for Human Resource Development, had exhorted the Azad Institute of Asian Studies in Calcutta in 1998. The Babri Masjid destruction was beginning to have its fall-out in the Indian establishment's views about Indian cultural interests, north of the Karakorams, setting aside age-old links with Islamic culture and Urdu.

India was groping for links with Vladimir Putin, soon to be President of Russia. By the summer of 1999, the Russian star was once more in the firmament and the Central Asian Republics, economically insecure and culturally threatened by pulls between Western globalization and Islamic nationalism, had been relegated to a much lower place than they had commanded when India had been ruled by the Congresss party.

The old *Soviet-Hindi Bhai-Bhai* spirit was evoked, indeed, in May when Rabindranath Tagore's birthday on the 25 Baishakh (celebrated by our Government on 7 May the date of the Christian calender when he was born) was observed in the Indian Cultural Centre. Its principal activity, to trained young Uzbek girls in Kathak and classical tabla on its own as well as dance accompaniment, was done with considerable devotion and had gained popularity. This was done in a capacious dacha, just past UWED. It also housed a well-stocked library of Indian and Russian books on India; private classes were also organized in Yoga.

The Director requested my wife to help out at a function on Tagore. She found the girls so well trained by their Indian dance teacher that she put together a variety programme of Rabindra Sangeet dance performances and recitations from his poems. There was an old Soviet tradition of translating Tagore into Russian, and from Russian into Uzbek. The girls from the Institute of Oriental Studies vied with each other to be allowed to recite. Not one of them knew good Bengali. One had only studied the alphabet in addition to her studies of Urdu and Hindi, yet her Bengali recitation of one of the spiritual poems was remarkable. So was the verve with which the students danced. The affinity with Bengali culture, though it was based on the Indian Renaissance, and perhaps because of that reason represented an era of modernity, was to be replaced by 'post-modernist' reaction.

A BBC correspondent came to interview me about why Raj Kapoor was such an icon for the Uzbeks. That year Karimov had decreed that the old Soviet Day of Victory over fascism would be renamed a Day of Remembrance of national and world personalities, among whom Raj Kapoor had been included. He had made Indian modern values of the common man far more familiar to the Russian and Central Asian popular imagination than any other Indian had. This includes Satyajit Ray, who, contrary to intellectual belief, was hardly known among our friends in Tashkent. Raj retained his charm for middle-aged people, aware of the Indian renaissance, who had seen his films. But the youth had replaced him by Mithun Chakrabarty, known to them as Jimmy, and by Shah Rukh Khan.

ISLAMIC CHALLENGE AND SECULAR RESPONSE

Just after I reached Oxford to spend the 1999 summer vacation there, there was a seminar on the Central Asian Environment of Business and Investment in St. Antony's College, to which Dinora

Azimova had drawn my attention. I requested participation in it. It was a pointer to the changes that were in the offing about perceptions of Central Asia in Europe. The seminar was different from ones I had attended. For one thing, I had not been invited to it and heard about it from someone who read about it on the Internet. There were no free lunches. More significantly, it was commissioned by South Koreans, competitors of Daewoo through the Asian Development Bank in Manila, for information sharing about the political climate. It was event-managed by a previous British Ambassador to Tashkent and his wife acting as consultants for the seminar organization enterprise.

This new look of market friendliness dominated the entire proceedings. Practically all papers emphasized corruption and weak democratic environment. Most concentrated on the peculiarities of Central Asian social structure, which contributed to such unfavourable competitive conditions. An Indian educated in the USA who taught in London, Bhavna Dave, had a good anthropological paper on the Juz, or geographically ranked clan patterns of kin and affinity in Kazakhstan, and its bearing on power cliques in the Nazarbaev regime. Her senior colleague, Shireen Akiner, had a grim evaluation of the Karimov regime's choices. Without condoning the increased authoritarianism, she emphasized that there were few alternatives for an economy without innovative potential, and with high threat perceptions from, what she saw as an, increasing type of fundamentalism. Another paper by a young couple on irrigation and the salinization of the lower Amu Darya in Uzbekistan had a similarly specific approach as well as pessimistic prognosis. The twentieth century was closing with the West's relegation of Central Asia into the backwoods as a difficult business prospect. Perhaps it was a case for a World Bank salvage operation, if its dictators were prepared to play ball and accept neo-colonial conditionalities. This was still all very muted and implicit. The region was good enough for backpacker tourism, but hardly even B level for major injections of capital.

Being in Oxford was a wonderful opportunity to use the resources of the Bodleian Library and the scholarly help of John Gurney of Wadham College, a friend in Iranian Studies, to get a clear picture of the literature of the Islamicate in mediaeval Turan, away from its local manufacture of fantasy and concocted history. Meanwhile back there the cultural threat erupted into violence on the mountain borders of Ferghana and the Surkhan Darya. Forest rangers, involved in local squabbles over timber and other hill resources had been murdered, south of the Chimgan area itself, where intensive repression was said to have been launched. In August, there were attacks in three separate areas. One was in the Alai range between Tajikistan and Kyrgyzstan: here Kyrgyz troops had been murdered and Japanese geologists were abducted for ransom, in a way reminiscent of the Hizb-ul-Mujahideen or Harkat-ul-Ansar kidnappings of Western tourists in the Kashmir ranges earlier in the 1990s. The other two were in Chimgan and the southern mountains between Tajikistan and Uzbekistan. The civil war in Tajikistan had once again impinged on Uzbek public life, as it had threatened to do in the mid-1990s.

To appreciate the significance of this, it would be useful to recapitulate the story of Juma Nomongani's Islamic Movement for Uzbekistan, and the insurgency that he had started in the Garm and Karategin mountains in Tajikistan. Readers interested in good investigative journalism on this, will get precise details of Juma and Tohir's ideology, contacts and local bases from Chapters 5 to 10 of Ahmed Rashid's third book on Central Asian contemporary affairs, published in 2002, to which reference has already been made. What is presented here is a view from the Tashkent sidelines. My interpretation of the media construction of the fear of *jihad* will be evident to someone who has already read, or is interested in reading, Rashid's far more alarmist version, based on the moderate Pakistani position of General Musharraf or General Colin Powell in the USA, which was played up by US propaganda from the middle of 2001.

Narrow Tajik valleys, easily guarded from southern passes, run up towards the Alai, pointing towards Ferghana as well as Chimgan, and, by implication, Tashkent. The southern side in Tajikistan is bottle-like. It can be guarded from inspection by government troops by watchers on high cliffs on either side. To the west of these valleys lies the ancient town of Khojent (called Leninabad in Soviet days) on the Syr Darya in Tajikistan. It has ethnic and political affinities to Uzbekistan. Tashkent is not more than two hours drive through a once industrialized set of towns in lower Kokand. Khojent had shown signs of Uzbek-sympathetic intransigence against the once communist forces of the southern Kulyobis, led by the present President, Emomali Rachmanov, who had come to power, subordinating the Islamic fundamentalists of Haji Turajonzodeh and Sayyid Abdullo Nuri in Dushanbe (once called Stalinabad). Islamic extremists radicalism who refused to accept this new order, whether Tajik or Uzbek, and whose sympathies lay with Mujahideen extremism, and ultimately with the Taliban in Afghanistan, were in control of the valleys and popular minds in Garm and Karategin. Juma, who, as we have said, had been indoctrinated during the Afghan war in which he had fought as an Uzbek soldier, wished to read the Koran in its pristine purity in his home country. He may, as Uzbek propaganda alleged, have worked through people sympathetic to the anti-modern Puritanism of the Hizb-ut-Tahrir. This had been spread, perhaps with funds from the Saudi Arab international organization, the Rabita-i-Alam. The Rabita's zeal in spreading the Koran in once-Communist Turan had grown from the late 1980s.

The kidnapping of Japanese experts in the mountains of Batkent in south Kyrgyzstan caught the attention of the world leading to the despatch of Kyrgyz reinforcements to hunt for the hostages and their captors, and to the isolation of the Islamic rebels in the triangle of the three Republics. Although the kidnappers were able to gain a reportedly large ransom in much needed dollars in exchange for the release of hostages, they had not been able to break out of the mountains into the plains of Uzbekistan. Their action had alerted the national security interest of the three Republics, behind them the Russians, and even further the multinational business lobbies concerned with Central Asian investment, about Mujahideen seepage north from the Pamirs. This appeared ominous for the West world, panicky about growing Islamic diffusion and the threats against America by Osama bin Laden in Aden, Mombasa, and Dar-es-Salaam. That had the effect, counterproductive for Juma's gang, of uniting the powers against them. Thus, instead of being a sign of fundamentalism on the rise, the act took away any advantage of surprise, which the Hizb-ut-Tahrir may have collaterally gained from the February bomb blasts. It led the West to enter the struggle against political Islam, directly.

When I came back from Oxford at the end of summer, the Day of Independence—from the Soviet Union in 1991—1 September was just over. All educational institutions start a new session after this: there would be a new batch for my classes on International Relations History. Tashkent was as familiar as ever and calm.

Deceptively so, we would have thought, given the panic accounts of Batkent in the English press. No signs of turmoil were visible. This was when I started thinking of parallels between Indian Kashmir and Uzbek or Kyrgyz Ferghana. What happened, up in whichever valley was certainly a problem for the national security people. The masses and the upper classes in the plains, however, had other agonies to keep them busy. Already, the zone from the Syr Darya to the Jhelum, encompassing territory from Ferghana to Jammu, had become isolated, in a hermetically sealed sort of way, in popular imagination.

It was still enjoyable, and a novelty, to explain international relations in Asia in general and South Asia in particular, to young people who had no idea about this, beyond the rigid Communist syllabi about progressive movements, imperialist machinations, and non-aligned states teetering between the two. That was essentially all that the new international relations ideas of Moscow, propagated by Georgii Arbatov, Alexander Yakovlev, or Yevgenii Primakov amounted to, beyond the 'mutually assured destruction' (MAD) theory, which guided their nuclear security experts. I still thought Central Asia was on the verge of transition to the sort of sovereign bargaining between the two power blocs, the NATO and the beginnings of Sino-Soviet cooperation sponsored by Jiang Zemin: and that a path similar to what Jawaharlal Nehru had practised in the first decade of Indian Independence would be the way taken by Uzbekistan. I wanted to help in this process in whatever small way I could. There was also the fact that my wife and I were beginning to come to terms with the admittedly boring tranquillity of life in Tashkent. It would take more than a year more to realize that anodyne is also a tranquillizer.

The summer before we left had been more eventful than the first winter. The new friends we were making had introduced us, not only to chamber concerts, but also to the pride of Tashkent, the Opera House. From Swan Lake we had graduated to more modern ballet. One of them, Romeo and Juliet, done by a recent Soviet producer, choreographed in harsh red and black hues was very powerful. So was Spartakus. Another, called Soni Mahiwal, was based on the Punjabi story, with the variant that the youth was a young merchant from Bukhara travelling in the Lahore kingdom: its dances were strongly influenced by folk and modern popular Indian dance forms. Then, we went to an antiquated old theatre hall, the interior of which reminded me of the old show houses of north Calcutta in British Indian days. We were accompanied by a young Uzbek musicologist and scholar of Indian classical styles, Diloram Karomat.

The play was called Super Kainona, Kainona meaning mother-in-law in Uzbek. It was a very explicit social farce against the practice of families, including elder women, of treating young daughters-in-law as chattel, having them divorced at will, and getting compliant sons to contract multiple marriages with corrupt Kazis acting as marriage registrars and minting fees. The audience, largely traditional looking ladies sporting headscarves and ankle-length Uzbek dresses, with little children in large numbers, were in splits, following the verbal badinage and rough and tumble, particularly when female youth got on top and proceeded to knock the corrupt old gentry around. The message was an interesting rehash of Soviet style social transformation. Polygamy had been attacked in this way in the late 1920s, particularly by fervent secularists like Hamza Niyazi, who had indeed been murdered by mullahs in Ferghana for encouraging women to tear up their *paranjas* or veils. The principal modern theatre in Tashkent is called the Hamza Theatre. The collapse of communism and the brief triumph of Islam at the end of the Afghan War had raised the spectre of superstition and obscurantism once again, particularly in the traditional cohorts of Muslim Central Asian society. Here again will be seen the interplay between continuity and change, which is the warp and weft of any social transformation. We could recall how in the Bengal Renaissance of the nineteenth century, the young radicals of Hindu College in Calcutta had challenged a range of conservative social practices. Apart from the great epic recensions of Michael Madhusudan Dutt, such as *Meghnadbadhkavya*, he wrote skits, such as *Buro Shaliker Gharey Ronh* (Down On The Old Sparrow's Neck, a semi bawdy critique of an old man's lechery). Uzbek cultural performance had the same strong flavour of the tension between the reformulations of modernity and of Islamic tradition. It was interesting for us to get a chance of being part of an actual process of social transformation, that we still hoped might be like the one in which we had ourselves grown up during the 1940s and 1950s. The possibilities of social stagnation, affected by globalization had not yet entered our imagination.

RECONSTRUCTION OF 'NATIONAL' HISTORY

The Director of the Indian Cultural Centre informed me that he had sent my name to present a paper on a theme of nationalist interest for Uzbek historians, which was to be celebrated in Khiva in October in memory of Jalaluddin Mangubardi (or Mankbarni as historians in India are used to read about him). The invitation from the Uzbek Academy of Sciences giving the theme of the seminar was intriguingly post-modern. It clubbed together the last ruler of Khwarezm before the Mongol conquest of 1219 with a mythical folk hero, who was said to have lived and fought a few centuries before, at Termez, further up the Amu Darya, Alpomysh. The invitation stressed the aggressive imagery of heroes, who had defended the territorial boundaries of Uzbekistan, as it was defined in the twentieth century, way back in its presently defined legendary past. This encapsulation of memory to satisfy present needs, as a classic example of 'historical construction' for a particular national interest, has always interested me in the exploration of nationalist ideology. In Oxford I had soaked up what I could about 'myth and reality' (as D.D. Kosambi called it in the context of the rhetoric of Indian national culture)[1] specifically the Khwarezm prince. That enquiry was a fascinating entry into the translated sources for mediaeval Turkestan history. The Ambassador left for India instructing that either the Director or I be delegated to go. The Director went. But what I read in the English translations of thirteenth century history may be interesting, as part of the geo-strategic fantasies which permeated Central Asian national-populist policies.

Many Indians reading history in my generation, had heard of an ill-fated prince, from the desert edge of Central Asia, chased by Chingiz Khan from his domain (conquered from the Ghorids) in Afghanistan to the edge of Punjab, where with the river Indus at his back, he turned and gave battle in 1221. Defeated decisively by the Asian conqueror, Jalaluddin left his wives and family to the latter's army, turned his horse's face to the raging river, and swam across it to his own safety. Here, gathering his broken bands, he proceeded to loot and pillage the local people. He sent word to a fellow Central Asian, Sultan Iltutmish who had come to power in Delhi that he should be granted shelter and refuge in the dominions of Delhi. The figurative word used in their common Turki language, was *yurt*, which means space for building large felt camping tents. Nomads of the time still lived in these. Perhaps they still do in Mongolia.

The canny Iltutmish was not hospitable. He feared the competition of the last titular Emperor of Khwarezm, whose father had ruled from Khiva up to the Kazakh steppe and the Indus, and who himself had governed Khorasan and Afghanistan for the previous decade, after his father had extirpated the last Ghorids, whom the Delhi sultans had served. The prince, whose surname Mangubardi meant in Turki the gift of God, thus turned south, hoping to rule Sind. After cruelties to its people, he was ousted from it in three years by Nasiruddin Qubacha. This was another ex-follower of the Ghorid conquerors of Delhi, who ruled Multan, till he in turn was defeated and killed by Iltutmish. Jalaluddin left India along the desert route through Baluchistan by which Alexander's foot soldiers had retreated, fifteen hundred years before—not a very pleasant man to know (not that his adversaries, or the hooligan times in which they lived, were any better). What had interested me in the seminar invitation was its braggart assumption that the man Uzbeks wished to celebrate had once 'conquered' Central Asia, Afghanistan, India, Iran, and even Georgia. The boast that Uzbeks were the inheritors of imperial consolidation from the Black Sea and the Caspian to the Arabian Sea, seemed as pregnant a fantasy as that of Mussolini's boast, still engraved in a stone map near the ruins of the Roman Forum, that the Mediterranean was *mare nostrum* (our sea) because the Romans had once held it from Tyre in the Levant to the Pillars of Hercules.

It seemed that, after leaving some stragglers behind in Sind—one of them with the interesting name of Uzbek Pai (which can literally be translated as self-lord-foot man), ruled part of Sind, till as late as 1249, as a part of the jumble of adventurers pushed out of their homes by the Mongols, into what is now Pakistan—the prince proceeded to briefly raid large parts of Iran and also Ajam (between Iran and Iraq) and then used this as a springboard to the Caspian shores and thence up the valleys of Georgia, where he carried off and wedded its queen, but was driven out by a local uprising. By 1229, the Mongol hordes had tracked him down. He was cut down by a common peasant in northern Iran. His father, Alauddin Muhammad Shah, had died miserably in the Mangyshlak (*ming kishlak* or, in Turki, thousand villages—rustic villages are still called *kishlak* in Uzbekistan) Peninsula, west of Khiva, which juts into the Caspian.[2]

What came out of these mediaeval geopolitical details was not only the realization that in their dreams of past glory, today's Uzbek intelligentsia thought of the entire desert and mountain space between Caucasia and Pakistan as *terra nostrum*—our land, over which their glorious ancestors had roved. From roaming and roving, it was one imaginative jump to conquest. Of such stuff, as we have noted before, is populist historiography fashioned. One need not be condescending about Uzbek colleagues. In the early twentieth century, merely on the basis of fables that a prince called Vijay from Lata in either Gujarat, or Rarha in Bengal, had colonized Sinhala, the Bengali poet Satyendranath Dutta had sung lines familiar to every Bengali child which can be roughly translated in English, 'once, where (a Bengali prince) Vijay (or victorious) troops had conquered Lanka with ease, where once Bengal's sea vessels had roamed all over the Indian Ocean'. Or, closer to the present, India's then Minister for Human Resource Development, Science and Technology, on an admonitory visit to the Institute where I worked in 1998, when I told him that we were interested in Bukhara, the ancient *vihara*, and also Bamiyan, had admonished us, no, we must look at India, all the way from 'Bamiyan to Borobudur', i.e. we must propagate the Hindu concept of a Greater India stretching from Afghanistan to Indonesia, in place of common earlier roots of Hinduism and Islam in those tracts today. Historicist chauvinism grows when there is no future to plan for, and people fall back for alternatives to the abject dreams of a fantasy past.

Mangubardi does deserve research. He is an example of the plurality of classes and forces, seeking shelter as well as new forms of lordship in an age and region where notions of territory in the inner Asian landmass were fluid throughout the early centuries of Islamic diffusion. This approach, however, had very few takers among post-communist Uzbeks. At one time there had been analytical studies by Soviet historians looking at Persian and Turki sources from the point of view of social sciences to chronicle processes of urbanization and state formation in Mawar-an-Nahar. When the papers presented in the Khiva seminar, which had been presided over by President Karimov himself, were published, all but one wrote of Mangubardi in the hyperbole devoted to a great patriot fighting to save his capital and his mother from invading hordes. Defence against foreign aggression was the common theme. Only the paper by the senior Uzbek historian, Rosia Mukminova dealt innovatively with the sources, to mention, though in a cautious low key, that it was the common people of Khiva who had cut the ditches in the delta, to protect it from the invaders. This difference from orthodoxy, which now sought to project that heroism, was the personal virtue of leaders, rather than the led, was a remnant of Marxism.

My friend Professor Goga Abrorevich Khidoyatov, who had joined as Professor Emeritus in our department, later invited me to speak on Mangubardi in his seminar. I sought to bring out some of the implications of hero worship and imaginative romanticism. Only Professor Khidoyatov appeared to see my point and picked them up for discussion. So did one or two students who were curious to know, as if they had not heard about it before, about possibilities of differences in interpreting the significance of a historical personage, in terms of differences in viewpoint, i.e. whether the historian was an Uzbek or an Indian or a Pakistani. History had been taught to them as the Truth, not as the present interrogating the past from particular and pluralistic presumptions.

SOUTH-WEST TO BUKHARA

The autumn of 1999 had come to Tashkent. The trees thronging the roads, briefly flared into a blaze of colours—yellow, brown, red and russet, all in the space of a fortnight. Tashkent seemed friendlier and more familiar than when we had arrived here in the depths of winter.

The calm of public opinion always surprised us. It was not just the fearful whispers after the bomb blasts, or after the Batkent events. Nor was it the gloomy prognostications of a colleague, about the untrustworthiness of humanity, for instance, when he told me that I should not talk frankly even in the presence of the driver who brought me back and forth, or his repeated glances at the ceiling, meaning even light bulbs could hear. All, or most, office rooms in educational institutions had a benevolently smiling Karimov, and in our department, also a large national flag splayed across the wall. It was my practice not to mention the President, but just flick a glance at the portrait! This was only half in jest.

It was more than that. In the middle of an unusually quiet night, while my wife and I were chatting, she noticed that the bed had tilted and slid away and then rocked back. When we realized it was an earthquake, it was our Indian reaction to look out to see if others were coming out of the houses and whether there was any commotion. There was not a peep from our neighbours. That it was a heavy earthquake was confirmed only when Indian friends rang to ask whether we were all right. The next morning we heard that the shocks had been more than 6 points on the Richter scale. We thought that the reluctance to not express their fears vocally had been beaten into the people in the communist era. Later we learned how after the massive earthquake of 1966 in Tashkent, the city rebuilding had led to the great apartment blocks being built on foundations so stable that they would take shocks of anything up to 9 Richter. Whether this was the cause of the present placidity we do not know. It is certain that public expression did not appear to be the norm in Tashkent, except, so the story went, when Islamic fundamentalism had briefly expressed itself in religious rage, from 1989 or so, till Karimov and his henchmen soon firmly crushed it.

So, as the people spent their time worrying whether computers would crash and planes dependent on electronic controls would be left dangling over runways as the changeover took place to the new 'millennium', there was little concern that was openly expressed about either regional or international politics. The year before had seen most people talking about USA and Britain bombing Iraq, and then the NATO powers browbeating the Serbs over Bosnia and Kosovo. At the end of 1999, there was a mood of resigned acceptance not only of super power dominance and NATO tutelage, but also of the Russian President's battering of Muslim intransigence in Chechnya and Daghestan. Opinion had begun to harden in favour of toughness against radical Islam. Men like Putin who represented conservative toughness were the obvious heroes of the hour. The renewed bomb blasts in central Moscow increased the toughness.

In November our son travelled for his fieldwork in India from Oxford and visited Tashkent for three weeks. We took this opportunity to go, via Samarkand, further into the country to Bukhara, its twin in the historical consciousness of most people who have heard of Turkestan. Samarkand up on the mountains is cosmopolitan and open; Bukhara, further west, as the steppe peters into the desert, between the Aral and the Caspian Seas, is narrow and introverted, more wrapped in its own history, and inward looking in its narrow lanes and dusty old houses.

The road from Samarkand to the west follows the course of the channels that come into the Zarafshan River. It is quite fertile in the lowlands up to Katta Kurgan (which in Uzbek means big palace). On a later trip, our driver mistook the turning and went by a parallel road, which dipped and swung up a series of switch-back low ridges, quite arid, on the southern flank of the river base. This is the character of oasis settlement, all the way from Chirchik below Chimgan to Khiva, the oasis snaking along small rivers between barren steppe on either side; where the ground is fertile, cultivation is intensive, water being injected by a network of channels from the rivers and ground water. The water soon becomes scarce. The only instance of crop diversification that came to our notice was viticulture, which is intensive.

Along the road were villages where important saints associated with the Sunni theological heritage and Sufi *khankas* (hospices) are buried. The most important of these is the little tomb, and the extensive precinct built around it recently by President Karimov, of Imam Bukhari, an early exegetist of the Koran in the immediately post-Arab conquest period. His text is considered an authoritative analysis of the different accounts of Muhammad's views by the Companions (Sahiban) of the Prophet. Immediately after Independence, Suharto, then President of Indonesia with a reputation for anti-communism had visited Uzbekistan, and expressed a desire to pay his respects to the Imam's memory, as part of Islamic solidarity with the new sovereign states. The new authorities were dismayed by the dilapidated condition into which the shrine had been allowed to fall during the Soviet neglect of Islam. Karimov made a mark by starting a massive restoration, involving international agencies including Oxford's Centre of Islamic Studies. With renovation and expansion of the sacred area visitors at the end of the decade even went so far as to refer to it as the Mecca of Central Asia.

The car journey to Bukhara takes three and a half hours from Samarkand. The road becomes straight and wide as it comes down the steppe, following the main branch of the ancient Silk Route from China to Europe. The monotony of the drive pushes the imagination back to the caravans, which must have trudged along it, for more than a millennium. Villages on either side are unremarkable. The highway bypasses large towns. Outside the factories of Navoi there was a large hatchery from where the driver said much of the country's eggs are produced. Soon after this, the drowsy traveller on the Golden Road from Samarkand is suddenly jolted awake by a high arch with thick walls on the right: standing stark and empty, like the ruin that the Romantic poet had visualized, of the statue of Ozymandias, this is Rabat-i-Malik, the King's Well.

The actual edifice, sunk on the left of the road, is also in ruins. The structure was part of the caravanserais, built at regular intervals, of the roads, by the ninth-century Samanid rulers of Bukhara, who brought the culture of Arab and Ajam into Turan. Walking through the arch, all that can be seen is a low stone plinth, square in dimension, as all courtyards still tend to be in Central Asia. The chambers to which the gate leads may be visualized: camels, horses, men and produce, all herded in for night time security and from the cold. These were moments, extremely rare for me, when I caught myself thinking of the fantasies that stir Western readers of James Elroy Flecker's neo-Romantic ditties about journeying on the golden road to Samarkand. The place had a powerfully forlorn ambience. Coming back along the road the next year, we were painfully surprised to find that the President's restoration campaign to refurbish deserted ruins for tourist interest, had taken over the arch and the well. The activity around it was enough to make it look like a cheap replica of what it had once been.

Another hour bypassing historic towns like Ghijduvan, where Ulugh Beg had built another madrasa with mosque, and where the Safavids and Shaibanids in Babur's times had once fought a notable battle, and we were driving in the dusk into the Bukhara oasis. This was once swampland, after which the Zarafshan loses itself in the western desert. It was the beginning of winter in November: the dark comes early. Not still having heard of the large numbers of boarding houses for guests, we had booked into the Intourist Hotel in the centre city. This was the usual Soviet style monumental monstrosity: an ornate mural in the public lounge downstairs, small rooms, with hot and cold taps but no hot water in the elementary toilets. Without a shred of apology, we were informed by the lady, who by Soviet tradition controls entrance to each floor, that the heating system could lift water only to the second floor. It appeared that the hotel had not been meant for the many floors that had been piled above. We came down to dinner to find that we were the only guests in this vast dump. Rates for the rooms were reasonable, but the meals, which had to be specially cooked as in an Indian dak bungalow, were not. The official accreditation cards that we held permitted us to pay in soum, and not in hard currency. For our son and Rustom (who was Uzbek), there were different rates. The latter's charge was even less than ours. This complicated system of accounting, advantageous for those with diplomatic privileges, was taken away by a ukase in early 2000, meant to mop up whatever hard currency the cash strapped Uzbek Government could scrape away.

A foggy haze shrouded Bukhara the next morning, when we came down very early, to meet Nigora Bozorova, a young Uzbek assistant lecturer in Bukhara University. A friend had requested her to give us an idea of what we should see. She spent the day taking us to the principal monuments. When she later came to Tashkent for her M. Phil degree, she was to become a friend of our family as did several young Uzbeks whom we began to meet. Nigora took us out of the city in the chilly, grey cold, to an area far outside. This was the shrine complex of the early mediaeval Sufi *pir*, Shaikh Bahauddin Naqshbandi, who had been followed by many others in his *silsilah* or traditional line of followers with their practice of quietly conducting meditation without advertising it to all and sundry. The complex itself, though large and obviously antiquated in its rough style was not particularly impressive. Its extensive graveyard and square ponds, with the usual stunted trees and trelliswork, had a reputation for sanctity. We came out with traditional long Uzbek knives, the usual present from this country to foreigners. Nigora insisted on my hearing some of the couplets about worldly life as the saint's followers should practice it. A few months later, the Embassy's abstract of the daily news gave a quotation of one of these couplets by President Karimov himself, as a conservative alternative to fundamentalist propaganda about Islam.

Naqshbandi Sufis have time and again shown their capacity to motivate the revival of Islamic authority at the state level and were often king makers in the Muslim states. In Mughal India they led the seventeenth-century return to orthodoxy, away from the Emperor Akbar's eclecticism. In the modern period they were at the root of the quiet, private maintenance of orthodoxy, which has time and again consolidated the Islamicate, even without Arab influence. It has been shown by Alexandre Bennigsen and Stanley Wimbush that Naqshbandi mystic practitioner branches, scattered across Eurasia from the Uzbek lands through Turkey to its old dominions in the Balkans, have contributed to modern Islamic revival. This had repercussions in the assertion of the faith and communist repression of it, whether in Tajikistan, Chechnya, or Kosovo. It was interesting to be at one of the old nerve centres of a scattered, global, religious revival.

The sun was coming out weakly as we came back to the nodal centre of the city, the old fortress of the Emirs, called in the local usage for such buildings, the Ark or Arg. The broken mud ramparts at the back stretch for a long distance. The imposing stone façade over two storeys high, unbroken by any windows or embrasures in the front, stretches for about 500 yards. The Bukhara fortifications in one form or another are reputed to go back two millennia. Halfway in its frontage, rises a steep and narrow entry ramp, for horsemen only, winding in a dark tunnel (now full of guides and the trinkets they sell) and with nasty little guards' cells: in which dummies of inmates have been kept. In one of the cells, entrance fees are taken and a lady guide attached to visitors. Her patter of folklore is enough to frighten away any one genuinely interested in the history of the place.

This history can be found in several books beginning with ones by Wolff and Vambery in the nineteenth century. However, these accounts are specifically from the British colonial point of vision. They focus on one of those events of imperialist defeat at the hands of Asians, which has long moved Britons to bursts of sentimentality: the incarceration of two British military spies and their execution in the Registan, or open space fronting the Ark. Like the Black Hole of Old Fort William in Calcutta in which Sirajuddaula's officers stuffed their white prisoners in 1757, or the Afghan massacre of the British Army of occupation in the Khurd Kabul Pass, leading down to the Khyber in 1839, or General Gordon cut down on the steps of the Governor's Palace in Khartum by the Sudanese followers of the Mahdi Pasha of Omdurman in 1871, the fate of Colonel Stoddart and Captain Conolly at the hands of Amir Nasiruddin of Bukhara at the time of the British disaster in Afghanistan has a tragic place in British historical minds that the rest of the world, let alone the Uzbeks today, do not accord it. The

Ark's significance is different; it is the remnant of a dingy palace of a petty Asiatic despot.

Beyond the entrance tunnel is a plain and dignified mosque for the palace, on a bit of an eminence, with good woodwork and no ornaments, disused today except for exhibitions. Close by was the seat of power: first the quarters of the minister of the Amir, dingy rooms in an undistinguished alley, then the enclosure for the throne, a raised platform with lower stone platforms on either side, and a high wall blinding the entrance, so that outsiders could not view the ruler's face—and finally a slightly more imposing building of two storeys, in which the ruler lived with his harem (now a museum of Bukhara history). The throne hall is imposing, even in ruins. The platforms were meant to be covered with carpets and rich wall hangings. It is possible to imagine supplicants escorted by the Minister to pay respect to the Amir, expected to back away towards the baffle wall, bowing low as they went. The English books talk of the mutton headed Colonel Stoddart, refusing to take his shoes off on the carpet, believing as his colleagues did in India that that would be a mark of respect to the inferior Asians, and thus annoying the Amir, who ordered his imprisonment. When we went back later to Bukhara, in 2001, the place was being restored and in this case with an attempt to conserve the old woodwork. In 1999, I had asked to be shown the fearsome prison well, or 'Bug Pit' (so called by Captain Conolly in his prison diary found after his death) which was shared with rats and insects. The guides then said they did not know about it. In 2000 the guides, when she found we had lost interest in her lectures in quaint English, offered to show us 'prison chamber' ten minutes walk away. We did not have the time.

What was striking was the roof of the entrance tower. Here, Bukhara carpets, knives, the famous lambskin Karakul caps, and hand painted blue ceramic and textile handicrafts were spread out in the sun. So few tourists go to Bukhara that the vendors become importunate. They plead for purchases, though unlike eastern markets, they do not know how to respond to bargaining. In this simplicity or perhaps because they are on government property, they deal in soum and did not demand dollars, as in the carpet market outside. The Bukharan, wherever we got the chance of interaction in the three years we went there, was quite different from the relatively sophisticated and modernized people of

Tashkent. Tashkent has a more obvious Russian veneer. The last of the northern cities, Tashkent is more confident of its contacts with the wider world, passing through to Moscow, Germany, or Delhi.

In Bukhara, the global south is far more evident; darker skins, proximity to Tajik culture on the borders of Iran, and an excited welcome to Indians, who had, till 1917, a famous sarai close to the Ark, and who carried on a flourishing trade with British India in rugs, dried fruit, and fur caps. Bukharans are warm and simple: but perhaps more narrow and conservative in their outlook and dress. The flavour was conservative and yet friendly, like the non-metropolitan palaces and markets of old Hyderabad in the 1960s or Kathmandu, even today, both seats of princely power in colonial times, as Bukhara had been in the Russian Empire. We could sense the difference in the driver's unspoken assertion of separateness from the men of Bukhara, a somehow more timid lot. He was a Tashkentlik, he let us understand. These were people of the south, a gentler sort.

Slightly to the north, beyond the unmarked graves of Stoddart and Conolly—cut down in the public square or Bukhara Registan, after the news of the British defeat in Kabul, when they refused to convert to Islam—lie two much more ancient monuments. The Chasma Ayub or Well of Jacob is a very distinctive conical tapering dome, reminiscent of the more western Khivan style not found further east. It is associated with a spring inevitably sacred in this desert terrain, perhaps with other ruins underground. Next to it is an old bazaar, much filthier than the clean marketplaces to which we had become used. It was closer to our own Indian type. Beyond, in a shady modern park, is perhaps the oldest and most valued monument of ancient Central Asia. This is the tomb of Shah Ismael Samani, of the dynasty that ruled Turan after the Arab conquest, long before the Saljuqs and the Ghaznavids. This ninth-century structure is built of bricks, light in colour and placed in juxtaposition in a simple mathematical design to give the appearance of a cube with a domed cupola. It is quite small. The intricate fretted symmetry and the simplicity of its location in a sunken ground, from which it was excavated intact, give it a distinct charm. The guidebooks say that it glows in the moonlight. As is common in much of Muslim folklore, our Bukharan friend said that circumambulation of the tomb was common for people who came to have their wishes fulfilled: we did so and then drove back to the venerable part of the old city.

Ancient woodworked stalls line a road of carpet sellers. Past it rises the old Kalon Mosque, a great edifice with arched entrance of halls and a magnificent courtyard leading up to central prayer halls. Broken by conquerors and rebuilt by rulers, its lineage goes beyond Chingiz Khan's invasion of the thirteenth century. Angered by Bukharan resistance, the Mongol ordered his cavalry to desecrate the temple, trample the Koran, and raze the older building on the spot. We met here the Head Imam walking across the courtyard, a grave and simple young man with a neatly cropped beard (beards are not common in secularist Uzbekistan, being a mark of an Islamic theologian) to whom Nigora introduced us. He politely enquired about my work and requested me to take his greetings back to Hindistan. Among the mullahs whom I met in religious establishments in the country, the Imam of Kalon spoke like one with a broad vision of his vocation.

Adjacent to, but separate in structure from the mosque, is the Kalon Minar. A thick and broad primitive version of the soaring edifice from which the Faithful are called to prayer, it could well have been one of the models for the later, taller, more fluted and elegant Qutb Minar in Delhi. A work of considerable art with a splayed platform on top (from which a beacon fire would be lit at night to guide travellers into the city), the Minar escaped Mongol destruction. The story, once again, has it that standing before the sacked mosque with his notables, Chingiz was shown the height of the pillar. Craning his neck to look up, the conqueror's cap fell off his head. 'Let it stand', said the Khan, chastened by the height of the edifice. Much later, the minar acquired a ghastly reputation. The Shaibanids who drove out Babur and his Mughal kin, were succeeded as Uzbek rulers by the Mangit dynasty in the eighteenth century, who lasted till Said Alim Khan's collapse of 1922. This set of princes was noted for brutality. One of the punishments for heinous crimes, which was more dreadful than being dumped for years in the bug pit of the Ark, was to throw convicted persons from the high platform of the Minar, to be dashed against the paving before the mosque.

Symmetrically opposite the Kalon Masjid at a distance of about fifty yards is the Mir Arab Madrasa, named after a minister of the

Shaibanids, who commissioned it as a college of theology. Bukhara is a city of *madrasas*, often built with arched portals to face each other in the distinctive *kosh madrasa* layout of twin colleges, similar to that of Ulug Beg and Shir Dor in the Registan of Samarkand. It would be necessary to live at least a week in Bukhara to trudge through the colleges' square courtyards and blue and gold tiled interiors, with cell-like classrooms on two floors to get an idea of the architectural and old theological heritage of Central Asia. These complexes carried over some continuities of the old Buddhist *viharas* after which Bukhara is said to be named. The difference was that the cells of Ellora or Kanheri or Dunhuang in China are open to the landscape; the Central Asian Muslim seminaries faced inner cloisters. They have more privacy, similar to the mediaeval Oxbridge college courts and quadrangles. The Mir Arab gained pre-eminence in the twentieth century as the principal theological focus of local Islam, back to the wall in defence against repression of its religious practice. Along with the Barak Khan Madrasa in the old town of Tashkent, it had been one of the two where Alims and Talibs could still keep alive the study of old Muslim texts, going back to Imam Bukhari, and beyond it to the Koran itself. Its students travelled for higher studies to Al Azhar University in Cairo and then graduated to teach as Imams in places such as Dushanbe. A Russian diplomat in the 1990s, Trofimov worked out the background of these teachers and the part played by the Mir Arab College in the spread of revivalism in the 1980s.[3] When we went in to gaze at the tiles, there were a few students in the standard long robes.

Beyond the high walls of the *madrasa* is an open space. Here begins the series of *toks* or mushroom domed market plazas (with radiating stalls), so distinctive to early mediaeval Bukhara. These have been recently replicated in the great edifice where dried fruits are sold, built in the Chorsu market of Tashkent after the 1966 earthquake. On one side is the site of the old Sarai Hinduon, where Indians from the valley of the Indus and further east would settle, often for several years, in rented lodgings for their mercantile activities. Indeed the Jadid liberal educationist rebel against the last Emirs in the early twentieth century, who ended his years as an eminent citizen of Tajikistan, Sadruddin Aini, who had studied in the Bukhara *madrasas*, wrote in his memoirs about a book seller called Banerjee or Banaji, who would carry on largely secular discussions about contemporary political literature before the First World War from his room in the sarai—an interesting case of a (perhaps) subversive Bengali or Parsi taking the power of the book to reactionary Bukhara. Right behind the Mir Arab is the Tok Zargaron, the Jewellers Market, where a variety of craft goods are now sold. These include carpet shops, tourist books, and best quality fur caps. We were to become familiar in later journeys with one carpet vendor. The exit from this Tok opens to a broader space, with two large madrasas (one built by Ulugh Beg in the fifteenth century) asymmetrically facing each other. Their portals are massive, but crumbling, and sadly in need of conservation. And so it goes on, the narrow roads widening up to high religious edifices, accumulated by the social piety of Bukharans, which lasted over at least five centuries, and which gave the city its distinctly orthodox reputation of Bukhara Sharif, Bukhara the Noble, second only to Damascus and Baghdad; equal perhaps to Shiraz and Isfahan in Iran and certainly not inferior to the more secular Samarkand.

Bukhara has a Chinese-puzzle box-within-box urban layout. The city plan on a map may appear simple, but one moved from one open place with public buildings constructed in different centuries to another, through a maze of ancient-looking mud tenements, at various ground levels (i.e. some built on the ruins of earlier ones). It is easy to lose one's way in a car. The place reminds you, in this aspect at least, of north Calcutta or old Varanasi as it stretches along the Ganga down to its myriad Ghats. We could sense this most on each visit when we tried to move from Kalon and Mir Arab to the little curiosity called the Char Minar or four (domed tower) minarets. I had seen pictures of this style of building, either the one in Bukhara or of a similar one in Khiva, and was interested in looking at a prototype of what the Nizams of Hyderabad, themselves descended from a Bukhara Turani migrant in the Mughal Emperor Aurangzeb's time (Ghaziuddin Khan Firuz Jang), had built in their new city outside Golconda, next to their Mecca Masjid where the Nizams lie buried.

Turning for the umpteenth time out of the rabbit warren of low buildings, one comes across a sunken rectangular space, with a little *madrasa*, the centre piece of which is an absolutely foreshortened structure, which does look like a prototype of the far higher, larger, and more classical Char Minar at the four point crossing in Hyderabad. But here the four towers are in different styles and irregular in height. The ensemble does not straddle any junction. Nor is it particularly old, having been built in the Mangit period. We came away with a feeling of disappointment since we had seen the mature version, before seeing this oddity of an embryo. But the search for it every time we went to the maze of old Bukhara was worth the sensation of losing one's way in a really old town.

On that first visit, we were really hungry around four in the afternoon. So, we went to the Lyab-i-Hauz (Lyab pronounced in the local vernacular as Lubb) quarter or the Vicinity of the Tank. (Writing 150 years ago, the Hungarian traveller, Arminius Vambery, who went disguised as a wandering dervish through the Turkoman deserts to spy out Khiva and Bukhara for the Europeans, describes how in the hot summer evenings, all and sundry in the city would make their way to the low mattressed couches, spread around a deep, stepped tank with two *madrasas* and a sarai reared on its side.[4]) One side opened to a narrow channel, which took water along the road to another market and sarai as if in a tunnel with shops on its side. People reclined on the mattresses, drinking tea and gossiping. That winter there was nothing outside, except a sizzling shashlik stall. There was of course Bukhara's famous statue, facing the tank, of the folk hero of Turan and Iran, Mullah Nasiruddin Khoja, riding his donkey. Mullah Nasiruddin is the centre of a host of stories, all sly and stupid about the resources and the plight of the common people, which still come out when there is a point to make in friendly conversation. A modern sculpture, this is a pleasant example of Uzbek affection for common people and their humour. One of the madrasas, known by the name of its founder, Nadir Dewan Begi, has handicraft stalls inside.

The restaurant by the tank is a cozy building, on the second floor of which excellent but simple meals are served. This was when we were introduced to a new Russian meat preparation they called *langet*, the closest thing to which is a well-done escalope, with French fries. In the Russo-phobia and Turkophilia then rife in Uzbekistan, we were tired of eating the standard *manti* or *somsa*, or *shashlik*, *plov*.

We quizzed Nigora about the election of the Oli Majlis (Parliament), which was due that day: we had been surprised that she was not attending to cast her vote. The elections were meant to bring in a group of representatives to be guided in training themselves, for changes from communism to a democratic regime.

They would prepare a new presidential election, in which Karimov was a candidate for re-election. He had a brand new party, the Fidokorlar or Trusties, which had come out of the post-communist chrysalis of the People's Democratic Party. Nigora said it was all right, her vote had been cast in the morning. We later gathered, back in Tashkent, that lazy people did not have to bother. The *mahalla* arranged for votes to be collected from the homes and cast at the booths. Decisions about who would be voted were communally taken and organized by the *mahalla* leadership. For those in India who raise eyebrows at this travesty of democratic practice, as it had been defined in the modern West, it may be recalled that, only half a century ago, *basti* dwellers were being brought together with their lunch packets in lorries or rickshaws for voting whoever their 'dadas' or 'didis' (respectable people, not necessarily elders, of both sexes) had told them, would be good for their interests.

In a country like Uzbekistan, in a century that was just ending, there had been transition from the closest that Asians have come to despotism to the violence of Civil War, then peasant revolt against socialist expropriation in the 1920s, which Stalin called the Basmachi or 'bandit' uprisings, then the liquidation of Jadid nationalists by plebeian supplanters of the 1940s, and, finally, socialist chauvinism of the generations of Sharaf Rashidov and Islam Karimov. In these circumstances democracy was a hybrid with very weak vitality. Nigora said her mother was a ruling Party functionary in Kagan, the new Russian cantonment town and railway junction a few miles from Bukhara, and her father was a doctor. Her brother was trained in jurisprudence and had begun to practice the law in Samarkand: her mother was looking for a bride for him. Nigora's generation had begun to look to the West (whose language she had learned from Scots missionaries and which she taught at the University). It looked for better opportunities to get the material benefits of democracy. In South Asia, following the West, democracy had been a plant watered by middle-class care and had not nourished the poorest in the land. In Uzbekistan, democracy was guided still by the nomenklatura, while the best of the middle class were already thinking of migrating to the north, or if possible further west.

Bukhara had been a new experience. The city represented something quite new after the north—more suburban, less obviously affluent, less immiserized, with fewer gypsies or beggars on the roads. But it was certainly more grey and grim than Samarkand or the capital city for which the Bukharan hankered.

ISLAM AND ETHNICITY IN END-CENTURY TASHKENT

The next morning, the mist that we had looked down on from the hotel lay even heavier over Bukhara. We drove back along the highway through a haze which only slowly began to shimmer over the fields, as the sun weakly shone through it. After a brief halt in Samarkand for a greasy lunch—the usual menu—in the bazaar, and a look at the sights, we headed for home. It was dark. The highway was shrouded in mist, which began to thicken as we came down the Timur Gates into the Syr Darya plain. It was here that I realized why Babur called this tract 'Ha-Dervish'. A dense fog lay all across the plains, up to Tashkent. A line of cars and trucks crawled, soon bumper-to-bumper, drawing courage only from the extremely hazy backlights of the vehicle ahead. As we crossed and re-crossed the check posts of the Kazakhstan strip, and then the district boundaries on the road, Rustom was quiet and ramrod straight at the wheel, with sweat pouring down his face in the cold night. By the roadside, trucks would suddenly loom out, overturned across the verges. He seemed to be fully conscious of his responsibility for our safety. It was not till several hours later as we were driving past the better lit, though still hazy, environs of the outer boundary of Tashkent, that he could be heard emitting a low sigh of relief. We had been nervous too. It was touching that just then his cellphone beeped. His wife was asking for reassurance that he had got through the fog, which the radio had announced was blocking the southern highway. We were all relieved when we got home.

A day or two later we took our son and a friend to hunt for the snow in Chimgan, as after a brief show of snow one day in late October, the skies had been clear. We were lucky. As soon as the road wound past the police check-post, still very suspicious of travellers to the mountains after the summer attacks, and on the lookout for speed money (so that our official accreditation cards had to be produced), a blizzard began. Snowflakes came down, slanting hard across the windscreen, but the driver seemed more cheerful than he had been in the fog. The road, ski slopes, and everything else was white when we got to the resort area. Snow ploughs were already out, creating narrow lanes of tarmac, but it was a losing battle. Chimgan was deserted and the cable station shut; the shashlik stalls cluttering the road at this point were closed: it was a weekday and out of season. Already it was apparent that poverty was stalking the mountains in the way that we had sensed in Humsan. The only person moving about was a halfwit, who urinated on the road, to watch it solidify immediately. But then he was always around on all our trips, pointing to his mouth for food.

Other places in and around Tashkent that our son visited with us included notably the fairly impressive mosque of Zangi Ota (the dark father) and the tomb of Babur's maternal grandfather, the actual Mughal from whom the Baburids' Indian title is derived, Yunus Khan, and also the theological seminaries beyond Chorsu bazaar. Zangi Ota is a shrine-cum-hospice complex to the south of the city, a bit distant from the Yuzhnii Voksaal or South Station and the road to Samarkand. It has the usual complement of beggars in old-fashioned local dress that you find in every Muslim shrine here, as indeed you do in Hindu shrines in India. Beyond is a minaret separate from the mosque, said to have been built by Timur himself, to honour an old fourteenth-century *pir*. This pious person had married the widow of a more famous *pir*, Yasavi. The portal of the mosque has striking blue tile work. Around it the ubiquitous modern restorers of wood-work were refurbishing the precinct.

Restoration of what had earlier been disused, and sometimes ruined, holy places was becoming rapidly apparent in the country as the new century dawned. In Chorsu, a large *madrasa* facing several main roads near the Samarkand Darwaza (one of the many portal gates which marked the quarters surrounding the old city) was being renovated to house handicraft and curio makers. Next to it a rundown little place of worship was being enlarged with multiple domes gleaming silver above the bazaar to accommodate a much larger congregation. When I had visited it in summer, a couple of bearded men hurried up to find out who I was. Told that I hailed from Hindistan, they placed their hands on their hearts in true polite Uzbek fashion and desired me to convey their *salamat wa aleikum* to all Muslims in Hindistan. Informed that I was no Muslim, they smiled abstractedly and moved away, disappointed. This enthusiasm for faith re-discovered was also found in the library where the Koran of Caliph Usman is kept. It is evident in the modern buildings, close by, of the Islamic University in Tashkent with its classrooms, decorated with maps of the Islamic world in Asia and Africa, in Arabic script. The caretaker of the campus speaks proudly of contacts with Al Azhar in Cairo. The University is far from fundamentalist and is supposed to keep Uzbek scholars in touch with trends in contemporary Islam, with domestic religious practice, and with scholarship with a strong secular bias.

In its library there is a massive tome, published in English in Islamic Deobandi seminaries in Pakistan, of their versions of commentaries on Imam Bukhari, seen as being relevant to the daily life of the faithful. Such books were important sources of the Taliban revival, sponsored in Pakistan by fanatical preachers, trained in the theology of the Indian Islamic college at Deoband Dar ul Ulum between Delhi and Hardwar, who had started their own schools at places like Akora Khattak near Peshawar or Binnauri near Karachi. These very teachers, also trained their students or Talibs in the use of modern arms and fed ideas into the *jihad* of people like the captains of Mullah Umar of Kandahar, or the hoodlums of the Lashkar-i-Toiba in Jammu and Kashmir. With their beards and round headgear or turbans, they were to leap into prominence the next year, when Afghanistan returned centre stage. Even today they are the intellectual force behind the Majlis-Muttahida-i-Amal, which has become a force in the North-West Frontier's anti-American reaction to the toning down of political Islam in Pakistan.

Tashkent Indian acquaintances would often quote all this as instances of the creeping spread of 'fundamentalism' among the Uzbeks as well. Look at the spread of the round headgear, of their belief in the tenets of Imam Bukhari, and the treatment of his renovated shrine as 'the Mecca of the East', at the proliferation of mosques and at sickening maintenance among women of reactionary practices, like virginity tests, they would say. We, meaning tolerant Hindus, interested in the common security of India, Central Asia and the Western world, could never trust Islamic clannishness. Look at even the educated young women. If they went to India, they took to wearing the *burka* to emphasize their distinctive purity from lewd men in the *mufassil*. At home in the Uzbek provinces they still had the practice of mothers-in-law searching for hymenal blood on the sheets of newly weds and of throwing the bride out of the house if the sheets were clean. All this in hushed tones.

It was true that some sort of revivalism was indeed rife among many Uzbeks. Young girls, and matronly ladies such as the middle-aged person who came to our flat as domestic help three days in the week, were turning to the practice of *roza* during the month of Ramzan because the *mahalla* had persuaded them to do so. With a memory of Soviet precept, she was a bit embarrassed to tell my wife this. In explanation she added it was also good for the health and the figure to eat less one month in the year. She had lost quite a few kilos. Younger girls, if quizzed, would tell my wife that fasting during Ramzan was a social duty. In Uzbekistan such observances were expressed in a familiar traditional idiom of the country. The country happened to be ethnically Uzbek, in transition from the collapse of Russian overlordship, as well as religiously Muslim. Islam was a badge of social ethnicity not just an undifferentiated 'religion' to be read off from the Koran, as the Taliban would like it to be. What was being reasserted in Uzbekistan was social practice, not theological identity, which the Taliban were asserting in Afghanistan.

In Uzbekistan open conflict was controlled by the political system. Conflict was also controlled by the manipulation through schools and colleges under Party regulation, of a strong secular ideology. Above all it was controlled by the *mahalla* micro-leadership. This retained the social content of Islam while campaigning against the fundamentalism of the Hizb-ut-Tahrir, which played the same role among backward sections of society, that the Jamat-ul-Islami with its cheap tracts and pamphlets play in countries like Bangladesh, Indonesia, and the Philippines.

The tomb of Yunus Khan is part of a precinct in the middle of the city that does not attract any attention, from citizen or foreigner alike. Our younger friends in UWED like Dinora, or Nigai, had not even visited it, behind the buildings of the architectural restoration institute at Shaikhantaur, between two of the broadest thoroughfares of the city, and close by the procuratorial courts, where the trial of the bomb blasts accused still dragged on. If, showing your visiting card to the guards at the main gate, and speaking to them in your broken Russian laced with Uzbek, you could wheedle your way in, it was a rewarding experience.

Yunus Khan had been a cosmopolitan figure of the mid-fifteenth century, when the power of the Mughals of Turkestan had been at its lowest ebb since the days of Chingiz, a century and half before. Eastern Turkestan had lapsed into domestic rivalries and warfare up to the Sino-Tibetan-Kashmir borders, while Islam itself did not extend beyond the Timurid dominions. Yunus Khan, an exile from what is now Xinjiang and Southern Kazakhstan, had wandered through Ajam, Iraq, and Misr, and educated himself in the Arab lands. He was brought back to Tashkent as a loose vassal of Timurid princes who followed Ulugh Beg in Samarkand, to hold the borders against his own nomadic people, a sort of 'indirect rule' later practised in the British Empire through the 'native princes'. There is a fascinating account to be constructed of him and his relatives, intermarrying, trying to keep culture and learning alive in a far frontier of the mediaeval Islamicate in its time of troubles, and also of the generation after his death. When Babur was a small boy, his uncles lapsed into warfare, betraying one another, princes taking each other's wives and sisters into their own harems, and sending them back to relatives after the ravisher had died in battle; in general keeping borders in turmoil from Kashgar to Khorasan and Tashkent to Bengal. This account can be constructed from the *Tarikh-i-Rashidi of Mirza Haider Dughlat*, another one of Yunus Khan's daughters' sons, who for a while served Babur, fought for Humayun in his defeat by Sher Shah at Kanauj, and ended up having conquered Kashmir briefly, killed in a local ambush. His history of his ancestors and masters is a fascinating and detailed narrative of the fluctuating fortunes of tribal authority in Turkestan and north India in a 'time of troubles'.[5]

The mausoleum of Yunus Khan is a pleasant dome, set in garden surroundings. Next to it is a mosque with intricate woodwork. Turn down a lane past a student hostel, and you will come to three structures in a little garden, very well tended. One is a historic *madrasa* also in woodwork where students study traditional learning. Opposite it is a little tomb built round a tree, which, legend has it, grew at Alexander's touch. The tomb is older than that of Yunus Khan and was probably a sacred spot already when he died. Past it is a slightly older one, of Shaikh Khovandi Takhur, from whom the whole locality gets its name, who is reputed to have been a Kazakh of the same *juz* (extended clan) as that to which the present President of Kazakhstan, Nursultan Nazarbaev, claims affinity six hundred years later. A large visitor's ledger, which you will be asked to sign, appreciating the maintenance, bears Nazarbaev's comments during a visit. Like the Imam Bukhari shrine, the precinct received its facelift during Nazarbaev's first visit here after Independence. It marks the careful post-communist turn towards ethno-religious identity.

In 1993, when the Maulana Azad Institute was set up in Calcutta, the powers that be suggested I stay in touch with the Ministry of External Affairs in South Block, New Delhi, through an Additional Secretary who had been deputed by the Foreign Secretary, then J.N. Dixit to help in the Institute's interests. This very polished diplomat who soon left to become our most senior Ambassador in South Asia, at that time travelled in a international group, which briefly visited Tashkent, and had discussions with Islam Karimov. He narrated a conversation with the President, who had expressed his admiration for our Prime Minister, then P.V. Narasimha Rao who, Karimov thought, had very adroitly managed the nuances of demolition of the Babri Masjid. This, the President had been informed, had been causing tension between majority Hindus and minority Muslims. The Prime Minister had neither toppled the Masjid, nor repressed the topplers, beyond taking necessary steps to separate the contestants. The President thought that this was the policy of equidistance from elements of tension, and of secular regulation of the material aspects of religious practice, that he should emulate in a situation where fundamentalism had to be held at bay. But there was the social aspect of spirituality encouraged in the vacuum left by the retreat of communism and Karimov certainly had gained a mechanistics view of the problems of political religion in end-of-century India.

I was continually reminded of the nuanced elements of this anecdote. True, the problems would grow as the Afghan crisis matured into its final tragedy, impinged on Uzbek strategies, and drove it into the US geopolitical clutch. In the subsequent two years one would learn more about the Byzantine ramifications of those tragedies, twisting and turning away from the failing Indian Congress model of twentieth-century Indian non-alignment, into the globalized model of outright subservience to the West, which much of Asia suffers from today.

There is a seamless web of mixture between pre-Islamic practices and folk memories of the early preaching of Islam. In Tashkent the buildings are distinctly Islamic, domed and arched, without even the conical high spire of the Khwarezm variety of the Western Marches, as in Chashma-i-Ayub in Bukhara. But the legends around them are of a sort that can be found anywhere in the non-Islamic world. holy men, settled for meditation and prayer in a particular spot, whose mausolea become the nucleus for later piety, seminaries where ancient learning and substrata of old theologies or primitive science are continually reinterpreted in a mélange. Syncretism has been the core of the transformation of popular Buddhism and pre-Buddhist beliefs (as for instance in Tibet, Assam, or the Tai-Ahom linguistic cultures of Inner South-East Asia) into Hinduism or into Later Mahayana Buddhism, as the case may be. The return to Islamic fundamentals does not take place only in the language of the Jamat-i-Islami or its more extremist clones. The latter depend on textual versions, like the Bible thumpers of the American Midwest, among whose following may be included today's Texas oil barons.

One may, however, visualize an Islam that is low key and socially rooted. Karimov and his administration encourage this when they publicize their selective restoration of the monuments associated with local men of piety, or when they reorganize *madrasas* as craft ateliers for miniature artists seeking to restore the arts of Bihzad and his contemporaries next to such monuments—and when they seek to build these complexes into quiet places for reflection about spiritual elements in the local heritage. This is an emphasis on 'spirituality', about which Karimov speaks in his propaganda brochure 'Islam in Our Hearts and Souls'. This tract in English was available and could be read in UWED in 1999, but was unavailable in the bookshops I later went to. This was neither 'Karimov's repression' that Ahmed Rashid caricatures in his recent book, nor did it necessarily create militant *jihadis*, whom the world press set up as a scarecrow in the next two years, as the bloody prelude to Bush junior's attack on Iraq.

NOTES

1. D.D. Kosambi, *Myth and Reality: Studies in the Formation of Indian Culture* (Bombay, Popular Prakashan, 1994 edition.)
2. For an Indian account of the Khwarezmian episode in Afghan and Indus Basin history, see Muhammad Habib, 'The Asiatic Environment',

Sections III-V in Muhammad Habib, Khaliq Ahmed Nizami, *A Comprehensive History of India*, vol. 5, *The Delhi Sultanat* (AD *1206-1526*) (Indian History Congress and People's Publishing House, New Delhi, 1982), Ch. 1, pp. 37-83.

3. Dmitri A. Trofimov, 'Islam in the Political Culture of the Former Soviet Union: Central Asia and Azerbaijan', in *Hamburger Beitrage zur Friedensforschung und Sicherheitspolitik* (Hamburg University, Falkenstein 1, Hamburg 22587, n.d. is a fresh account of the revival of Islamic studies in the Soviet Union's last days, written without Ahmed Rashid's jargon about underground Islam, which takes a cool look at actual fundamentalist tendencies from a secularist perspective: D.A. Trofimov was attached to the Soviet Embassy in Tashkent during 1998-9.
4. Arminius Vambery, *Travels in Central Asia: Being an Account of a Journey from Teheran Across the Turkoman Desert to Khiva, Bukhara and Samarkand* (1st published 1864; Bhavana Books and Prints, New Delhi, 1996).
5. An authoritative English version will be found in N. Elias (ed. with Commentary, Notes and Map) and E. Denison Ross (translation)—*The Tarikh-i-Rashidi of Mirza Muhammad Haider Dughlat: A History of the Mughals of Central Asia* (Academia Asiatica, Patna, 1973). Along with the *Baburnama*, this book gives a feel for the Central Asian *Quattrocento* and *Cinquecento*, which was no less turbulent or culturally creative than the European Renaissance.

4

Dialectics and Contradictions

CULTURAL LIMITATIONS IN POST-SOVIET SOCIETY

1999 was drawing to a close. My wife and son left two weeks ahead of me for Calcutta. Waiting for UWED vacations, I could reflect on what I was learning from immersion in Uzbek life of the last year of the twentieth century.

The specificity of Uzbek culture within Russification, a century and half old in the north, (i.e. Tashkent and Ferghana), eighty years old in the south (the Bukhara Emirate), is something that was ignored in all the talk about the rise of militant Islam beamed out by CNN or BBC. In Uzbekistan itself, people spoke of dialect differences between Ferghana, the Tashkent region, Khwarezm, or Surkhan Darya in the south, near the Oxus, much in the same way that Bengalis before Independence distinguished between the dialects of Krishnagar classicality, Vikrampur vitality, and Chittagong, Barisal, or Birbhum brogues. Uzbekistan was as much a frontier of moderate Islam as Bangladesh had been in the last quarter of the twentieth century, and that in spite of the sterling effort to change East Pakistan into Bangladesh in the 1960s and early 1970s. Uzbeks were more concerned with regional identities than religious purity. The mix of the cultures of various dominating aliens, with subject people on the soil, whether the Sart (settled folk) of the plains or the Tajik of the south, was a distinctly frontier element.

Secondly, fear and a lack of dissent among the people seemed to explain much of the old Soviet dominance and its continuities in the present day. People were warm and friendly if you talked to them about any personal matter: children, homes, food, and so on. Talk about political issues or principles; a blank but wary veil dropped over their features. The conversation would dry up, or even among friends, be deflected. Unlike Indian diplomats, I was not treated as a person who might be reporting back home. It was realized, with sympathy, that if I did want to report, my own immediate authority, the Ambassador was not interested in what I tried to say. Even so, the polite curtain of privacy was general. People would not risk a political opinion about the present regime. Dissent was something we never actually saw; though I had seen signs of it in Moscow in Gorbachev's early days in 1987. On later occasions, the older, and once very powerful, retired civil servants we knew would snort derisively, if when discussing some obvious injustice in the land, we asked why people had not protested against it. Protest! They said people got shot for protest.

Here emerges a third Uzbek specificity. Bolshevik, and in particular Stalinist, repression was not the real reason for the fear of protest, though the brutalities of the oppression of the Basmatchis in the 1920s, and of the Civil War in general, as well as the liquidation of the national reforming leadership of the local Communist Party in the 1937 Purges, must have played an important part in creating a mentality of latent terror. Beneath lay the hideous superstition and obscurantism of the Emirate and Khanates of Khokand and Khiva. Their aristocracies had been co-opted by Russia much as feudalism was co-opted by the British in their Empire in Asia and Africa, for instance, when they recruited their Gurkha or Hausa levies from Nepal or Nigeria. Naturally, there were differences between the reaction of Russians, Tatars, Siberian tribes, or Kazakhs, to Soviet hegemonization. All we could sense was the fear of voicing protest. The only exception that I would hear about was in 2001 summer. That was in Ferghana where dollars and Korans were seeping in from Juma and Tohir's last hideouts in northern Tajikistan.

If there was no tradition of democracy from below, in this society layered for centuries by the forces of domination and subordination, there is to our citybred amazement, a strong sense of the dignity of labour. It is almost trivial to describe this feeling today in South Asia. In our societies, class has become so deeply impregnated by caste that the well to do cannot dream of performing certain household chores, without the physical activity of what are still unfortunately called 'menial servants'. It is not as if many among them do not remember the values inculcated by people such as Mahatma Gandhi, or by an entire generation influenced by the broad ideas of the Congress during the freedom struggle, about the dignity of all work from ploughing the soil to wielding a hammer or cleaning a latrine. Half a century has elapsed since then. The edge of that ideology has been blunted by embourgeoisification. The fact that in the Western countries, equality of labour practice now exists, has to be seen in the quite different context of a general transformation towards available technology, even in the domestic sector, in such matters as sanitary appliances or kitchen equipment. In the old USSR, the level of technology was nowhere as high, nor was it easily accessible to average consumers. Even in 2001, in as much of a marketplace for Central Asia, of consumer durables, as Navoi Avenue in Tashkent had become (it was later reputed to have been much curtailed due to anti-smuggling measures) only the very rich or the easy money mafias of crony capitalism could afford to buy such products as Japanese or Korean large refrigerators, the costliest airconditioners, or the vast home cinema TV sets, which were being displayed, row upon row. Equality of opportunity leading to equality of labour practice is still a far off dream in Central Asia. Here, dignity of labour means what it meant in India in the middle of the twentieth century in the last days of the freedom struggle a state of mind and a belief that doing any work by using one's own hands was not a matter of shame nor of ritual impurity, but of self-respect.

Our driver was a member of as good a family as any other in a respectable *mahalla* of Bodomzor in north Tashkent. His late father had been a director of a state cooperative. As the youngest son, he lived with his mother according to Uzbek practice. The elder brother had moved away to his own house, and he remained in his parents' house. After army service and a diploma in mechanical engineering from a technical institute, he had worked through the 1980s in a machine tool factory. After Independence he had chosen to use his savings to be a driver with his own car. He hired it and his services out for income. His wife is a pediatrician. If asked why he chose this form of self-employment, he would say he loved his *mashina* (car) and was happiest in it, except in the evenings when he loved the company of his three children or his friends in a billiard room or good café. He never had any problems in hunkering down to fix any appliance, whether it was our flat's water system or its commode. This was always a friendly gesture, never asked but granted as a matter of course. Or, our maid, apart from her assigned work would not hesitate to fix the wooden racks in the sideboard, which had become loose, or the screws, which had come adrift in the hinges of the furniture. All work was interchangeable. The concept of 'menial labour' made no sense to the late twentieth-century Sovietized Uzbek.

What socialism endowed the Uzbeks with by way of dignity of labour, it took away with in its approach to mass education. The Russian higher education system had not permeated to the Muslim territories, beyond perhaps Tatarstan. Historically speaking, Jadidism, the growth of modern reformism among the young, and the national democratic intelligentsia in towns like Karshi between Samarkand and Bukhara on the southern road, as well as in the cities, had sapped faith in the outmoded old syllabus maintained by the Emirate. If the Revolution of 1917 had stopped in March, and Kerensky (who had grown up in Tashkent, where his father had been a government official) had remained the social democratic prime minister of a reformed Romanov dynasty after the First World War, modernization may have spread in Turkestan, as it was earlier spreading in British India and its Native States. But this 'if' of history was never a probability, not even a possibility.

The imperial nobility was in a state of collapse after the defeats by Germany. The defeated armies streaming back home were in no mood to compromise with reformism. The small Russian working class in Turkestan—mainly railway workers—did not sympathize either with nobles like the Governor General Kuropatkin, or the disgraced Romanov prince who had been allowed to build a palace in Tashkent (both were shot) or with the Uzbek Sarts and the Kyrgyz of Semirechie who had risen in revolt against forced conscription into the Russian army in 1916 and massacred Russian peasant settlers. The bloody civil war for four more years destroyed Jadid moderation. Liberals like the northerner, Mustafa Chokaev, fled west to Europe after the Khokand massacre. Many Jadid like Faizulla Khojaev worked for the communists.

Uzbek education thus went the Bolshevik way. The indoctrination of *proletkult*, the denigration of elite excellence, the reduction of independence of thought among the brightest to a uniform average level of formal competence in passing standard examinations, the acceptance of instruction and the rote learning of simple messages, all these contributed to the reduction of even higher education to the creation of cadres, trained to carry out orders; picking cotton, or in technical institutes turning out machinists. Two universities grew in this period—Samarkand, which looked after Tajikistan and Tashkent, with its emphasis on linguistics and pedagogical training in the interests of Party workers. Other universities like Bukhara or Andijan were secondary. So were yet others where purely technical matters like soil science, irrigation, or law were given importance. Until the 1970s, Russians dominated the faculties, the older professors whom I met in UWED, who had all headed university departments elsewhere or institutes, were completely Russified. They spoke little Uzbek, except for colloquial or domestic purposes. They had often married Russians; some of their children had done the same, or gone north. Their newfound patriotism was that of a rootless Party elite, treated with contempt by the new social groups who pushed their way up with the indigenization policies of Sharaf Rashidov in the 1970s and early 1980s.

Ahmed Rashid, following recent US scholarship, has romanticized the present character of the Jadid heritage. He says, 'in 1991, Uzbek intellectuals attempted to republish and popularize Jadid writings, but they were quickly suppressed. Uzbek President Islam Karimov discourages all attempts to renew interest in Jadidism, although the movement has immense relevance in today's discussion of the way Islam, nationalism, and democracy can co-exists in Central Asia'. Later he repeats himself 'after the 1917 revolution a few Jadids attempted to combine Islam with communism, but they were crushed by Stalin. Jadid ideas returned in 1991 in the planks of nationalist opposition parties like Birlik and Erk, both of which President Karimov immediately banned. By this move Karimov ensured that there would be no democratic outlet for the revival of Islam and Islamic nationalism.'[1]

The Jadidism affected by liberals like the Pulatov brothers or even Muhammad Salih, in the brief flowering of Birlik and Erk, had democratic potential: it is also true that the recently communist Karimov crushed these groups. The real danger to the Uzbek state was however not the weak intellectualism of the liberals. Nor was the latter any alternative to the militant Islam of Adolat, or the Hizb, or Tohir Yuldashev and the ex-soldier, Juma. The Islamic groups were closer to fundamentalism, and would have had little sympathy for Jadidism. In the conflict between open democracy of the Pulatov variety, and guided democracy of the Karimov variety, Jadid ideas had no chance. But that is not all. In 1999, the Academy of Sciences, the apex body that controls the intelligentsia, organized a high level seminar with the Konrad Adenauer Foundation, a conservative liberal German organization, to help the President in his Academy for State Reconstruction, where his administrators were being trained in conjunction with the Islamic University people, for historians and philosophers. The seminar was meant to rehabilitate the Jadids as pioneers of the intellectual renaissance of Uzbek nationalism. It was attended by scholars from Holland, Italy, Germany, and France, brought together by the Institut Francaise d'Etudes Asie Centrale (IFEAC) under the Directorship of Vincent Fourniau. The presence of these scholars ensured the availability of simultaneous translation. Professor Fourniau invited me to follow the discussion.

The Uzbek scholars of the older generation were frank about their confusion. They had been taught in Soviet days that the Jadids were bourgeous nationalists. Why were they being resurrected today? The younger generation of historians was less questioning. If Jadidism was fashionable in the West as a sign of liberalism, then they were prepared to go along with it. What was most important was not the debate, or the papers by the scholars, which lacked common focus, but a lavishly produced collection of fullface portraits of Jadid leaders, intellectuals, newspaper writers, teachers, poets, who had contributed to Uzbek literature in the early twentieth century, and many slaughtered in Stalin's liquidation campaign of 1930s. After their formal inauguration, the pictures with long life histories were turned into posters in Uzbek language. A full set remained on display in the corridor of the UWED library, as no doubt in other academic institutions also.

Rashid incorrectly sees President Karimov as a brutal suppressor of liberal or Jadid ideas. The truth is more nuanced. What Karimov has done in recent years is to appropriate liberal rhetoric, to draw its fangs against authoritarianism, and marginalize its more vocal proponents. In this he has been no different from many populist Right wing politicians in more democratic parts of the world. The result of all this has been that the students with whom I came into contact, are being pulled into the official way of thinking. Only those who believe in extreme Islam turned to dissent. Many more just accept the rhetoric of the West for a chance to move into Europe or, better still, America. Most of those to whom I lectured either in international relations (an utterly new subject without the analytical sophistication that it had developed in the West and not far removed from Soviet geo-politics)[2] or at the Tashkent Institute of Oriental Studies, or in the Alberuni Institute, were young people with limited minds. I may be quite unfair. I did not speak either of their languages of instruction, and they did communicate with me in English, or in the Oriental Institutes in Hindi. They suffered from lack of books and textual scholarship, beyond the most simplistic textbooks or selected works meant for the edification of common people. The sophisticated and complex scholarship, in which Indians used to take pride was completely lacking. Lack of funds, lack of encouragement from higher authorities, and over emphasis on language training, as distinct from depth research in the social sciences and humanities, was certainly the reason for this. I have considerable admiration for some of the people who continued their mission as teachers despite these constraints.

However, the fact remained that in Uzbekistan there was no incentive for fresh enquiry about changes taking place in the world as a result of globalization, about new developments in democracy, or about the transformation of relations between the Asia-Pacific rimlands and the Atlantic civilization. It was these circumstances that created President Karimov, not Karimov who was alone responsible for the repression of dissent or fundamentalism.

KANDAHAR 1999

Classes had just come to an end and I was preparing to leave for Calcutta to join my family when the television came alive on Christmas Eve with the news that an Indian Airlines plane, flying out of Kathmandu, had been hijacked on its way to Delhi. Matters came closer to us in Tashkent, when it was reported that the plane had landed for oil at Amritsar airport, that the authorities there had failed to move with stealth and block its wheels for fresh takeoff, and that it was on its way through the Middle East, with commentators guessing about its destination. Many of us were glued through the night to the Doordarshan commentaries. What added a tinge of urgency was the geographical ignorance of a BJP legislator from Jammu, who informed the media that the hijackers would land at Tashkent. Uzbekistan and Afghanistan were, for him, not much different, Muslim tracts of the north. Our Embassy officials—the Ambassador was away—spent the night at the phone in the office, on the alert, in case the plane did land in Tashkent. It had already been heard that one of the passengers had been separated from his newly-wed wife, and knifed in cold blood, when he tried to raise his head to look at the criminals. A Christmas night party for all Indian residents in Tashkent, at the home of an Indian businessman, went off in sombre mood. At dawn there was snow on the ground and trees. One wondered what was happening in the freezing plain, surrounded by Taliban, due south in Kandahar.

Let me pass very briefly over the next month, when a range of personal happenings, quite unexpectedly tragic, left their mark. The Kandahar events were moving to their climax. There was an air of inevitability about the outcome that left no scope for cheerfulness. Foreign Minister Jaswant Singh flew with the three convicts to be exchanged for the plane and all its passengers. Precious little remained to be done, once our authorities had failed to prevent the hijackers leaving Amritsar, after the pilot had actually succeeded in bringing the plane down there. The horse is difficult to bring back once the stable door is left open.

The Government of India's policy with regard to terrorist threat, now that it was out in the open, was pitiable. In the 1980s it had not been capable of dealing with General Zia-ul-Huq's policy of Islamization, which had paid rich dividends against Russian and Indian influence in Afghanistan. That policy had been switched to create a milieu in which the demand for *azadi* could be voiced in Kashmir by the fronts for Islamic Kashmiriyat (as distinct from secular Kashmiri regional identity within the Indian Union, the policy of the National Conference).[3] This lack of initiative in the 1980s was partly remedied in the early 1990s, when the Ministry of External Affairs cultivated warm relations with the new, Muslim and strongly secular, republics of Central Asia, where the heritage of Indo-Soviet peace and friendship was still alive.[4] The Congress party's failure to retain even its tenuous control over the Central Government in the late 1990s, and the slide of the country towards the Hindu fundamentalist ideological outlook of the Bharatiya Janata Party had alienated our foreign policy from its positive support of secularism and tolerance for all faiths (what Abul Fazl four centuries ago in Akbar's time had celebrated as *Sulh-i-Kul*, peace of all). The fact that a Indian Foreign Minister had to be sent to escort his captives to a foreign destination for a hostage swap, without trusting officers of the Foreign Service and Research and Analysis Wing of the Cabinet Secretariat to do their job, sent a new message, not only to Pakistan and the Taliban, but also to the neighbouring Central Asian Republics, like Uzbekistan.

The message was that Indian foreign policy lacked the confidence and initiative that Indira Gandhi (whom they still admired greatly for her strength) used to show. Kandahar marked the decisive sidelining of India in the lands from the Indus to the Syr Darya in the next few years, during which all power equations were to pivot round fundamentalism and oil resources, and would radically change.

UZBEKISTAN TURNS THE CENTURY

Meanwhile, we came back to Tashkent in February 2000. The rigors of the winter had passed, though we were sorry to have missed the snow. The even tenor of Tashkent life was becoming familiar on this second return, but my wife suddenly became ill on the plane. When we reached home, friends had summoned the emergency medical service, always on call for any inhabitant in the country. Nothing serious could be found that did not improve by the next three or four days. However, the brush with the medical system in contemporary Uzbekistan was instructive.

A year before, we had a good experience of this, when soon after arrival, we had to take treatment from an orthopaedist at the New Tashkent Medical Institute, way outside the city, past Chorsu as well as Universitet Gorodok or the main Tashkent University settlement area. The massive building on the fifth floor of which was located the excellent Uzbek specialist was clean and well organized, quite unlike hospitals we are used to at home—broad, antiseptic passages, medical staff in white uniforms and constant politeness even though we could not speak their language except for a few broken words. The therapy was distinctly Spartan—the young lady specialist did not believe in anesthetics or any frills. Her injection into the finger bone was very painful but meant to be borne with a smile. What helped was the nurse on duty, who seized the opportunity to start a conversation with my wife in Hindi, her second language in one of the many Hindi schools which used to flourish in Soviet times. She had done a stint as a nurse in the Steel Plant Hospital at Bokaro on the Bihar-Bengal border, that had brought India close to many presently middle-aged Uzbek professionals. She even said friends there had given her an Indian name. She became very upset, when at the cash counter, we were asked to pay a small sum and that too in soum for the therapy—*mehmaans* (guests) deserved full hospitality and Indians were national *mehmaans*. The specialist, of course, refused to take a single soum on the several visits we made, every time giving the excuse—how can I, you are Indians and our friends.

On the stairs of Novy Tashme (as it was abbreviated in local parlance) one day, we were greeted by a large group of young Indian doctors. They were the last remnants of the exchange beneficiaries who had come from many parts of north India to take degrees from Tashkent hospitals, until after 1991, the system was discontinued. Many were Muslims, mainly from Kashmir (which has old affinities with Central Asia, Srinagar having been on the trade route through Leh and Kashgar to Osh and Andijan, in Tsarist times)[5] or from Lucknow. Since their course was six months shorter than the Indian MBBS, many had been stranded in Tashkent and some had married here. Each came up and asked if there was anything they could do to help us. There are not too many Indians left today in Tashkent: the ones that are, can be very friendly in chance meetings.

The emergency practitioner and nurse who turned up at our flat on our return were, however, pretty elementary. They promptly put three injections into my wife, without even waiting to hear in Russian from our friends about what had happened. We later gathered that this is standard sedative practice in Russian medicine! They left her to sleep it off. Embassy friends and other expatriates had previously told us that Uzbek medicine, whatever its virtue in the past, had collapsed, since funds were cut in the 1990s and the better doctors (often Jews from Bukhara) migrated to Moscow or the West. Without going into the dubious mercies of local diagnosis, we chose to go for consultation to the International Clinic under UN auspices. Uzbek therapy, *per se* can be very misleading, as we shall later have occasion to describe.

Our health problems were then going through a somewhat bad patch. My eye pressure tension had to be checked each month and optical perimetry done every three months. An Indian eye specialist, working at the Stara Tashme, the Old Hospital very close to our house, a rambling collection of Tsarist style buildings, in a park like area (reminiscent of Calcutta Medical College as it used to be in pre-Independence days) was a moral support throughout our stay. He admitted that local methods were primitive for diagnosis and medication. For instance, eye pressure is tested the world over by modern machinery. The Stara Tashme, had no funds for this, so a primitive method of measurement had to be used with a considerable margin of error. Dr. Khera's father, an eye specialist in Pathankot, used to throw up his hands in horror when he heard from his son about this method, which had gone out of vogue decades earlier. Later Khera directed me to a clinic where this new equipment had just arrived.

The Soviet system of medicine, excellent as it was in many areas, and highly routinized as well as clean, had been, like all other public utility services in the USSR, dependant on a top-heavy system of centrally determined state subsidy. The pushing-out of the Central Asian Republics from the USSR had meant the collaps of this system. Each Republic had been thrown back on the extremely limited resources. What Uzbeks were doing to maintain the organization of their hospitals and public polyclinics, at the low cost prevalent in the past, was impressive. This, however, was the force of inertia. Routinization had no inner strength of analysis or imagination necessary for humane, individual diagnosis. Few people remained to read and interpret what the modern machinery signified, in terms of advancing therapeutic techniques. Common disorders were treated well, as if on a factory line. It was becoming inevitable to increase the cost of treatment to cope with the funds crunch. This was not done, because the government feared popular discontent and talk of fundamentalist alternatives, among a population already hard hit by the pervasive economic crisis. An acquaintance who had a gall bladder disorder needing surgery would not go for it, because he did not have the funds to cover the cost. In the Soviet period, he said, this question would not have risen; charges would have been remarkably low, cheaper by any currency standards than what the average Indian has to pay in a government hospital, let alone private nursing homes.

This is the classic dilemma that Asia faces at the turn of the twenty-first century. Either the state exists with rigid totalitarian controls over democratic liberties for the benefits of average equality, or it minimizes its function, and by permitting the privatization of public utility services, enables the affluent to get access to comfort, while the poor are deprived. Relative deprivation and a return to nineteenth-century scales of immiserization are the wave of the future in the capitalist development of Asia today. We have not had the chance to see how people live in China, where the first alternative used to be strong, but there is now a decisive turn towards the second. Until 2001, among the Uzbek intelligentsia an undertow of affinity for the Chinese path to democracy was growing. At the same time (and this was a principal contradiction rather than a minor one) the same intellectuals hankered for the Westernized advantages of market-friendliness, with its distinct benefits for the average consumer. Yet the universities, devoid of genuine innovative talent and as routinized in such disciplines as technical education and health care, lacked any core which could develop a new outlook on the dilemmas of political economy that face Asia as a whole.

Obsolescence is of course a part of the aging process in any organic activity. Lévi-Strauss in his great anthropological travelogue, *Tristes Tropiques*, wrote at the beginning about the rise and fall of the cultural landscapes created by colonial industrialization, Calcutta, Minas Geraes, Sao Paolo. Whether it is old Bengal or Brazil, these are metropolitan areas which have flourished and now lie sterile and derelict with sick or obsolescent industry and with other regions in the country opening up. Savouring the lotus-eating life available to the expatriate community in Tashkent with its hard currency, one uneasily wondered whether what Bengal thinks today, Uzbekistan will think tomorrow. Tashkent had been the high water mark in the modernizing thrust from the Russian north into Mawar-an-Nahar. Today that moment seems to have passed. The lack of surplus to invest in even maintenance of civic facilities, let alone diversification of the old machine and textile technology; the manifest lack of innovation in any thing except financial speculation and the food and entertainment industry, spreading into vice rackets, which inevitably grow around nodal points in drug transfer routes, such as Bangkok, Goa or Tashkent, the mushrooming of mafias; the feelings of frustration among the older members of the once highly-productive classes; all these add up to this sense of individual comfort but social unease.

The city was beginning to develop a reputation for prowlers and sneak thieves. Not that we were ever bothered, even if on rare occasions, we walked back home late at night along the roads to our lane, on which there was always a remarkable absence of people after dark. But we had heard, right from the beginning, that there was a propensity for hooligans and drug addicts to barge in and demand money, if one was negligent enough to open the front door without caution. Never open the door when you are alone in the house, never trust the local doctors if you fall ill, my wife had been admonished by an expatriate young lady, when we first arrived. Without going so far, it was true that in our once fashionable locality, Darxon, right in the centre of the city, hit-and-run drivers in the middle of the night, led to even our own leafy street being barricaded at the point where it debouched into Pushkin Boulevard. The weird pantomime of the presidential convoy of black cars streaking down this and other arterial 'Presidential Roads' on the way to work and back became increasingly common. In Tashkent, the roads would suddenly be blocked by the militia, with the driver sighing 'President coming', with infinitely amused patience. When the procession went past, it was like a scene from a central European film. First came the goggled motorcyclist, then the pilot van. It was followed by a car, then, driving three abreast, three cars. There were more all going at high speed. We gathered the President and his look-alikes sat in each of the three cars, and rarely in the same, to deflect sharp shooters who might try to knock him out, as they had tried to do in Tbilissi in Georgia with Shevardnadze in the summer of 1995. What was perhaps more bothersome was to see the opposite pole of the new authoritarianism. At the dustbin vats, where our street joins the main road, veterans of the Second World War, medal ribbons on the lapels of their frayed old gray suits, would poke among the refuse for scraps of food to supplement their meagre and devalued pensions.

ACADEMIC AND CULTURAL DIPLOMACY

From February to March, the last of winter, is when UWED classes have their busy season, before the examinations for the second and final semester. The final year undergraduate students of the 1998-9 batch had now began to study in what the university authorities were calling their brand-new Magistratura course of two years. Pro-Vice-Chancellors had convened meetings, one after another, to give pep talks to their faculties about how necessary it was to upgrade standards of teaching to world levels, and how this could best be done by devising new courses with material more than what was provided in courses at Baccalaureat level. Asked to attend a general meeting, and after several venerable emeritus professors like Kuchkar Khanazarov, once a very powerful Director of the Institute of Philosophy, and Goga Khidoyatov had spoken in Russian, I was requested to say a few words. I sought to sound a note of warning.

The gist of it was that questions of upgradation were totally dependant on the availability of new books and articles in current journals. Nothing of merit was available in Uzbek. In International Relations, the material in Russian was basically factual and not up to date with the recent transformation of the world scene. The English language material in the library was dismal. A small collection of books on Central Asian economics, in the late Soviet periods, that used to belong to the late Ann Sheehy (sister of a Patrick Sheehy, a very senior executive of British American Tobacco) had presumably been donated to the Foreign Ministry about the time UzBAT gained its factory concession in Uzbekistan and the university was being set up. There was none of the explosion of materials since the late 1980s, except some books on international trade and marketing, presumably presents from one Embassy or other. There was no attempt, beyond my classes, to encourage students to use the library of the Indian Cultural Centre, surprisingly well stocked by previous Ambassadors. Unless library stocks were radically expanded, with careful planning by a committee, studying catalogues of books in print and new publications, the mere replication of supposedly more advanced courses on the same subject would make no sense at all, I said. They would merely fritter away the resources of extra teaching time, which should be better utilized by making the existing lower Baccalaureat courses more intensive and qualitatively sounder. All this was met by the usual indifferent, but quite polite, silence that one got used to in speaking at Uzbek gatherings. Smaller discussions among one's own discipline colleagues often evoked questions, though of very simplistic nature. The little I could follow of post-presentation discussion in this general meeting appeared to be acrimonious, with orders by the seniors to carry out this or that task, and counter charges about insufficient clarity of the instructions being parried back and forth. Neither of these of course applied to me as a guest, who was to be heard out politely.

Now that the Magister classes had begun, two of the students who had come up from the BA, attached themselves to me after lectures on the subject of political and economic trends in South Asia after 1947. They were not really concerned about the secular tendencies of post-colonial patterns of change and the impact of these trends on national developments and regional variations. One student was keen to know about Yoga and the various schools of Indian philosophy! He was surprised that Indian scholars were not, everyone of them, well up on spirituality, that hallmark of Indian culture to the outside world. It was no use referring him to the works of Radhakrishnan in the Cultural Centre in the hope that this would interest him to read further about rational explanations of Hinduism, and also later about Indian Islam. He had met, he said, one or two Hindu religious practitioners and wished to know more about the texts, which they told him were a clue to mental peace. I was reminded of the links between the Institute of Oriental Studies in Moscow and the Ramakrishna Mission Institute of Culture in Calcutta in the late 1980s, and of Russian-Indian interchanges on practical Yoga teaching, by reputed Russian orientalists and the Swamijis. It was this image of Hind as a land of *sadhus* with supernatural powers, and a set of philosophical texts whose potency for tranquillity had to be unlocked by a world which had become too materialistic, that was uppermost in the minds of the average Uzbeks. It was an image that genuinely frustrated someone from a modern, rationalist, Indian background, trained professionally to teach from secular texts, and without any pretensions to higher spiritual truths. Once again, I learned of a new contradiction in the contemporary world. The quest for modern quality hardly meant anything to this primal search for the elixir of mental peace.

The other student's set of demands for further enlightenment was equally irrelevant to the content of my lectures. He was a probationer teacher in the school for small children (many of them children of the university teachers) opposite the UWED's main building. He wanted some lectures, he said, introducing India to the little ones. Making knowledge of India common to the Uzbek people was supposed to be part of the work of the India Chair.

The mind of the child was where it could strike root. I was reminded of traditions set up by Rabindranath Tagore in Santiniketan, where advanced teachers were expected to spend time with the tots in Patha Bhavan there, to make their professional knowledge compatible with popular use. So I spoke in English for two or three class hours to the ten to twelve age group which Utkir was teaching, and sought to hold the children's attention on unity in diversity, composite culture, and pluralistic socio-economic levels of development. The pupils were well behaved, more so than their elders. These children seemed more familiar with the English language than the first batch of college students whom I had faced in 1998. This may have had something to do with the fact that my pronunciation and explication was simpler and more slowly put for their age group than I felt necessary for their elders. For the latter, more complicated concepts had to be used, for which perhaps their training in English had not equipped them. Utkir's purpose was different. He wanted to expose the pupils to someone who could go on teaching in fluent English. This was what the children needed to get on in the century to come. The failure of my proposal to the Indian Foreign Minister that our Embassy sponsor competent spoken-English training by linguists will be recalled. The memory halted my enthusiasm in its tracks. I reverted to the less popular aspects of contemporary South Asian history for the magisterial students.

The Embassy, in fact, had been working at its own pace, without any reference to the India Chair, on another project of the Foreign Minister: Indo-CIS academic collaboration at the highest level to revive interest in the pre-Islamic roots of culture contact between India and Central Asia, on which much work had been done in recent years by Russian and Central Asian scholarship in the fields of archaeology and linguistics, and their historical interpretation, more recently by scholars like B.A. Litvinsky and G. Pugachenkova as well as their successors, some in collaboration with French or Japanese scholarship.

The roots of India's interest in this field go back to the early twentieth century and to two distinct strands of academic and popular research. The first represented by Prabodh Chandra Bagchi, collaborating with French scholars in Santiniketan, the second by the socialist traveller, Pandit Rahul Sankrityayana, who delved deep into Indo-Central Asian, particularly Buddhist culture, contacts from the Volga to the Ganga, and who wrote in Hindi. These roots had never really been nurtured in India after Professor Bagchi's early death in the 1950s and Rahulji's retirement. In 1967, the Russians had organized a Seminar on the Kushan Culture and its Find Spots, at Dushanbe. Since then, the subject had been studied in depth in Europe and in Japan. Unfortunately, knowledge of the Brahmi and Kharoshthi scripts in which the texts of this period as well as the Asokan edicts of an earlier pre-Christian age were to be found, had radically decreased in India, along with the decrease in the knowledge of Greek or ancient Chinese. Only Bratindra Nath Mukherjee keeps this linguistic skill alive in our country. The same can be said of his older fellow antiquarian, Ahmed Hasan Dani in Pakistan.

Scholarship about cultural artefacts and texts, common in antiquity for the region from the Jaxartes-Syr Darya to the Jamuna and the Ganga, as well as up to the Gulf of Cambay, regained political prominence. This was distinct from its merely cultural eminence in the brief honeymoon between the post 1991 Muslim Republics of Central Asia, and India on the one hand and Pakistan on the other. The new Republics maintained the academic norms of secular interest in all stages of their cultural past—and not just of Islam in their nationalities. They sought cultural affinity with both Pakistan and India as moral ballast in their search for credit lines from these countries to salvage obsolescent industries. In the age of P.V. Narasimha Rao and I.K. Gujral on the one hand, and Benazir Bhutto and Nawaz Sharif on the other, it had been open to the SAARC countries to develop an imaginative strategy of cultural coalition with the Central Asian successors of the Soviet 'knowledge of the East' to back up the sort of understanding, which India and Pakistan in their separate ways later developed today with the United States of America.

That was the time when China under Jiang Zemin and Iran under Khatami were putting forward the concept of 'dialogue of civilization'. South Asia, however, in the era immediately after the death of Rajiv Gandhi, was still too close to Pakistani rivalry with the Central Asian Republics' regimes, which had been inimical to Islamization. And, India's trauma of foreign reserves crunch and liberalization initiatives put constraints on the magnanimity that could have brought such a South Asian cooperative coalition in the great, mid-rimland peninsula into its true stature as a force for best use of resources, markets, and human capital in conjunction with a culturally similar part of the Asian heartland. The final seal was set on the loss of this opportunity, when Brahminical Hindu chauvinism came to central power in India in 1998.

In the brief interlude of groping attempts for new understanding, our Embassy in Tashkent was developing a cultural strategic vision. When Ambassador Bhadrakumar asked me to lecture in 1997 on Indo-Central Asian culture contacts, he stressed that enough had been propagated about Mahmud Ghaznavi, Muhammad Ghauri, Timur, Babur, and Sufi migrations. Fantasies about Muslim conquests would not appeal to either the Indian people's national interests or create comradely good feeling in India or Uzbekistan. This was the time when Pakistan was utilizing the name of the second conqueror, Ghauri, for a nuclear missile, obviously meant to threaten India. The previous Indian missile had been called Prithvi, recalling Prithviraj Chauhan, who defeated the Ghauri once, but according to one story was carried off after the second battle of Tarain in 1197 to die in captivity in Afghanistan. It was politic in the conjuncture of the mid 1990s, when the Bhutto encouragement of the Taliban (as well as of the Lashkar-e-Toiba and the Harkat-ul-Mujahideen in Kashmir) was growing, and was directed against both India and its Panjsheri allies in Afghanistan, to emphasize non-Islamic as well as Islamic elements in the heritage of coalition.

In 1997, when I had spoken about these subjects, I had preferred to bypass political and strategic forces and to merely emphasize continuities and discontinuities from ancient times to the present day. In Pakistan, the cultural strategy was clearly one of religious politics. Professor Dani, an eminent UNESCO expert on ancient inscriptions on what is now the Pakistan-China Karakoram Highway through difficult Indus gorges, had recently chosen to emphasize more than his old research on the Buddhist links of the Kushan period, the Muslim links of Sufism and ethnicity that creates special affinities between Central Asia, Afghanistan, the Pathan frontier and Punjab.

When I first met Professor Dani at a French seminar in 1986 on cultural aspects of Islam, he was speaking with passion about the diffusion of mosque styles in the modern world. When I met him in 1995 for a UNESCO group working for cultural peace in Georgia, he was caught up in discussion with Professor Asimov of

Tajikistan (whom hooligans would shoot in 1996) about prospects of Dushanbe's cooperation with Azad Kashmiris in joint veneration of an early mediaeval Tajik Pir Hamadani, who is said to have proselytized in Kashmir. The implication of this regarding the politics of anti-Indianism in Kashmir and its potential for disturbing the famous syncretic Kashmiriyat of the Srinagar valley will be evident. Dani Shaheb, as his one-time students in Bangladesh (then East Pakistan) call him is a firm Islamist. He hails from pre-Independence Jammu and Kashmir, is a Sanskrit scholar, and speaks Bengali and Urdu, as well as Darri, which is his mother tongue as well as being the mother tongue of Tajiks. This cultural mix shows the ethnic force that cultural Islam has within itself for the region.

Indeed, Professor Khidoyatov, invited to lecture in Pakistan at that time, had brought back from Peshawar a large wall map, depicting in green, Central Asia as a region which included Pakistan up to the river Sutlej. This was the Taliban geo-politics for the establishment of a Muslim bond above all. The CIA and ISI strategy of exporting Arab versions of the Koran across the Amu Darya to trap the Russian Bear had left its mark on Pakistani ideas, which did not tally with the Indian. That negated the idealism of any SAARC coalition built without US mediation.

Indian cultural diplomacy of the period was mainly concerned with linguistic affinities. The Minister-Counsellor at Tashkent when I had been there in 1997 went back to Delhi as Joint Secretary in charge of the Central Asia Division of MEA, which he was to remain till 2001. Unlike the bulk of officials whom MEA posts to Central Asia, Alok Sen's foreign language specialization is not Russian but Turkish. His prior service in Bangladesh and Turkey had given him a greater comprehension of contemporary Islam and its cultural network than our Russian trained, anti-Islamic-fundamentalist diplomats have. He was aware of the many differences between modern Turkish, and the archaic Turki of Central Asia, of which Uzbek language and culture is a part. This makes Uzbeks closer to the Tatars or the Uighurs than to the Turks of Ankara and Istanbul. He did not over emphasize, as senior Indian diplomats of the time were stressing, the idea that Turkish economic contacts (much thinner on the ground than what Turkey's mentor, the USA, wanted people to believe) were a danger to Uzbek-Russian secular and foreign policy affinities within the CIS overall context. Indian foreign policy thinking at the end of the century sought to maintain recently established links between Russia, Central Asia and India in a north-south axis, as distinct from the east-west axis from China via Pakistan to the Middle East, which the ruling powers in Delhi now see as the hub of the Islamic world.

The new seminar, which Jaswant Singh (who had been accompanied by Sen) enjoined the Indian Embassy to organize, with Uzbek and Russian cultural cooperation, was a product of this north-south axial culture contact perspective. It was limited to the pre-Islamic centuries. Presumably this was for diplomatic safety's sake. The Uzbeks perhaps feared the Indian discussion of Islam—the Indian Government after 1998 treated Islam as an external interactive and often conflictual force 'outside' the heritage of its imagined Hindu India, while the Russians are better in analysing Hindu spirituality, which is not the same sort of danger to them that militant Islam has become.

Diplomatic management of this discourse became clear over time. A Tashkent scholar of ancient history, a Georgian non-Muslim settled in Uzbekistan, Edouard Rtweladze, who had worked on ancient art and epigraphy, with eminence in that field was entrusted with finding the best specialists of the CIS. Neither the Embassy nor the Academician could contact any Indian. Sen ultimately telephoned me from Delhi and later invited Prof. Bratin Mukherjee to submit a paper, the only Indian to do so. Except for the limited translating capacities of the Russian-Kyrgyz lady in the Embassy, the proceedings were in Russian. Only Professor Mukherjee spoke in English. Invitations were sent to Indologists in Uzbekistan. I got a card the day before the seminar. Embassy officials were instructed to sit on the dais with one or other CIS scholar, quietly, without taking part in the esoteric debate. The idea seemed to be that Indo-Central Asian culture contact was specifically Avestian, or Buddhist, or Hindu. Scholars of later periods were not even expected to be interested. Professor Khidoyatov, a 'world historian' of the Soviet variety, was not invited, much to his chagrin, since he prided himself on his old contacts with Indians and the policy of non-alignment. In a speech at an Indian Cultural Centre seminar in the previous summer, he was reported to have spoken from a pacificist and nuclear disarmament position warning against India falling victim to Pakistan's policy of increasing the heat of proliferation. He had called for a return to the diplomacy of Nehru and non-alignment. This was seen as a challenge to the present assertive stand in nuclear postures. Indeed we did not meet him any more in any of its gatherings, and he became coldly aloof from an India for which he found it increasingly difficult to feel any affinity, nurtured as he has been in the traditions of Tagore, Nehru, and secularism.

The seminar was obviously rich in stocktaking facts on the ground. It lacked awareness of the research being conducted at that time by French scholarship. IFEAC (the Institut Francais d'Etudes Asie Centrale, located in Rakatboshi street in Tashkent itself) had contacts with Dutch, German, Italian, Kazakh and Japanese scholarship. Its Director, Professor Vincent Fourniau, and his research staff, were not invited. To my embarrassment he quizzed me about this when I next went to study in his Library: he had made it a point to come and listen to my own lecture a year earlier in the ICC at my invitation.

The diplomatic community must have been used to each other's information gathering. Each nationality has its own guiding presuppositions and its channels of informal sharing of knowledge. These labyrinthine subtexts did give me a sense of alienation from the diplomatic milieu of the politics of knowledge, which was remarkably different from open, democratic, academic interchange in a free country.

A TASHKENT SUMMER

Spring is the seminar season in Uzbekistan, much as winter sees a crop of such gatherings in our country. The air becomes balmy, the shoots begin to sprout into a dense cover of leafy trees, shading the roads and avenues, there is a crop of flowers on the trees and vines, pink and white on the apple blossom and then red dog roses, though there are fewer flowers than one can see in a European spring. The gardens and pleasure parks grow fuller with people boating and buying the standard shashlik, or even dancing in open-air arenas in the evenings, as the sunlight stays on quite late into the night.

One such park grew up before our eyes. Close to our house, near the main road from the airport to Chorsu, which bisects Pushkin Boulevard under its great flyover, is an area which had old houses when we first went. Swiftly torn down in the next few months, the trees were left intact, rubble cleared by bulldozers, and then in the summer when we were away, turf was planted, a slope terraced by flights of steps, and an artificial boating lake fashioned out of swamps at the base. When we came back in the autumn, a giant ferris wheel had been installed, with smaller roundabouts, and area for a roller coaster, cars to bang each other, a toy train, and a gymnastic area for toddlers. In 2000, the same thing was done to the slope on the other side of the highway, so that within a short space of time, the city had developed yet another lung, where youth and children could enjoy themselves, and older people like us could go for an evening walk. This concern for the common people, the constant building of a clean environment, and that too with exemplary speed, reminded me of all that I had heard about the social virtues of Soviet transformation. This was the other side of the medal of Stalinist authority and of the fear of condign punishment on which it is based.

Evenings are long and nights are brief in summer in Tashkent. With younger acquaintances from the Embassy and their little children, we visited several parks. In the Hotel Intercontinental surroundings, there is an assortment of electronic whirligigs on which Uzbek youth and children ride, to the accompaniment of the usual shrieks. On open-air stages the latest pop is blared out with flashing psychedelic lights. An open-air disco springs up as night falls. Girls, very pretty, in the skimpiest imitation of nightclub life, are found swaying to the beat, along with their partners. It is almost as if the Battersea Fun Fair, in London, to which one of us had gone, way back in 1955, has come back like Rip Van Winkle struggling to keep pace with the new millennium. Small wonder that the fundamentalists in 1991-2 tried to shift the focus to masculine control of public display. Summer in Tashkent, ten years later, gave us the feeling that Puritanism stood not a ghost of a chance in Central Asian Islam.

Summer brought this tension of social mores into the forefront of even university life. Some of the emeritus Chairs of UWED, the oldest Party functionaries of the hoary Soviet past of the 1970s, were heard in faculty meetings (chaired on Saturdays, by the then Foreign Minister-cum-Vice-Chancellor, Komilov son-in-law of the late Sharaf Rashidov) complaining that girl students' skirts on campus rode too high as they clattered on their high heels along the tree-lined, concrete path, which linked the main buildings. The Minister, a younger and very quiet man was seen to smile broadly, and heard to murmur that to tamper in such matters was tantamount to decreeing that trees should be less green in the spring. While Islam retained its solid base in *mahallas*, the winds of change were blowing in from the West into Eurasia. This, after all, was the time when Iranian liberalism rallied behind Muhammad Khatami against bigoted Hizbullahs. Social convergence was taking place in the new Asian market societies.

About this time, we were invited to Chimgan, not the resort but the little hamlet that nestles below Malo Chimgan, along slopes coming down a mountain stream. Our hosts were the Mirkasymovs, old friends of India from their Calcutta days in 1971. They had come to our city to initiate work for the well-known Gorky Sadan on Lower Circular Road, the USSR cultural centre. Its language classes, film shows, and sponsored chess tournaments became a part of Calcutta's life and earned them many friends in the city. There is still a lady doing research in the Asiatic Society, who proudly says she learned Russian from Mirkasymova. With independence in 1992, Sureth Mirkasymov was appointed Uzbekistan's first Ambassador in New Delhi. He lost no time in getting in touch with me at the Maulana Azad Institute of Asian Studies, and in encouraging our interest in Uzbek history. They returned in 1997. He was a lecturer at the President's Academy for State Reconstruction and Development, a thinktank training presidential staff. Along with Fetih Teshabayev, another old India hand and later Uzbek Ambassador, first to the USA and then to Britain, Mirkasymov stood for the *Hindi-Russi Bhai-Bhai* fraternity.

These values were solidly grounded in the hard verities of the pre-Gorbachev epoch—pragmatism in foreign policy, Andropov-Gromyko style, intellectual trust in the Westernizing enlightenment that had taken place in the Russia of Pushkin or Chekhov, or the India of Rammohun and Rabindranath, as distinct from Victorian or Bonapartist capitalism. Like their contemporary, Goga Khidoyatov, they hankered for a return to the Nehruvian policy of non-alignment, and primacy in Asia on the basis of peace, popular prosperity, and progress. This policy had worked in building up a third force in international relations between 1950 and 1970. The Arab oil price rise, the USA's tilt to the Pakistan-Chinese axis and its disentanglement from the Vietnam fiasco, and the colonial collapse in Indo-China halted Russian infiltration towards the warm waters south of the Indian Ocean. Pakistan's ISI-CIA link-up through Zia-ul-Huq's Islamization strategy of building a Saudi-

Gulf-Pakistan axis, tied in with the Sino-Pak strategic relationship. All these made even the positive aspects of Nehruvian non-alignment out of date in the 1980s. It was this new turn in international relations, as much as the implosion within 'actually existing socialism' that took Central Asia beyond the Indophilia for which our older acquaintances in Tashkent stood. Their growing isolation and bewilderment could be sensed in their old fashioned eulogies of Indo-Russian relations, which at the end of the century they bravely thought could continue without change as Indo-Uzbek relations.

The Mirkasymovs are warm hosts. Their dacha in the decaying hill village had been lovingly renovated in their retirement by personal physical labour, driving up and down from the city, planting fruit and flower trees round the house, installing sanitation room by room over months and years, plucking seasonal fruits for gifts and preserves, and making wine for abstemious consumption. We made trips there on several occasions. Pride of place in their living room was taken by a picture of Sureth Saheb driving in state to present his credentials to the President of India. Outside the house was an open stove made of brick and earth, on which he prepared a lunch of *damdama*, a sort of casserole, with summer vegetables mixed with the ever-present meat. Accompanying this would come several delicious Russian and Uzbek salads prepared by Nelya Mirzoeva Mirkasymova, herself once a senior bureaucrat in the Uzbek educational system. Homemade wine was served, followed by homemade sweets, leaving guests somnolent, till they were roused at teatime with the farewell plov. This would be cooked with fanfare, younger guests encouraged to participate in the culinary efforts that always turned out well. Nelya left the preparation of plov to her husband, who, asked how it always turned out so tasty, said it was no thanks to him, he left it to the mercy of Khizr Bua, uncle Khizr. This is the saint whose shrine rises between Shah-i-Zinda and the Samarkand bazaar. Uzbeks are wont to entrust their efforts to him when they cook. If you take his name, whatever you mix together will come out well.

Walks around the dacha were always a pleasure. On one side one follows overgrown paths to a spot where once had stood a Kazakhstan Government Sanatorium, employing many people in the village. The break up of the USSR stopped Kazakh funding. On its other side, the village mouldered in decay. The roads steep and badly rutted, repelled cars in the winter snow. Snow ploughs did reach the main road above but bypassed the dwelling houses. The rivulet, coursing down the road, muddily, past a grotesque folly shaped like the old lady's shoe in which she lived in the fable, swerved past a dilapidated farmhouse to the brook. Occasional picnickers park their cars and play raucous music here. Once we heard Hindi filmi cassettes echoing up the glen. The decay included theft of unattended property by villagers. This had not been the case when employment had been provided by the previous regime, through massive central subsidies. To eke out a living, hill youths would move as guides to the ranges across the Ferghana valley, into tracts controlled by Nomonghani. They were coming back with dollars from Juma's foreign funds, gained by ransom in Kyrgyzstan; they also brought the message of fundamentalism as an alternative to government neglect. On a subsequent trip to Brichmulla, at the head of the Charvak reservoir further north in the mountains across from Kyrgyzstan, we found the same milieu as in Chimgan: a deserted sanatorium, forlorn picnic facilities, and a shuttered and impoverished village.

To travel to Brichmulla, the next year, we had to follow a lower road winding along the reservoir, up below the snow peaks. We asked friends whether the artificial lake was an old one and were told that it had been formed by damming the confluence of three mountain streams, the third one coming down from Humsan, which had submerged several hill villages, some thirty or forty years before. This was for the water supply of not only Tashkent but also the military industrial complex of Chirchik in between. How had the people whose villages were submerged reacted, and where did they go, we enquired, thinking of our own Narmada valley and of Medha Patkar. That, they did not know. Did they not protest, I asked ignorantly, since I should have known better. Protest! Did they want to get shot? This was the elementary aspect of peasant insurgency in post-colonial USSR. The circumstances of previous provision of social welfare for the downtrodden in the hills, for instance, in Western Nepal or in Darjeeling in India, are so very different. The difference between a totalitarian and a more democratic regime comes out in the degree of hegemony of fear. Fear is greater in the post-communist as well as the semi-feudal regime. It is less in the Indian hills than in the insurgencies of Nepal today or Central Asia till 2001, when those were crushed only after US intervention. But, in 2000, what already struck us was the disparity between popular warmth and the country's simplicity, and, on the other hand, the stark grimness of the social norms, which have been silently accepted by the Pioneer camp guard we had met in 1998 in Humsan, or by the poorer villagers of the deserted tourist camps of Malo Chimgan and Brichmulla.

NOTES

1. Ahmed Rashid, *Jihad: The Rise of Militant Islam in Central Asia* (Yale University Press and Orient Longman, India, 2002), pp. 31 and 79.
2. The best historical account of Soviet studies of Asian geopolitics is by Milan Hauner, *What is Asia to Us? Russia's Asian Heartland, Yesterday, Today* (London, Unwin, 1990).
3. Barun De 'Geopolitics and Regional Identity: South Asia's Northwest Frontiers', *Economic and Political Weekly*, XXXVII, 14 September 2002, pp. 3812-17.
4. J.N. Dixit, *My South Block Years: Memoirs of a Foreign Secretary* (New Delhi, UBS Publishers, 1996).
5. A catalogue of bare archival facts about this will be found in K. Warikoo, *Central Asia and Kashmir: A Study in the Context of Anglo-Russian Rivalry* (New Delhi, Gian Publishers, 1989). The subject deserves broader and more contemporary multidisciplinary analysis.

5

The Uses of the Past and of Indo-Uzbek Cultural Relations

BABUR 'RE-CONSTRUCTED'

In the early summer of 2000, the University of Samarkand sponsored a seminar to celebrate Babur. The Director of the ICC, Prof. Qamar Rais, was invited to represent India. He suggested to the university authorities that they should invite me. I accepted the invitation to learn about the way Babur was discussed by academics. The Russian interpreter and the dance instructor would accompany the Director—the instructor, so that she could give Babur enthusiasts a feel for Indian art form. Professor Rais asked me to apply for being included in the official group. When I did so, the Ambassador told me that the official intellectual was enough to show the Indian academic flag. The Samarkand people were kind enough, however, to extend to my wife and me, full hospitality. A Lecturer from the History Department took a dawn bus to our house to escort us by taxi to the city. He spoke better English than many of his generation in Tashkent, was impeccable in the simple verities of historical materialism, and spoke with feeling about the legends and monuments of his city, which he later arranged for us to tour once again. A very comfortable boarding house had been arranged for our stay.

The seminar was more festivity than academic discourse. It was funded by a curious NGO called the Babur Foundation, organized by an Andijan entrepreneur, supposed to have been some sort of a technical person in Afghanistan, with contacts in India. He had led a group to look for the place of Babur's first grave in Agra, from where Sher Shah, who vanquished Babur's son, Humayun had later allowed Babur's Afghan widow to take the body back to Kabul, to be buried in a leafy hillside. In 1997, I had seen the replication of the Kabul graveyard on a slope overlooking Andijan, which vied with Osh in Kyrgyzstan for the tourist credit of being his childhood home. The Foundation had invited the US historian Stephen Dale, the author of a book on Indian merchants in medieval Central Asia and Iran,[1] who is now writing about the Turko-Iranian synthesis in Babur's personality on the basis of that talented prince's own text. The Babur Foundation was sponsoring the usual dinners and entertainments.

The ICC delegation was informed that they would have the honour at the first night's dinner, at a delightful little restaurant called Du Chinor (where actually two Chinar trees shaded the open air trestle tables) to present Indian dances for the entertainment of the gathering. Our instructor was thoroughly indignant. Kathak dance, to her represented devotion, not the applause of an audience partaking of wine and meat. Both Prof. Rais and the Pro-Vice-Chancellor for International Affairs succumbed; however, the next afternoon, in a packed university hall, the instructor presented a *Rama Vandana* or eulogy to Rama. Whether this actually meant the irony of Rama's revenge on Babur, whether the subtext of the Babri Masjid demolition peeped out, there was no means of knowing. What is not stated explicitly is not cause for concern in the simplicities of Uzbekistan.

I unfortunately overstated my own case in the paper I had prepared. It was about Jawaharlal Nehru's romanticization of Babur as a Renaissance hero, and the way in which Nehru's ideas were worked out in the period of glasnost in Uzbekistan (in the 1980s, before Karimov came into power) to create Babur's heroic image. As an Indian academic, my positions were inoffensive, analytical, aimed at revising the idolization of Babur as an *Uzbek* hero. The gist was that Babur's Memoirs showed his love for Samarkand, its quarters, its local heritage, and its people. He deserved to be celebrated. Yet, present categories of nationalities obscured the fact that he had fought Uzbeks with the help of his maternal Mughal kin, whom he detested, since as Mughals they were prone to desert him in any crisis. It was the Uzbek Shaibani who had chased Babur out of Samarkand. Actually, I argued, hero worship was a late development, a product of the rise of Uzbek national sentiments in the 1970s and 1980s, through novels such as *Starry Nights* by Pirimkul Kadirov (who had been invited to the seminar) and through references by the Uzbek national poet Muhammad Ali (who knows Hindustani) to Jawarharlal Nehru's historical writings. The latter writes to his daughter Indira in glowing terms about Babur's artistic temperament and joy of life. If any Timurid descendant deserved a high place in world history, in whose context the seminar sought to view Babur, it should be Akbar, the modernizer of Indian administration and centralization with its stress on composite culture and realpolitik, rather than Babur, who, after all, had claimed to be a Ghazi, fighting *jihad* against the Rajputs at Khanwa in 1526, and Chanderi in 1527. A rhetorical aside was to be my undoing; that it was not necessary to either show adulation for religious fanaticism, such as Babur showed in his comments on Hindu princes, any more than condone the breaking of the Babri Masjid, which I emphatically stated had been a barbarous and uncivilized act.

There was complete silence in the hall. Coming out, I was accosted by an Afghan refugee from Mazar-i-Sharif. She was a member of the Babur Foundation and connected, she later told me, with the Afghan-Uzbek General, and ex-communist, Abdul Rashid Dostum, then fugitive in the Middle East, having been driven out by the Taliban two years before. She was furious. She had always known that Indians admired Babur. Here was a person from India actually criticizing him, treating him in the same way as people who pulled down monuments by which he was remembered. Her rage had nothing to do with objective history as I understand it. My understanding had nothing to do with the politics of historiographic chauvinism as she understood it. We were clearly on different trajectories. It seemed sacrilege to her understanding of History as Truth, which her teachers had passed down to her. Thus would have thought from the opposite angle an RSS volunteer, who believed from his pamphlets that many thousand battles had been fought to save Ramjanmabhoomi in Ayodhya, and that one last push was necessary to protect the historical truth.[2] The matter spiralled further when our ICC Director sought to caution me about resentment regarding what had been seen as my iconoclasm. It was not necessary to contest any claims about Babur, in a seminar celebrating him. If Babur's associations with Mughals had not been emphasized, Uzbek sensibilities would not have been hurt. An 'apology' on my part would solve the matter. The past had obviously dropped its historical mask and the present was coming out. I told him that there was no question of my apologizing for my academic opinions.

At the end of the day, the Pro-Vice-Chancellor took me aside; he amicably told me the same thing. In the winding up session, next morning, a resolution would be mooted, expressing strong resentment about the reference to Babur as a Mughal. With a very faint, and sadly cynical, smile playing on his lip, the administrator said that, as historians, we both knew the relativity of truth. In the older days people had been clear about Babur's Mughal help and maternity, as well as Timurid heritage. He did realize what the term Mughal meant in India. But the present situation—by which he meant post-Independence and contemporary history—required that it would be wise, did I not agree, to not hurt Uzbek national sentiment as it was today. A clarification from me, not an apology of course, pre-empting any general resolution, would ensure that the matter blew over.

At no stage did this very sophisticated gentleman, the epitome of politeness, refer to the politics involved in concocting national identity through idol-worship. The metal had to sensed, latent beneath the veneer. Reflecting on the episode that evening, while watching a most indifferent and eulogistic *son-et-lumiere* about Timur and Ulugh Beg in the Registan, couched in the same present-day nationalist jargon and in which ironically Babur's defeat by the Uzbek Khans on those premises themselves are discreetly left out, it became clear to me that the tissue of fantasies about the past, selecting parts of it and forgetting others, permeates Uzbek minds. I was fighting against shadows.

The next morning I asked to speak first and pointed out that I was aware of the verbal distinction between Baburids, as the modern Uzbeks called them, and Mughals as we Indians have called them, and also of the actual distinction between Mughals who marauded Mawar-an-Nahr as Babur's maternal kin, and Baburid Mughals like Akbar and Shah Jahan, who had based themselves on Timurid culture. I ended by recalling that it was a Mughal, Yunus Khan, whose tomb stood in Tashkent, reminding present Uzbeks of the Mughal heritage of Babur's maternal grandfather. The same stony silence prevailed. There was no resolution, which might have created problems for the University with cultural censorship. Instead, Prof. Rais made a speech. He said that Babur was not a *jihadi* in India, but a man under whose pillow, after his death, had been found a will, in which he enjoined Humayun to never slaughter cattle in Hindustan and to win the love and respect of Hindus! Stephen

Dale was sitting next to me. As a specialist in Persian and Turki texts, I asked him what this will was all about, as I have never heard of it. He said there was indeed a Bhopal document, but of very late provenance. Current sensitivities, relevant to present controversies had been tranquillized. But the historical baby had been thrown out with the analytical bath water.

The matter might have ended there. Such are the Byzantine ways of Missions abroad that this was not to be. After a journey back in a university van with the Afghan lady and her taciturn husband, as well as Stephen Dale (with whom we discovered many common acquaintances) in which the lady, her Baburic pride assuaged, regaled my wife and me with little pamphlets presenting pious Islamic verses, that Babur was wont to write after his exploits or his drinking bouts, all the way from Syr Darya to Ganga, and talked about how he was a glowing example for Afghan post-communist Uzbek refugees from the Taliban, we came back home over the weekend. On Monday there was a phone from the Ambassador's P.A. Would I see H.E. at my earliest. 'What made you bring up the Babri Masjid in Samarkand?' he queried sharply. I slowly responded: that I supposed I had got emotional. I was going to explicate that I was distinguishing between Babur as a historical figure, and the political use of his memory. The Ambassador had no time for what I suppose he considers casuistry. In a no nonsense tone, he explained that emotions were all right in private, but a government servant had to follow public norms. This meant nothing could be said that could even remotely be construed as criticism of government in public. Without leaving time for me to point out that it was not the existing government, but parties now dominant in it, which in opposition to the Central Government then, had taken part in pulling down the Babri Masjid, and was still being legally proceeded against—he went on to sum up that, in case I repeated a criticism of government measures, he would have to warn me about the consequences and ask me to show what I was writing for public consumption. I said no one had been upset by my reference to the Masjid, but rather to my reference to the Mughals without calling Akbar a Baburid. To this he replied, 'I have told Rais that's a historian's opinion'.

Till then I had been feeling that his information was from Samarkand. I said I stood by what I had said since I believed in it, but would, since he had brought up my terms of my appointment in which I was under the Head of Misson's interpretation of what I should lecture about, write to Samarkand, deleting the one clause in it, which referred to the Masjid destruction, in case my paper was published: also that I had no intention of creating an opportunity for him to read what I would write during the rest of my period of service. The paper, revised, and in original, was immediately put up for his office.

We have moved far from 'The Place of Babur in World History'. The entire episode shows the distinction between what my generation of historians of the mid-twentieth century called scientific or academic history which tried to be analytically objective and what a newer generation calls 'popular history' or 'plural pasts'. The political premises and personal biases of the historian remain as strong as R.G. Collingwood and E.H. Carr thought they were. The burden of science, however, which historical materialism placed on history is showing cracks. The element of rhetoric has recently been emphasized in statements purporting to be historical. One person's history may turn out to be another's poison. Discordance and tension is as much a part of the present looking at the past, as synthesis and composite harmony. What Babur stood for in his own age is indeed important. Scholars have presented data and interpretations of how they analyse him from the time the Memoirs have been translated and edited in various languages and one looks forward to Dale's forthcoming version about strands in the personality of a wandering conqueror, never at home in the new lands, which he always ruled as an alien. How Babur's memory is used for an ever-changing present is, however, something else. Varying uses can be inferred from different purposes, determined by faith, sentiment or policy. Plurality in the uses of the past is something we have learned to our cost in India in the last decade.

An advantage of this episode was getting to know a new historian. Stephen Dale had been taken to Andijan for further junketing in Babur's name. He stopped overnight with us in Tashkent before leaving for his classes in the USA. He represents a sort of scholarship in Islamic studies, without which it cannot continue to flourish, but which has been slightly marginalized by the jargon and popular dramatics of the fashions of subalternity and, later security conservatism. The older modern scholarship had developed after the end of the Second World War, along with new democratic forces as well as the growth of new types of modern dictatorship, and revived absolutism, spread across the Middle East and the Maghreb from Turkey to the Sudan and from Pakistan to Morocco. New forces were explained sociologically rather than theologically—as in the older Islamic studies. The disciplines of historical geography, growth economics, literary analysis, and Weberian approaches to the study of religion, legitimation and state formation all fused in a new cultural materialist understanding, whose archetypes were scholars like Marshall Hodgson, Clifford Geertz, Ernest Gellner, Maxime Rodinson, Michael Gilsenan or Timothy Mitchell in the Atlantic world, or Muhammad Mujeeb, Syed Husain Alatas, Anouar Abdel Malik, or Anisuzzaman in Asia and Africa. This sociological approach, which relies as much on the insights of European sociology or local literary traditions as on indigenous sources, has found greater favour with the Western historians of Central Asia.

Dale is very much a part of this trend. Ranging from Islamic merchants of Malabar to Indians travelling through Khurasan and Iran towards Astrakhan, he now seeks to understand the problems of culturally hybrid members of a ruling class, who were alien to the countries to which they migrated, or who were part of a recent diaspora. Instead of the fashionable focus called 'post-modernism' so dear to Non-Resident Inhabitants of affluent countries, he chooses to look at the contexts of the pre-Christian domination of Asia: in particular the interweave of Persian and Turki, as distinct from the better known Persian and Arabic. This interweave explains much of the nostalgia for Inner-Asian lands of origin, which will be found in the Persian or Urdu *rubais* and *ghazals*. I could learn much from him in that one day of taking him around old Tashkent about the cultural dimensions of what Dale's friend, Richard Eaton has called 'cultural frontiers' such as Turkestan or Bangladesh.

In the summer vacation that soon followed, we were to see another cultural frontier, quite distant from both these lands. Our home leave gave us the opportunity for a brief personal journey to Hyderabad. I have visited this city many times. I always made a point of sitting on the stone bench in the Mecca Masjid where the Nizams are entombed. The guides will tell you that the seat will bring you back to the city. On each occasion, I climbed the fortifications of the earlier Qutb Shahi Sultans of Golconda and felt part of that composite culture, now fragmented into what its regional politics call Telugu Desam. There certainly were separate Muslim and Hindu components, but there was concord among the components in the regional identity.

In the summer of 2000, a different human ambience was sharply evident. In Golconda Fort itself, there were crowds of sightseers. Most women were veiled in burkhas up to their eyes. The men had cropped crescent beards and round skullcaps, not unlike the common Turki or Uzbek ones. But Hinduism had reared a *trishul* and a Shivalingam close to the highest point of the rock, where the Sultans used to go up for the cool evening breeze. This is a new trend in India. Where Islamic banners were once flaunted as signs of past conquest, the trishul and the saffron flag (*bhagwa jhanda* of Shivaji) are now being raised under cover of piety. Perhaps this explains why in the imagination of the common people and the poor, Islam too reacts to the challenge by emphasizing fundamentalist dress codes; a sartorial distinction that is to be found also among the more Muslim elements in Uzbekistan and Tajikistan.

All through the densely crowded thoroughfares of the city from Abid's junction to the Char Minar, the *burkha* darkens the streets. It would be simplistic to explain this as the spread of Arab money from the Gulf, eager to look for pure brides from Hindustan. That would not be a sufficient explanation. All over South Asia, as much as in West Asia and the Central Asian borderland beyond the Oxus, Islamic cultural identities have made a dramatic comeback after the encouragement of Mujahids against Russia in Afghanistan by the US-Pak axis. Organizations like the Jamaat-ul-Islami have proliferated, extremist wings like the Hizb-ut-Tahrir work at the family and domestic levels. These are clear, pan-religious and counter-Islamic movements, which convert secular regionalism into embattled religiosity, subsuming frontiers in globalizing counter-dependence. Living in a predominantly Muslim country like Uzbekistan and comparing it with social change in Hyderabad, opens one's eyes in a way that Kolkata or Mumbai, where Muslims are ghettoized, cannot. At the same time, one must live in cities like Varanasi or Kathmandu or Dharamsala to realize that Hinduism or Buddhism today perhaps has the same effect of overarching regional identities. Even in the average Indian group, or city, the growth of the *tika* on the male forehead, or the saffron scarf draped over both shoulders of men, or the image of Hanuman wielding a mace, can be seen far more than in the more secular and less macho late twentieth century that we have left behind.

GLOBALIZATION AND ITS DISCONTENTS

When we came back to Tashkent in September 2000 a day or two after Mustakillik Den or Independence Day for the opening of the new academic session, life in the city appeared embedded in its standard groove. Autumn is a beautiful time. The heat of the *chilla,* or high summer of forty days, had slid down from 45 degrees of dry heat in the shade. Fruit and vegetables were found in their last weeks of plenty. The evenings were still not chilly. From this time, if you stand under the trees lining the roads, you can expect to hear a faint rustle, as large yellowish leaves drift down like confetti on your shoulder and head. The Alaiski market goes through a change of colours from the green vegetables of summer with its abundance of tomatoes, patches of red capsicums and deep mauve aubergines, to the reds of strawberries, raspberries and plums, as well as deep, blood red and succulent cherries and yellow peaches. All this is available for so little money that one wonders why a flourishing fruit canning industry has not developed in Ferghana, Zarafshan, and the slopes coming down to the Amu Darya. After all there is a decent industry in wines and vodka in which Uzbekistan appears to be self-sufficient with very low priced vintages that deserve publicity in the wine-imbibing West.

The preservation of perishable foodstuffs is a major domestic activity in the country. Central Asia is a land in which fruits and vegetables are in plenty in spring, summer and early autumn. From November to March, there is dearth of them, startling to those of us who are used to a profusion of winter vegetables. Meat there is in plenty, from the pastoral economy, and from the nomadic tradition of living off herds for food, clothing, and even shelter (in cured skin *yurts*, or bell-shaped felt tents, once commonly used, and in the still continuing carpets and wall hangings to keep the houses warm). All this is very strong in city as well as countryside. Eating meat three times a day, though not in large amounts, but to flavour the bread or the sweet and round rice or plov, is common. Men and women alike are addicted to fatty foods (perhaps to keep warm in winter). Even the lissome and occasionally remarkably beautiful young women become in middle age square and stubby, as do the hefty men in their long robes. Through the months of plenty, housewives—and practically every working woman is a housewife even while she plays a second role as hard labourer in the interest of the lazier menfolk—busy themselves in storing sacks of potatoes, large gourds in numbers, onions, etc., and they bottle in large glass jars, enormous amounts of tomatoes, capsicums, cucumbers, or gherkins. The sacks, sealed bottles of pickles and quantities of sweet jams from a variety of fruits are placed in the underground cellars found in most houses. These are consumed along with meat and cereals in winter, when fresh food becomes extremely costly, and the markets bare. The domestic economy relies on preserves to such an extent that it was amusing to find ladies making strawberry jam, unwilling to waste even a small segment of foaming scum rising in the boil, scooping it off, and savouring it. No wonder obesity is a common gerontological situation, throughout the land.

Some slight changes are visible with globalization. A few multinationals have ventured past the corruption and the unimaginative currency practices of the cautious Uzbek market regime. Mushrooming little supermarkets stock some tinned stuff, and also limited quantities of vegetables and fruits grown in summer houses. The few Indian entrepreneurs who have ventured capital into the Uzbek economy encourage vegetable gardening for their employees' domestic consumption. They distribute or disseminate knowledge, and create demand among Uzbek neighbours, on such exotica as bitter gourd or ladies fingers. Market farms are being set up by Turkish companies such as Demir. However, diversification along these lines, and a greater consumer choice (that great utopia of globalization), depends on higher purchasing power, more capacity for employment creation, or infrastructure development, and far less antiquated management techniques. None of these are long lasting in the backward, primitive accumulation conditions of Central Asian crony capital.

People are indeed trying to cash in for short-term profits. Five years ago in Tbilissi, at the UNESCO peace meet mentioned earlier, I had sat next to a US businessman at a dinner in a private house. He recounted his use of the opening of Soviet markets to the West. He had bought a vineyard for the famous Georgian spirits and wine. The product was refined and matured and sold in Germany, bought by retailers in the Netherlands, who bottled and sold it in the European Common Market. Speed money, protection rackets, and mafias within Georgia creamed off 50 per cent of the profits. Another 25 per cent went in his West European dealings. What was left was fun enough for him to leave his family in the USA and carry on business in the Caucasus. No doubt such people exist in the multinational communities of the Uzbek towns.

We met enough Indians who fitted this bill. It was not an easy job for them. A young Punjabi couple was at that time located in Andijan. They came frequently to Tashkent where we would meet them at a friend's house. The husband was working on behalf of his brother, a Punjabi merchant in Delhi, to set up a plant to market mineral water from Ferghana. The bulk of his time was taken in dealing with officials in the capital to get the permits necessary to make the new plant an actuality. By mid-2001, they had packed up and gone home. Business was getting worse.

On the other hand, the ones we knew with palatial mansions as well as spare apartments in the city, did assorted odd jobs, reputed to range from selling detergents to Kazakhstan and travel agencies for journeys to Khiva, all the way to acting as guides, translations or compradors agents for multinational enterprises, public and private. Sometimes, these transactions were said to shade off into the shadows, including perhaps transfers and purveyance of commodities that may not have been legal. I used to recall the 'agency houses' of late eighteenth-century India, Ferguson Fairlies, Russells, Palmers, Parrys, who were only later replaced by the Managing Agencies. These venture merchants, or 'portfolio capitalists', had flourished in the transition from Mughal to 'White Mughal' to British rule. Their contemporary successors in Central Asia did not have the independent or extra territorial leverage that the Levant merchants or service compradors of the politically sovereign East India Company used to have. Not, unless they represented US capital. That would become evident only after the 11 September of the next year. Productive utilization of the agricultural surplus of Uzbekistan in such enterprises as fruit canning was not encouraged by a regime that saw Western-style enterprise, by any but Americans and Germans, as milch cows for raking off cash and graft.

The glorious russets turned fast to brown, then to yellow, and then to carpets of mould on the green verges, ubiquitous on every Uzbek *kocha* or *torkocha* (road or byelane). Just before we had left India, in August 2000, the European press apparently had published snippets about 'fundamentalists' armed with 'the latest in modern firepower', making their presence felt around Tashkent. Contacting Tashkent, one learned that these were the old veterans, Juma and Tohir, with young men, up in Ferghana and the Surkhan Darya fastnesses in the south. Troublemakers in the Uzbek valleys had been wiped out by the time we returned. The old Batkent salient of the Kyrgyzstan snows had been again reactivated by the guerrillas to probe Tashkent and the road to Afghanistan. This was obviously part of a Taliban strategy to encircle Khojent with its secularists in Tajikistan, and isolate Tashkent from Samarkand via western Tajikistan, striking terror into Central Asia. Fighters had appeared in villages around reservoirs, including as far north as Brichmulla at the head of the Charvak Lake about which we have already spoken. I gathered that the intelligence community had been suspicious that they might cut urban water supplies. The Uzbek army sealed off the areas and itself terrorized villagers. They were suspected of having sheltered the militants. Numbers differed about the people who were dead on both sides. The balance of force was clearly with the anti-fundamentalist regime.

We had become quite blasé by this time. I had predicted to an International Relations seminar on Central Asian strategy in Jadavpur University, Calcutta, and to friends from Oxford who were to visit Tashkent in October and had rung to enquire about security, that the trouble was much overrated, and that repressive stability was firmly in the saddle. In the long run, this was correct. However, such predictions always run the risk of being toppled by contingencies. In Afghanistan, the Taliban had not yet embarked on the suicidal path of increasing tension against the liberal forces of world opinion, or of not heeding, first Pakistani and then US warnings to cool off. So, it was possible for Ahmed Rashid and his strategic studies fraternity, whom he quotes in his recent books (written before the Bush lobby began to bomb Afghanistan) to predict that Ferghana would become a world trouble spot if the USA did not act. The disasters of the following year changed the equations explicitly. This turned the Uzbeks, still on the saddle in 2000, into horses on which the US rode into Central Asia and Afghanistan in 2001. That was something I could not have predicted.

TALES FROM BUKHARA

When our friends did come to Tashkent, we went with them on an autumn journey to Samarkand and Bukhara.The road was familiar; the hill village selling fruits and honey by the road as hospitable. The scarce and stinking latrines had not improved. Their stench of disinfectant will probably stay with us forever. We used to be surprised that the Uzbek intelligentsia in various institutes whom we met, were by no means as familiar with the road and with sights in both cities, as we were to become. They were surprised that we went back to places like Shah-i-Zinda or the Kalon Masjid. Young Pioneers of the Soviet regime, they had grown up trekking or roughing it out by the streams along the mountain sanatoria with which Russian rulers had been so lavish. Since Independence, their savings went into travel to Germany, Turkey, or the USA.

In Samarkand, we went back to Irani *mahalla*, where a whole block of restaurants catered to the meat-loving populace. Each restaurant had an open space in front, where glass cases sometimes, or open tables mostly, displayed chops, steaks, or other kinds of cut meats, from which visitors were supposed to take their pick for grilling. One then proceeded to an inner square with rooms around, to be served, in privacy, along with Uzbek wine or vodka, lipioshki bread, and salads, and the dishes of your choice. The one we went to on that occasion had a vine trellis, with a Mediterranean ambience of shade. It was autumn and there was neither fruit nor leaf on it. The following summer we found its vines fecund with succulent grapes, green or light mauve, clustered just above our heads. As we ate the abundant food, regretting the amount of local bread that would go waste, by the window, looking out on a side lane a group of little children passed and stretched out their hands for a share. We passed some bread, rather shamefaced to give doles to the poor. No, said our driver, there was nothing demeaning in accepting bread by the wayside, it was given and taken as an act of social camaraderie in Uzbekistan. They had seen us as travellers: on their way back from school and had come to share this good feeling with us. This was one of the many occasions when Inner Asian norms revealed a rustic simplicity, with which our blasé urbanism was unfamiliar.

Driving along the road to Bukhara, we took a wrong turning and found ourselves off the main highway. Instead of going through the fertile irrigated villages of antiquity on the Silk Road, we were on higher ground, with a narrow sideroad switchbacking up and down across very barren steppe lands, with no cultivation or habitation as far as the eye could see. The few carts of primitive make, drawn by large nags, or the pedestrians plodding along, were quite taciturn when asked whether the road went to Bukhara. They didn't have a clue. This was one of our regrettably very few encounters with real rusticity. Ultimately the road moved into the main highway in the central square of Kattakurgan. Then it became clear security controls were tightening up. Every now and then would loom up the elaborate guardrooms and barricades of the Uzbek DAN (Davlat, state, Avtomobil Nazorati inspection) through which every vehicle had to weave. Tension about terrorism, as the state saw it in 2000, communicated in a far more centralized way than in our lax and far more democratic homeland. The Rabat-i-Malik past Navoi had lost its look of ageold remains. State patronage had moved in. Fancy surroundings in the shape of grass verges were being preened around it. They recalled Quwwa in Ferghana or the new gold inlaying inside the dome of Gur Emir. The prettification of archaeology always diminishes the flavour of the past and appears to be a particularly Russian habit.

Once again, night had fallen when we drove into the vicinity of Lyab-i-Hauz in Bukhara. We had been told to wait at a particular spot to meet someone who would guide us to a bed and breakfast in a very old *mahalla* on the outskirts of the main town. The route in would beat even the vintage mazes of Europe, with multiple choice, little alleys, crammed with the oldest possible, mud-walled residential dwellings, none of which were high, and all seemed to lead nowhere. After innumerable twists, we had started having misgivings about what we had let our guests into, when the car was stopped outside a big portal, set in one of the walls. A wicket opened and we stepped gingerly into quite a different element of open space. A slightly raised platform with wooden pillars on one side gave shelter from the sun. It overlooked the usual square courtyard with a vine trellis in the middle, and two-storied rooms on either side and one-storied rooms in front. The place was neat: the two rooms allotted for our stay, with one on top for the driver, were clean and spacious with the carpet wall hangings, common to the country. Our young friend Nigora, who in the meantime had come from Bukhara for her M. Phil level course in Tashkent, knew the young owner-cum-manager, Mir Farkhod, and his mother Maya. She had phoned arrangements for our stay. Her own brother, it so happened, was getting married on that day in Kagan, the Russian cantonment outside Bukhara, where her parents lived. She had specifically asked us to try and attend the wedding. Even though it was late and we were all fairly tired, we piled back into the car after a wash and a very welcome *chai* and followed Mir Farkhod to Kagan.

Uzbeks set much store by wedding receptions, quite a few of which we attended. The cold cuts on the table, the succession of the same pattern of dishes, brought after interminable intervals, punctuated by speeches made in honour of the newly weds and with fulsome praise added about their families and the hospitality, toast after toast and the regulation dancing, mostly by the ladies and then joined by the men, had become familiar. The proceedings are held in a large hall. At its head is a sort of high table meant for the bridal couple and their close relatives. Left and right of the hall are set long tables for the guests, the bride's family and friends on one side, and the groom's on the other. The groom's gathering are served first as the main *mehmaans*, the hospitality to them is profuse. The couple are ushered in with much fanfare, actually blared out by musicians playing the long curved Surnais and Tarnais, somewhat like Swiss alpenhorns or Indian shehnais and cymbals, whose noise is somewhat harsh in our ears. They perform jigs with their instruments in front of the couple as the latter are escorted to the high table. Here the marriage register is signed. This begins the public reception: marriage vows have been solemnized before a Muslim Kazi in family privacy earlier in the day. In the reception, the bridal dress is like any Western wedding dress: the groom is in a dark suit with a deep coloured long robe with brocade embroidery and an ornate turban, which is taken off after the registration, while the lace veil is pushed back from the forehead of the girl. We have never been invited to the Muslim ceremony, but only to the civil ones, presumably mandatory since Soviet rule. This leads one to wonder whether the private customs became completely internal to the kin of the couple getting married, since these had been frowned upon by the Party bosses before 1991; so much so that after that the families never dreamt of including outsiders into what had, under communism become traditionally private. There were a range of such private gatherings at weddings and funerals;

morning ceremonies for the men to partake of plov along with the *sehri namaaz* at the crack of dawn to start the gathering on a pious and social note (rather like *dadhi mangal* among Hindus or *guru ka langar* of the Sikhs). Attendance was scrupulously maintained by the menfolk. Such private festivity is the core of any social group of rituals in any ethnic community.

What is remarkable in the public marriage reception is the showering of the bride with currency notes, when she comes on the floor to join the dance with her husband, and the way in which menfolk and senior matrons in the gatherings present notes with a flourish to ladies who participate in twirling round. The traditional musicians soon leave and hired modern pop bands take charge. The hostess would call my wife to join the festivities. On early occasions she came back home with a big smile and about a thousand soum or more. We knew no better. It was in Bukhara that she learned, after getting nearly more than three thousand soum, and feeling very embarrassed, that the cash was meant to be passed on to the band, in appreciation of their efforts. One leaves these sorties completely deafened by the cacophony.

On this occasion in Bukhara we had arrived late and left late, but the speeches were still in full flow. On the way back I joined Farkhod in the taxi. I got to know the interesting tale of his growing up in the last days of Soviet power. His mother, Maya, was a teacher of mathematics, his father a pilot in the Air Force serving on the Kandahar front in the 1980s, when Mujahideen shot down his plane. The plane and body were not found. The higher authorities suspected that he had gone missing, as many Uzbeks were doing, deserting to the Mujahideen, out of shame in fighting co-religionists. They promptly arrested the mother and young child and kept them in separate prisons near Kandahar, interrogating them to get information about the pilot's contacts and whereabouts. Utterly bewildered and isolated in a time of great sorrow, they pleaded ignorance. Farkhod said they were subjected to torture: the only evidence he gave was that his inquisitors would try to frighten him about dire consequences to his mother. I find it hard to disbelieve this, recalling the story of threats by Gorbachev's inquisitors in Tashkent at the time of the Sharaf Rashidov enquiry.

After a month of their imprisonment had passed, one of his father's friends, while on sortie, saw a crashed plane. Later the dead body was found. They were promptly released and the authorities offered substantial compensation to induce them to forget the harassment. Maya came back to her ancestral dwelling in the house where we lodged. Farkhod learnt English to start business as soon as he left the technical institute. He had met Nigora at a Young Pioneers' camp in the Crimea; an example of the wide links that the USSR could facilitate before 1991. Their common affinity had been the urge to do well in the English language. His mother's earnings in the teaching profession, highly regarded and with considerable emoluments in the 'good old days' (presumably of Brezhnev, even Stalin) were being reduced to a pittance. Forkhod told Maya he would bring her far more cash as a tourist guide and boarding house manager, operating out of the Internet on a global scale. He planned to set up in an apartment with his girl friend, and if possible, move to Tashkent with its vitality and bigger business. Bukhara with only its factory for natural gas was but a sleepy hollow on the edge of the deserts.

Next morning, the breakfast he served was a hearty one, with several types of dishes and beverages on the side. Well fortified, we left for the round of innumerable *madrasas*, great gateways facing each other, the Ark, and different sites we had seen the previous year. We moved on to the Kalon precinct, where beggars surrounded our guests, trying to sell *karakul* caps and hand-embroidered little pouches. We found our acquaintance, the carpet vendor, in his spacious stall. Then ensued a long haggle in which he had to concede a considerable over-pricing of two hand-woven silk carpets. The town struck us as very cold, without the fog that had earlier enveloped it, but somewhat dreary, and stuck in a time warp, in which there was no sign of change—not even the ferociously bigoted piety and scholarship that have been described with awe by Vambery or Sadriddin Aini. Once again, Samarkand the next day seemed so much more open, high and sunny, with clear skies. On our way, there had been an unexpected break for lunch in a large *chaikhana* outside Kattakurgan, beside a river. Freshly fried fish was served piping hot, with tea and lipioshki. Fish is popular along the riverside towns (few and far between in this country). Government prohibits the netting and selling of it during the summer months to improve breeding prospects. It disappears from the bazaar stalls at this time. Inferior varieties are clandestinely sold by fishwives.

THE PLACE OF BENGALI IN SOUTH ASIA–UZBEK RELATIONS

In the middle of the year, Professor Azad Shamatov had asked my wife for help in the training of Bengali translators. The background of this work is an interesting chapter in relations between Uzbeks and Bengalis. Immediately after Independence, India was further from the USSR than it had been to the USA. The Congress Party's affection for President Roosevelt's qualified understanding of its position during the War, took time to wear off until US foreign policy identified Pakistan as an ally against Communism and India as Hindu opposed to anti-communist Pakistan. In the 1950s, the policy of non-alignment grew as Nehruvian equidistance from the USA and the USSR. The Dulles line; of identifying all those who were not trusty allies as potentially suspect, pushed equidistance towards the ambit of friendship with the Soviets. Growing Himalayan border tensions with Chinese expansion in Tibet brought Indo-Soviet understanding into being. At this time, in 1956, Jawaharlal first landed in Tashkent. It is significant that he recalled his old liking for Babur's personality as a Renaissance type in his praise for someone whom Uzbeks were beginning to revere as a hero and not, as what their parents had been taught, a marauding Mughal. Uzbeks past middle age still recall with pride Nehru's words about Babur. They conveniently forget that Babur was an archetypal Mughal to Nehru. When President Karimov left for India on his second visit in summer 2000, the press reported his speech at the airport. He was going, he said, to the land of Nehru, who respected Babur.

Nostalgia for a composite Hindu-Muslim civilization and for the elite elegance of Urdu culture (the word Urdu, be it noted, derives from the Turki *orda* or camp of the horde, and Urdu is the language of the royal camp) is at the root of the specific secular ideology of Nehru. Respect for Babur as one of the founders—along with Ali Shir Navoi, the minister of the Timurid Sultan Hussain Bayqara of Herat—of modern Turki linguistic style and thus of Turkestan ethnicity, was one of the roots of the new subaltern nationalism inculcated in Uzbekistan. Uzbekistan with its developed plains culture and historical affinity with the Tukharians, the Kushans, the Khwarezmians, and the predecessors of the Mughal emperors, as well as the Late Mughal-migrant Turanian nobility in Hyderabad and Lahore, was treated in the

USSR as the republic that would further the USSR's affinities with India and Pakistan.

The late 1950s and early 1960s was the time when Soviet steel and other heavy industrial plants were being set up across India—at Bokaro, Ranchi and Bhilai, at Bhopal, and in Gujarat. The manning of these plants and the achievements and limitations of the transfer of technology involved, deserves a historical study of its own. Many nationalities from the USSR took part in it. One of the important functions in creating a professional community among them was training to work with Hindi-speakers. We met many Uzbeks of our generation or slightly younger, speaking excellent Hindi, indoctrinated with a clear though simplistic understanding of the progressive aspects of Indian nationalism and anti-colonialism in the nineteenth and twentieth centuries, and an affinity with the pop elements in Indian filmi culture. From the 1950s, Tashkent, Samarkand and other parts of their Republic had received special encouragement for linguistic training in Hindi. The Tashkent Oriental Institute became a nodal point for language training in Hindi and Urdu with teachers like Muhammad Rahmanberdiev, Azad Shamatov, specialist in Hindi and Dakhni Urdu, and Professor Tashmirza with his interest in the Urdu of Pakistan. The people we met had learned about India in the Institute. Some had spread out to the Alberuni Institute for research, or the civil and foreign services, or as doctors and nurses.

One of the hallmarks of this linguistic connection was that the children of that first generation who went to work with the Indian public sector, often studied Hindi and Urdu at the graduate level, continuing in their parents' line of work, or perhaps in accessible schools in India. This younger generation could speak much better English than their compatriots who remained at home. Bilingual like their playmates in India, they found it easier in the late 1980s and early 1990s to go for higher training, or for diplomas in management or international relations in the USA and Britain. Not only for these favoured children of diplomats, industrial managers or KGB staffers, but also for a broader group, who it was hoped would form international contacts, there developed a system of special schools, in which the second language, other than the medium of instruction in Russian, was Hindi (not French, German or English, which were equally, if not more, popular as languages of specialization). By the 1980s, the trilingual pattern of elite education in the USSR found Uzbekistan with a large number of Hindi specialized schools, principally scattered all over Tashkent. These were the wellsprings of Indo-Soviet solidarity. Its cultural expression was the marketing of Indian films and, briefly, Indian consumer goods. Raj Kapoor and Nargis had been Indian logos for the masses all over the Soviet Union. Elderly people speak warmly of Raj's trips to the Tashkent Film Festival. Professor Bakhtiar Abidov of the Alberuni Institute proudly recalls being a young translator for Raj, when crowds mobbed the latter, calling out to him all along the way from airport to city. In the late 1980s new film figures appeared, who also stood for the images of the common man and succour for suffering humanity, such as Mithun Chakrabarty. Along with this a taste began for Indian allopathic pharmaceutical products, Yoga, textiles and north Indian leather goods.

Hindi-Russi bhai bhai wore thin when Gorbachev and Rajiv Gandhi faced their traumas of internal dissent. As Russia looked towards Europe and the USA, and India sought to build itself into the regional big brother of the Indian Ocean littoral (neither with conspicuous success), Indo-Uzbek relations became secondary. This was the age of Manmohanomics, liberalization, and disengagement from public sector gigantism. More and more Uzbeks were coming home. The stream of Kashmiri, or UP Muslim, men going to study medicine in Tashkent began to dry up.

Completely new terms of Indo-Uzbek relationship were imaginatively attempted by the Ministry of External Affairs, after P.V. Narasimha Rao, himself previously Foreign Minister, came back as Prime Minister with J.N. Dixit as his Foreign Secretary. In his record of that service Dixit writes about the Central Asian initiatives. They included a state visit by the Prime Minister to Tashkent in which agreements were signed for the new Embassy to develop trade through a State Bank of India office and Confederation of Indian Industry (CII) bureau in the city to further the development of credit lines from India. Also the India Chair was located at UWED, presumably because of its Foreign Ministry status, and because the President's daughters were studying there. The Indian component of this was meant to be the Maulana Abul Kalam Azad Institute of Asian Studies, set up in 1993 by the late Professor S. Nurul Hasan, Governor of West Bengal, in Calcutta, with the active interest of the West Bengal authorities. Dixit mentions that the Governor's unfortunate demise only a few months thereafter led to drying up of central government interest in the Calcutta project.[3]

Responsibility for the sterility of the new package was something deeper, related to a whole generation's experience. The premises of Indian foreign policy, like those of its popular consciousness, saw the CIS being still Soviet; and even more than that, Russian. Whether Tashkent, Baku, or Kiev, everything is 'Russian' to the average Indian, although these three cities are capitals of three new countries. This included the average Indian diplomat of the new generation. They all spoke Russian, didn't they—at least till the year 2000. Indian diplomats who specialize in Eurasia are given a year's special course of Russian studies at Moscow and then posted to CIS countries. This is the same as if from 1947 to 1956 and the Suez debacle, Indian diplomats who would work in Canada or Australia was first posted to London, because that was the centre of the Commonwealth. The young diplomat who came out to Tashkent or Almaty received his briefing about these places through Russian spectacles. This included the idea fostered by Gorbachev and his Anglo-US contacts that Islamic fundamentalism was the main thorn in the Central Asian flesh, apart from Uzbek pride and laziness or Tajik submissiveness. Also, it was believed that the whole of Central Asia was 'oil-rich' and needed to be cultivated for oil supplies.

On the other hand, US diplomats from the time of James Baker III's Secretaryship of State under Bush senior in the late 1980s, with their specific interest in Kazakh and Turkmenian oil, had already developed the notion of Eurasia, as an alternative to Russia in the south of the CIS. They had a well-developed tradition of Uzbek area studies, fostered by scholars like Edward Allworth, William Fierman, and Gregory Gleason, not to speak of people studying the neighbouring republics. Along with this were intensive training programmes in the Uzbek language. Compare with this the limited Central Asian area studies in India: in only JNU and Bombay. The number of people who looked at it from the local angle could be counted on the fingers of one hand. Scholars educated in Tashkent like Devendra Kaushik, R.G. Gidadhubli or Surendra Gopal, and their junior colleagues like Ajay Patnaik or P.L. Dash took a Indo-Soviet perspective. One or two scholars in Aligarh, the Jamia Millia, and Jammu, concerned with Uzbek history, thought 500 years back about Timur, or the Shaibanids and their Mughal adversaries. The situation was better for Inner Asian, Tibetan, and Mongol studies, where Buddhist scholars like Dawa Norbu and Phuntsog Stobdan were competent in the local languages and sources. Without linguistic specificity, diplomats have to rely on the perceptions of the ruling class. In Uzbekistan, this made the Indian approach Moscow-centric in an era when Moscow itself was seeking European and US credit, enterprise, and initiative. India's vision of Central Asia remained the view from the north and the west, and not from South Asia. While some centres of study such as Panjab University, Chandigarh,[4] and, briefly, the Azad Institute in Calcutta, sought to inculcate a view from the south; this was an uphill struggle against lack of interest in Delhi. In the Calcutta situation in any case, this was firmly repressed; research work was diverted by Murli Manohar Joshi's governance from Delhi as Human Resource Development Minister from the Calcutta Institute for publication through Delhi networks after 1998.

The decline of Russia's interest in Asia was represented by the choice of not the old Asia hand, Primakov, but Russia's man in Bonn, Putin, for leading the transition to supreme leadership in the Russian Federation. This meant a corresponding lack of interest by Indians posted at the peripheries of the CIS. That included Tashkent. Our Embassy failed to diversify from a limited interest in Hindi studies at Tashkent to competition with purposive US English-language training. It looked—as we have seen—at only the pre-Islamic past of resurgent Central-Asian Islam through Russian studies of the ancient period. And, there was no interest in learning Uzbek, since Russian was sufficient for communication with the elite. Lacking Indian initiatives, the Uzbek academic authorities failed to respond with a concern for new dimensions in South Asia. Uzbek Foreign Ministry thinktanks in 1998-9 were apprehensive about nuclear proliferation and its fallout, both literally in Pakistan and Afghanistan, and figuratively in Indo-Pak strife in Kashmir. By mid-2000, Uzbek strategic planners were more interested in outlets to the sea, through Pakistan south of Afghanistan, and to China, Pakistan's ally east of Tajikistan, Kyrgyzstan, and Kazakhstan. On the other hand, the Indian establishment chose to focus on cross-border terrorism, vice traffic through Pakistan into the more sleazy parts of Delhi, and the views of assorted spooks funding the Northern Alliance in Panjshir, as guiding principles in Delhi's position on Tashkent.

One of the results of the change was a shift in the Tashkent Oriental Institute's sponsorship of students in the study of the languages of South Asia, as distinct from Hindistan, as the Uzbeks still popularly called India. Even before the 1990s, it had been interested in Bengali. As early as 1972, Purabi Roy (who later joined the Department of International Relations in Jadavpur University) then doing her Ph.D. on Russian language and philosophy in Moscow, had spent a few months helping Bengali-language study in Tashkent. One of her fellow students had been probably the first Uzbek to teach an academic course in Bengali at the Institute. After Independence, like many professionals in the city, with hopes of getting rich quick, he indulged in mercantile business with some north Indian fly-by-night operator. This led to his total financial disaster when the initial speculative bubble, which had blown up in Tashkent after 1992, burst. He died soon after of heart failure. One or two of his students had picked up the Bengali script. When Professor Shamatov came to the Azad Institute in 1995, and again in 1997, he sought an understanding by which we would help improve Bengali-language teaching. Two of the Institute's research staff visited Tashkent to work in its archives with just one month's allowance. All four weeks, they gave intensive lessons in the script and elementary Bengali grammar to a new student, Barnobek, and his classmates. When I went to Tashkent, I carried with me a Russian-Bengali dictionary as their special gift to these students. They took great pride in showing off their spoken sentences in my own language to me. As has been noted before, the great intellectual gift of Central Asian people is linguistic competence.

Barnobek left soon after to take up a long course in Hindi at a government institute in Agra. A young girl was asked by Azad Shamatov to keep up contact with Bengali. She was the one who had moved the Indian audience at the Tagore function on 8 May 1999 by reciting 'Where the mind is without fear and the head is held high' in Bengali and Russian translations of Tagore's verses. Nodira was a graduate in Urdu, obviously trained for Pakistan studies. For her M.Phil. dissertation, she was asked to check the Uzbek translation of the Russian translation of Tagore's writings. Obviously a case in cross-linguistic translation analysis, this was meant to see whether Uzbeks were reading free or literal versions of the original sources translated in the Soviet past. For this Azad Shamatov requested my wife for help in reading a set of texts with Nodira. After getting the full meaning of these as far as possible, the latter would then use her understanding for the cross-checking. The texts were well known, short stories such as *Khokababur Pratyabartan*, *Kabuliwala* or *Samapti*. This exercise lasted till late 2001.

When the requests were formally made to my wife, I had strong personal misgivings, purely of an academic nature. She had no formal training as a teacher; she made this abundantly clear by asking to meet Azad Saheb in his office and clarifying this, as well as asking him how exactly she was to proceed. He was relatively lighthearted: just come and help, and something will come out of it, he said. That something did was due largely to the fact that Nodira was extremely gifted, and partly because both of them persisted seriously in the project. The instructor knew excellent Bengali, good English, a smattering of Hindi, as well as a smattering of Russian. The pupil knew excellent Russian and Hindi and most exiguous English, and was, when she began, familiar with only the letters of the Bengali alphabet and some simple grammar. I never ceased to marvel at the doggedness, as well as the imagination, with which both welded their knowledge in a line-by-line reading of Rabindranath. By the time we left Tashkent, Nodira was reading Bengali quite competently. The sincerity with which young students in Uzbekistan take up appointed tasks and make do with totally limited facilities is utterly amazing. I concluded that a world of difference exists between the trained Oriental linguist of the old Tashkent Institute, and the dilettante-aspirant diplomats or bankers from well to do families, who come via government patronage to the far more 'hep' UWED, with its multidisciplinary mishmash and American-style courses. Next year I had made known to the Embassy that it would be better if the India Chair were shifted from UWED to TIOS. There was the usual indifference.

The Ambassador of Bangladesh, Mohsin Ali Khan, was interested in linking his country with the Institute's work. He gave some Bengali books to Shamatov Saheb's seminar library, and encouraged Nodira's interests. Uzbek scholarship and policy was at that point of transition caught in the dilemma of the partition of the sub-continent—without of course having read the literary effusions about South Asia which poured out after India's Golden Jubilee breast-beating in 1997. The Uzbeks see the partition as a religious one, not as the culmination of British 'divide and rule'. Contemporary Uzbeks ignore the fact that British imperialism in the last days of 1940s, seeking to build southern barriers to Central Asian communism, used the idea of Pakistan to create artificial tensions. For imperialism these would become festering sores, necessitating huge armament industries, and arms sales. Indeed this happened in the 1960s. The Uzbeks were confirmed in their prejudice by the Right religious reaction that began with Zia-ul-Huq's Islamization (with CIA help) in the 1980s, which has now come to roost not only in Pakistan but in India and Bangladesh as well.

Uzbek foreign policy probably does not see Bengali as only an Indian language but also as an internatioanl one. Let it be said again that, in these days of globalization, Indian cultural diplomacy would do well to give up the Hindi chauvinism so integral to all of Delhi's current transactions with its wider world. It should compete on open market terms with other nations, using our pre-eminent skills in the English and Bengali languages, not to speak of Tamil, Telugu, Gujarati, Punjabi or any other international language.

NOTES

1. Stephen Frederick Dale, *Indian Merchants and Eurasian Trade, 1600-1750* (Cambridge University Press, 1994).
2. Gyanendra Pandey—'The Civilized and the "Barbarian": The New Politics of Late Twentieth Century India and the World' in Gyanendra Pandey (ed.), *Hindus and Others: The Question of Identity in India Today* (Viking, New Delhi, 1993), pp. 10-11 writes 'A pamphlet called *Ramjanmabhoomi ka rakt-ranjit itihas* (the bloodstained history of the Ramjanmabhoomi) and other similar leaflets and pamphlets . . . were sold all over Ayodhya . . . list(ing) as many as seventy-six battles that the Hindus are supposed to have fought for the "liberation" of the janmabhoomi with considerable statistical detail and local colour . . . supposed to verify the "truth" of this Hindu history . . . the mythical and the historical came together wondrously in these accounts (in which) . . . Mughals established their hold over India in the "fourteenth century" this "history" has it. Or again that Rana Sanga with a mere 30,000 troops confronted Babar with his 600,000 on the battlefield—and of course gave as good as he got.'
3. Dixit, loc. cit.
4. See Madanmohan Puri, 'Central Asian Geopolitics: the Indian View', *Central Asian Survey*, Vol. 9, No. 1, 1994, pp. 45-56.

6

In the Eye of a Storm

MULTINATIONALS AND MARKET RESTRICTIONS

India was falling behind other nations on the front of relationships with Uzbekistan. Karimov's 2000 visit to Delhi and Bombay in search of new credit lines had not been followed up by any significant interest from Indian industry, even in pharmaceuticals. Hopeful cries that 'the Ranbaxys are coming' had petered out. Ideas about developing an Indian tea market at Karshi close to Turkmenistan had not been taken up by the CII. In default of credit lines, its Tashkent bureau staffed by young, or over-enterprising, people had been closed down by its sponsor, the Indian Commerce Ministry. The State Bank of India's office, set up with many hopes, had also closed down. The pharmaceutical industry people, Dr. Reddy's Laboratories, Ajanta, and Core Healthcare worked in a narrow market. Gufic, with a factory in Bukhara, closed down its liaison office in Tashkent. This was because of a lack of funds and convertibility. The hubris of Daewoo from South Korea was catching up with the Indian businessman also. Indian business had accumulated soum, but had not found ways to put it back into a globalizing market, dominated by the dollar.

The emphasis was shifting from bilateral country-to-country relationships to West-oriented multinational connections. Even here, the process was bumpy. Government and corruption was in constant friction with the market purity that Chicago has idealized. UzBAT had moved from its factory in the city centre next to what became the Intercontinental Hotel Plaza and amusement park area, to outside Samarkand. The headquarters remained in Tashkent. We knew some professionals from Bangladesh and India who worked in it. The expatriate community had had Uzbekistan declared a hardship zone, with foreign allowances rated higher than the standard diplomatic levels. In an economy in which the local bazaar rate was steadily becoming softer than a pincushion, this meant savings and opportunities for regular trips home and for foreign travel. Those who did speak Russian kept company with foreigners. The multinational manager and his family treated Uzbek staff as informal subalterns. The Uzbek bureaucracy was seen in much the same way as the 'indirectly ruled' natives of Central Africa, eagerly waiting for their palms to be greased. At best, the more highminded ladies involved themselves in aid and charity projects for the poor and the diseased.

Aid did come into Uzbekistan from a variety of NGOs. However, the government was not clear about its policy on them. They too were seen as milch cows to create employment prospects and dollar earnings for the local young people. But when the Calcutta based Missionaries of Charity put in a plea that their travel in and out of Uzbekistan should continue to be charged in soum, and not in dollars, so that they could utilize locally funded charity, their requests were turned down. We were told that government had no economic argument against the request, but it would be politically incorrect to accept that foreign agencies could be treated on a par with local citizens, even if the former were benefitting the latter. On the other hand, since salaries doled out by the multinationals in soum were more than double of what Uzbek school and college teachers were earning, the multinationals saw no market rationality to feel compunction about the low costs of local labour and services.

We knew a manager from Bangladesh who had been transferred back to Dhaka, while his family was allowed to stay on for a few more months so that the children could complete school sessions and then transfer the eldest son to a Indian boarding school in the Himalayas. He was fairer than his fellow expatriates in his judgement about the people among whom he had worked. He said he had been recruited to organize the laying off of those workers who could not be moved, or would not move to a new factory that was to be set up. I asked him, as a technical engineer how he had found the workers. Uzbeks were superb at taking orders, he said. If you lucidly explained a process to be carried out, a system to be set up, a job to be done, there would be no cause for complaint. If the preparation of instructions was shoddy, or work was delegated to them to carry out on their own initiative, then there could be serious flaws. Constant and watchful leadership was a pre-requisite for their competent performance of tasks. I had interacted with the very last generation of decolonizing British, as well as with the early generation of independent Indian managers in my teaching years, in the 1960s in the Indian Institute of Management, Calcutta. I vividly remember the way such people, for instance then at India Tobacco Ltd. a cousin of UzBAT, or in Metal Box, or ICI, spoke of Calcutta and Howrah workers in the days before *gheraos* and *bandhs*. Keep a firm hand on them or they are bone-lazy, was the way the Scots, Cockneys, Punjab Khattris, and Gujarat entrepreneurs used to speak of Bengali clerks and labour in those days; those were the days of the 1960s when enterprise went around grabbing the sick industries and the property connected with them.

The same latent neo-colonial feeling of domination yet unease permeates the multinational approach to Central Asia. The whole region is treated as a potential market to be customized for consumer goods, for which it still has very little purchasing power. But this is only because oil reserves in Kazakhstan and Turkmenistan have to be controlled to regulate oil profits. An article in a UNDP volume entitled *Central Asia in 2010*, by a consultant for the James Baker III Institute set up by the ex-Secretary of State of the senior Bush (himself a oil magnate and adviser to the present President on Eurasian policies) would have it that Central Asian oil is nowhere as competitive in the world market as even that of the Black Sea.[1] The implication for this is that no one should use this oil to create price instabilities, any more than any Kazakh general would have been allowed, at the turn of the 1990s, to create nuclear instability, by suddenly grabbing the plants for atomic power at Semipalatinsk or elsewhere (a favourite scenario for US film shockers such as *Air Force One*). The same logic on a smaller scale applies to UzBAT keeping a finger in Uzbek markets to keep out Philip Morris, which acts vice versa in Kazakhstan. Restrictive market control of potential buyers, whether of tobacco or nuclear armament or oil, and not of specific reserves alone but whole political region, is the actual name of the game. This is not so much a struggle for oil, as a struggle to restrict competition from dabbling in potential markets, and to use authoritarian subalterns in democratic disguise to keep the peace as wardens of the heartland marches.

Stories proliferate of how ruling groups pestered the Company for extra contributions to harvest the tobacco crop at Urgut between the Tajik border and Samarkand; of how meetings with the Prime

Minister on a one-to-one basis had to resolve such issues; and of how entire factories, producing machine tools, now in a state of obsolescence, just outside Tashkent were offered on sale for a song, to be rejected on the grounds that the Company made cigarettes and not machines. Of late, the officials took to living in a large housing complex, way outside the city, in designer houses, square and identical, with guards at the barred gates.

The new century's first year closed on a grim note. There was a sense of embattlement, which had been utterly missing when we came to the country. The people were still friendly to us if anything perhaps warmer. In Alaiski market, the robust ladies all called out to me to enquire why my wife had not come. When she did, they took turns to greet her. In the University, the students had moved from asking me for testimonials to attach to their application for German or US colleges, to requesting me for an introduction to the ICC so that they could read about India. I remained unhappy that they searched for books on Hindu spirituality rather than modern international relations. Diloram, Nigora, and Nodira were fairly regular visitors, calling my wife 'mama', and increasingly chatting about domestic concerns and aspirations. Their youthful urge was to get out and see the world.

Diloram Karomat, an academic if ever there is one, making trips to libraries in India through the past decade, was soon to leave for Lucknow to join the Bhatkhande College of Music in the Kaiserbagh. She later wrote lyrically about strolling in the area where Wajid Ali Shah had once played. Nigora, more practical, was teaching Uzbek to a political staffer in the US Embassy. Her friends from Bukhara had already found scholarships or teaching assistantships in the US. They were encouraging her to come over. She had no desire to go back to live at home and was making new friends in Tashkent. Nodira, eager to get a feel for any part of South Asia, was anxious to know about prospects in Santiniketan, or in Dhaka. The next year she would receive, sponsored by her Institute, a very interesting internship organized by the Indian government for computer training with Tata Infotech at Kasauli and Delhi. This was as normal as what our young people look forward to. One could sense the same lack of faith in contemporary domestic traditions, which had now become obsolete by the standards of Westernization, the deep structure that underlies the rhetoric of globalization.

The end of the year is a sort of festive limbo in countries once ruled by the Russian Orthodox Church (and then by the Bolsheviks who espoused the Gregorian calendar, giving up different Russian dates for Christmas and the New Year). Add to that, the revival of Muslim and pre-Muslim festive dates such as Nauroz. The last week of December and the first week of January till the Orthodox Christmas, which falls on 7 January, becomes a fortnight of winter vacation for Uzbek educational institutions. The crowds flock to Broadway on the night of the Gregorian New Year's Eve, as they do anywhere else. Perfectly secular Muslims in their domestic faith, Uzbeks celebrated Xmas Day for their children in their *mahallas*. This is the nub of the cultural hybridization that has been brought to Asia by latter-day colonialism by whatever name. A festival is a festival. Religion is not all that there is to it. This is one of the best insurances against fundamentalism finding deep roots in Central Asia, unless a sudden increase of unemployment, or sudden World Bank impelled higher prices and frustrations jolt the shaky balance. All that the communist version of the latest Russian influence had done was to desacralize the Christian content and give the festival a local folk form. Christianity had retreated to the remnants of the Orthodox clerical establishment. On the Russian date of Christmas, the Mass was celebrated by bearded and robed monks under swinging censers and candles in the old garrison church that stands near the Nukus Boulevard, for the small gathering of Russians who had 'Stayed On'.

A WEEK IN KAZAKHSTAN

I had been invited by Director Stobdan, of the ICC in Almaty to visit the city and lecture on India at academic institutions there. Himachal Som, Director General of ICCR had introduced him to me during our journey back from India at the end of August. The thought of being able to compare our Uzbek experiences with conditions in a neighbouring Central Asian country, closer to China and yet with much greater affinity to Siberia (and thus the Russian Federation), was quite exciting in our humdrum existence. We spent a week as guests of the Indian Embassy in Kazakhstan in January 2001.

Kazakhstan lies on the northern Asian interface between the colonized Siberian plains and Mongolia and China. One can sense from travel accounts the tension that exists between Europe and Asia in these marchlands. The Siberian waste perhaps has geographic similarity with Canada and socially with Australia. It was once sparsely peopled by small groups of herders and trappers, with a flourishing wild animal population. The Yakuts, Buryats, and other tribal groups were whittled down by Russian settlement, though perhaps not hunted down as systematically as happened in Canada and the US. The first cities of Siberia, such as Vladivostok, Irkutsk, Yakutsk, and Novosibirsk, came into being as outposts of Russian civilization, communicating across the Urals as much as Vancouver did with Quebec and Montreal, or Perth and Adelaide did with Sydney. By Stalin's time, the tribal element had been decisively reduced to serfdom. Urban expansion further north, in the defence and industrial establishment, was carried out by the Gulag method of encamping foreign or Russian forced labour to build settlements in the freezing conditions of the Tundra. The prison camps extended from the north of Mongolia to the Uzbek desert.[2]

The drive was to push the frontier of cultivation from the north of Kazakhstan towards Manchuria, in spurts of peasant migration from the Ural regions eastwards. A south-eastern spurt in the 1930s had changed the entire demography and ecology of what is known as the 'virgin lands' of north Kazakhstan. Ravaged by famine and by death among the herds, native Kazakhs were still fleeing through Chinese Turkistan, into Ladakh as late as the early 1950s. Similar trends have been going on through the twentieth century in China, south-east of Kazakhstan. The integration of Mongol tribal minorities, part of the forty-million tribal population along the inner borders of China all the way from Tibet to Szechwan, into the main fabric of the dominant Han civilization of China, has led to the encouragement of poorer elements of the Han population to move across borders, as labour or as peasant colonizers, into these open tracts of Inner Asia.

Much of Sino-Russian, as well as internal Central-Asian, tension stems from these population seepages along the eastern borders of what the USSR in 1924 demarcated as Kazakhstan, nomad territory, very large and almost the size of India, larger than all the Central Asian Republics (which except for Tajikistan, snuggle into its south-western flanks). The last example of this tension to come into world news had been conflicts between Kazakh, Uighur (the indigenous inhabitants of Chinese Sinkiang) and Han migrants from Xinjiang and Inner Mongolia, in the late 1960s.

China's diplomatic relations with the Russian Federation have much improved since Vladimir Putin came to power. At the unofficial level, however, the Han peasant frontier is believed to be still seeping north and west along the Kazakh and Siberian borders. Straddling the borders of Chinese and the Central Asian Republics, however, are the numerous local population of the Uighur race, mainly resident in Xinjiang and thus Chinese, but Muslim and ethnically Turki. In Uzbekistan, they are being Uzbekized. In Kazakhstan, however, there are also tensions with China about Uighur sentiments, and its sympathy with Uighur ethnicity, which the Chinese seek to control.

At the interface Kazakhstan is far more Russianized than one would expected, more democratic, and in its social behaviour more Eurasian and confident than the Uzbeks, with the public secretiveness and private confidences of the latter. We arrived in Almaty in the middle of January, the plane landing through an inch of snow on the runway, to find ourselves in a white world. As our plane crossed the Tian Shan, the land had seemed to be a white lake. The reception from the Embassy that followed for the next week was a marked change also from the Tashkent quirks, which were tense and jittery about being on the wrong side of power. Ms. Nurgul of the ICC Almaty, who was with us most of the time when we were not being escorted by her seniors, came from Aktyubinsk near the Caspian on the edges of Russia proper. She was dismissive of the ankle deep snow through which we drove into the city. In her home in the far west, she said, the doors of houses could not be opened because of the snow. We would soon see on the television, how far east, south of Semipalatinsk with its notorious atomic arsenal, the temperature was dropping to its fabled 40 degrees Centigrade, and the roads were being dug out of snow.

A small apartment just outside our Embassy had been organized for our stay. A lady would come in each morning and cook us a hearty breakfast. She worked at the Cultural Centre premises as a cleaner. She was a trained teacher who travelled several kilometers by bus into the city to earn the far greater sum of money than her training would give her in consequence of the communist collapse. The Embassy welcome was gratifying, given the marginalization of the previous two years. Stobdan himself is a scholar with contacts among Central Asian and Mongol elites and strategy experts.[3] His Ambassador then was Dr. Syed Raza Hashim, who had retired as Secretary of the Indian Planning Commission. He gave me a full hour, briefing me about Kazakh economics and politics and its concerns about Chinese growth.

China was not far south of Almaty. Memories remained of the Jungars who had marauded the land two centuries before. Kazakh dominant ethnicity along the southern borders had led to shifting the official capital far north beyond the deserts of Central Asia to Akmola, now called Astana, in the region, which had been wholly colonized by recent Russian emigration so as to reassure the Russian element. Only the diplomatic community remained in Almaty. Government officials commuted between the two cities.

From the Indian point of view, Kazakhstan represents the possibility of triangular trade with either Russia or China as a pivot. While Tashkent had been an extra-national metropolis for the Soviet Union, and a node between it and China, the present circumstances of the CIS give Almaty a much greater economic and metropolitan significance than Alma Ata used to have; which was dominated by towns on the Trans-Siberian Railway to the north, that bypassed Kazakhstan and went to the Soviet *dalnyi vostok* or Far East. Uzbekistan became much more of a sideline in the geo-economics of inland Asia, important for cotton no doubt, to be exported west along the TRACECA route, but pushed into backwardness, because of the cotton price slump. In the post-Stalin period, nuclear and cosmonautical policy (at Baikonur, just north of the Betpak Dala wastes), as well as heavy industrial plants more modern than the mid-century Uzbek types came up in Kazakhstan. The regime can bargain for trade with Russia and China. With the first, its large Russian population looks for friendship. With the second, practical interests, provided the Chinese are moderate, call for economic cooperation.

Cooperation along its borders appears to be the Chinese policy, competing with Japan as well as the European Community for investment in a variety of projects, including rail communication links, all the way to Tashkent, railhead for the west and the south-west of Asia. Almaty now becomes the node, creating access not only to the north, but also to the west, in this expansion of Chinese trade, which is a part of its development policy, and which is expressed by its positive role in the Shanghai Association for Economic Cooperation. Kazakhs also look to the staging points of Urumqi and Yarkand in Xinjiang, south-westwards of the Karakoram Highway between China and Pakistan, and thus for access to the Arabian Sea and the Persian Gulf, as a subsidiary of the Sino-Pak (north-east trending to south-west from the North China Sea to the Persian Gulf) axis.

This context became clear to me in two lectures I delivered in the next two days. One was at one of the universities, and the other at an Institute that specialized in strategic studies. The first had an old tradition of Indian history studies. I was pleasantly surprised when a part-time lecturer arrived, displaying a copy of a book entitled *Freedom Struggle*, of which I am one of the authors, which she had read in Moscow. The usual Soviet emphasis remained on composite Indian culture, on Hindu-Muslim syncretism, and on the glories of Central Asian settlement in medieaval India. I heard of the Kazakh adoption of Mirza Haider Dughlat as a Kazakh national hero. He had been a Mughal cousin, not a Kazakh, and a follower of Babur, who had been driven out of his land in Mughalistan proper, north-east of Andijan; he later sought refuge with Humayun, suffering the latter's defeat by the Indian Afghan, Sher Shah, in the battle of Kanauj in 1539. While the Baburids fled back to Afghanistan and Iran, Mirza Haider marched across the Pir Panjal and carved out a brief domain in Kashmir and Ladakh. Here he was killed in 1545 by a local uprising of Kashmiris, ever eager for *azadi* from alien repression. He left behind his famous account of the post-Chingizid Mughals in the massive *Tarikh-i-Rashidi*.

The professor who presided was so full of this hero—similar to members of his fraternity in Uzbekistan, who celebrated Timur, Babur, and even the unfortunate Mangubardi, as conquerors of Indians—that he kept referring to Stobdan who had accompanied me, and who was a Ladakhi Indian, as a 'descendant' of the Kazakh hero, Mirza Haider. Little did it matter that in Dughlat's own time, as today, Kazakhs and Mughals were supposed to be ethnically different and of course tribally distant. Nor did it matter to the professor that the staunch Buddhist from Ladakh did wince, albeit courteously, at being supposed to be descended from a northern raider from the Muslim frontier. In the same way in Andijan in 1997, Professor Samsiddinov had affectionately introduced me as a 'Baburologist' from India because my grandfather Brijendranath De, ICS (retd.) had translated and edited the *Tabaqat-i-Akbari* of Nizamuddin Ahmed Bakshi. Conflation of genealogy into nationality myths, I was learning, is very much a part of identity politics in Central Asia, in regions where identities had been brutally erased by the Russians as late as the twentieth century. Such fabrications will not lead to genuine national integration. That can come only when and if economic stability is achieved.

In the non-governmental private institute where the emphasis was on strategic studies, I spoke on Kashmir and Indo-Pak relations in 2001, in the post-Kargil context. Here I could sense a hard tone of cynicism about India's legitimacy in Kashmir. I started with Pakistan's reliance on Kashmiri separatism since the tribal raid across Domel and towards Poonch, foiled by the National Conference, following the Maharaja's accession in late 1947. I also emphasized the complex geo-cultural specificities of Jammu, Kashmir, Gilgit's Northern Areas grabbed by Pakistan (before the accession but after 14 August 1947), Ladakh and Zanskar. I suggested that the solution lay in Pakistan putting an end to cross-border terrorism and its camps along the Line of Control, before there could be any discussion about the LoC as an international border. The research students present had an opposite and radical view. They asked about the Indian Army and human rights: what about the need for a referendum, rather than state controlled elections among the disturbed people in Kashmir: what about the need for Indo-Pak dialogue, and a return to the Gujral Doctrine and the Lahore spirit?

In Uzbekistan, General Pervez Musharraf was seen as a military despot, shakily controlling a potential rogue state. Pakistan's control of the Taliban and thus influence with Juma Nomonghani directly affected Uzbek national interests. Kazakhstan, on the contrary, had Xinjiang and Central Asia as buffers between it and the Northern Areas held by Pakistan. It could afford to think less of Pakistan's present adventurism, and more of it as a trade outlet to the Arabian Sea. India became only an ancillary variable. Deep down, though courteously unspoken by the ever polite Central Asians, was a vague sense of alienation, which all adults who had grown up in Soviet times as well as young people who have experienced the revival of Islamic fanaticism must feel, when they think of an India in which Nehru's principle of secularism, and beneath that Gandhi's ideas of Satyagraha, are now in eclipse—along with the rise of counter-terrorist extremism as a part of Hindu nationalism. This as late as 2004 was expressed as much in the suavities of L.K. Advani, who reads Humphrey Hawkesley and David Halberstam on Natopolitical strategic ideas, as in Narendra Modi's crude rhetoric.

Kazakh scholars appeared more prepared for academic discussion than in Tashkent or Samarkand. My formal lecture at the premier Abai University of Almaty, a massive skyscraper in the central square of the town, where Ambassador Hashim was good enough to accompany me along with Stobdan, was attended by history and social science professors of the city. It was on the main currents in Indian historiography in the twentieth century, and was received with considerable awareness of the issues involved in my critique of imperialism, nationalism, and revisionism from general social science, as well as chauvinist, aspects. The Vice-Chancellor of the University expressed the desire to the Ambassador that more academic collaboration should be set up for more research from Kazakh and Indian points of view. All this was accompanied with most generous lashings of the best Caspian red and black caviar, fine bread and red wine.

On one of the evenings, Dr. and Mrs. Hashim at India House just below the snow slopes, invited the leading historian of Kazakhstan, Academician Kozyrev. He spoke about his view of Kazakh national aspirations. He was emphatic that these were not the views of President Nursultan Nazarbaev, with whom he disagreed—where, exactly, I never made out. I had mentioned a poster for the celebrations of a millennial and a half that I had seen that afternoon in the strategic studies seminar. Attila (whom in my childhood during the Second World War, the British used to execrate as the devastator of Central Europe and Rome) was depicted riding tall on a horse. Was Attila now to be another national hero of the Kazakhs, as Timur had appeared to be of the Uzbeks? Brushing aside any comparison with the Uzbeks, the Academician went straight to the Kazakh point. The Kazakh land had been home for many races and many heroes. The Huns had built an empire from the Amur to the Donau (which we call the Danube). This had to be celebrated and Attila was its image. He spoke with confidence of a resurgence in Kazakhstan's role as a cultural bridge between the Far East and Eurasia. There was no awareness that deifying an expansionist with a reputation for brutality would hurt the people of those lands that had suffered that brutality. National aggrandizement—without the strength to practice it—is a positive legend in this country, as much as in its southern neighbours.

In the excellent seminars bringing together Central Asianists from the European Community and Eurasia, which Vincent Fourniau organized from time to time through IFEAC, I had heard a Kazakh anthropologist, Professor Masanov, speak remarkably critically about Nazarbaev's use of direct lineage from one of the three hordes (armed tribal groups or Juz), which had ruled Kazakhstan. He was drawing the attention of scholars to the appropriation of kinship history into the present needs of clan dominance. Uzbek historians had uncomfortably stirred in their chairs, seeing analogies they preferred to ignore, given their own circumstances. A colleague from Germany said that it was all very well to talk of this in a land outside one's own: how many in Central Asia could afford to be so critical within their own country? Certainly not Uzbeks, unsure of academic job security. I made a point of requesting Stobdan to arrange an interview for me with Masanov. Not only this, he arranged for me to meet Academician Kozyrev and his colleagues in the Institute of Historical Studies, as well as mediaeval Indologists and anthropologists in other institutes, all in the great mansion that houses the Academy of Sciences of Kazakhstan.

The modern historians were more interested in the internal history of Kazakhstan. Their subjects were far more relevant than the Uzbek historians' eulogies of their Jadid heroes: Uzbeks elided the fact of liquidation of many Jadids in Stalin's purges. The Kazakhs were reconstructing the demographic eradication of large segments of their population in the 1930s at the time of the great famine. They planned to publish a Book of Martyrs. This has not been done for many countries in Europe and Asia, which suffered mass slaughter and death by starvation during the Second World War.[4] Ethnocide came back to the world in a big way in the middle of the twentieth century, not just in what Stalin did to Kazakhstan, or Hitler to the rest of the Europe, but also through the fratricidal conflicts in India and Pakistan in the late 1940s.

Masanov was erudite on tribal genealogies and lineage structures, over long periods of time, quite an orthodox subject of historical anthropology, from which he had come to his views about the political concoction of lineages for purposes of legitimating present power. He was a political activist and knowing my interest in the present political implication of his academic work, he had brought along several pamphlets about human rights abuses for me to pass on to whoever was interested. There was no problem, he said, about freedom of opinion in Kazakhstan. They could think or talk as freely as they wished. The difference from Tashkent was striking.

Almaty is much smaller than Tashkent but it is a bustling and apparently flourishing little city. Only seventy years ago, it had been a small-fortified outpost close to the Chinese frontier, called 'Big Apple' (Alma Ata) in Kazakh, or Vierny (the outpost) in Russia. So small indeed that Leon Trotsky and his wife had been exiled there, disgraced by Stalin before he was permitted to go to Turkey and thence Mexico to be murdered. It was growing. Monumental buildings, an excellent museum of national history from ancient times to the present day, well stocked departmental stores like Ramstor, some of them more reminiscent of the West than anything in Uzbekistan, and sprawling markets for consumer goods and foodstuffs, gave it an aura of prosperity, which of course belied the very real poverty growing among the common people. The aura was symbolized by the full convertibility of currency at standard rates without the hole and corner, sleazy, bazaar rate of Uzbek soft currency. Cash points and licensed exchange shops were to be found on the principal thoroughfares. For a minimal commission, the local currency could be bought with dollars, unthinkable for us in the previous two years. When we came back to Tashkent, people opened up to admit that Kazakhstan perhaps was on an upswing. One of them envied the academic access to foreign books, another the departmental stores where there was so much more free choice of commodities. Kazakhs had advanced since independence, whereas Uzbeks had remained isolated in their regime to permits, licenses, and regulations.

It is not necessary to be starry-eyed about the consumerist pleasures of Kazakhstan. We were not there long enough to know whether capital account convertibility is easy for business enterprise. It is this which is the real benefit of full convertibility, not the dollar cash-point at street corners. Nor did we hear much about the health, or prospects for improvement, of industrial regeneration. The armaments and heavy industry appeared to be stagnating, if not in crisis.

Perhaps it was the sheer pleasure of briefly being in a friendly environment in our Embassy, with people to talk to every evening in warm houses, with snow glistening all around, which gave a glowing picture, in contrast to the suspicious milieu that isolates people in the 'lonely crowd' in Tashkent. Almaty's snow was wonderful. Everyday it snowed, sometimes in a blizzard, sometimes in a thick steady drop, covering all that would be green in summer with a thick white sheet, and the trees with fat, fluffy wraps. My wife went out in it to take photographs: the snow blurred the camera lens and her spectacles, making pictures impossible. One evening we went to dinner with the Military Attaché and his wife. The grounds around their house were practically knee deep in snow. After sundown, which came very early, the snowploughs would be out on the roads, clearing tracks for the cars. The general conversation in the warmth of the gatherings was whether the temperature had fallen below minus 15 degrees or not.

Just to the south in the suburbs, seen from all over the city, was a range of snow peaks into which roads climbed to picnic spots with winter sports along the higher streams. The most well known of these, all over the CIS, is the Medeo winter sports stadium. Assorted resorts cluster around it. The Ambassador, his wife, and Stobdan with his father who was staying with him, took us in a van towards Medeo. It was Sunday and the road was blocked by a stream of cars, many with skis on top, heading out for the hills. These are regulated by chokepoints, beyond which only a fixed number are permitted at a time, to prevent overcrowding on the mountain roads, prone to landslips; traffic was held up till some cars would come down and make room for those in the queue. So, we detoured to another area. The road climbed past the usual earthwork dam common to Central Asian hill roads, which are meant to prevent landslides when the snow melts. It rose past frozen meadows where people were ice-skating or just enjoying themselves, to the upper reaches below the crags themselves. Here we trudged through the snow to a spot where the stream came out as a spring. The water trickling out of rocks had frozen hard into a broad conical pile.

The skies were clear and blue, the crags ashen where they were in the shadow, the ground feathery with ice, and a silent whiteness enveloped the world. The only soft murmur was of the senior Mr. Stobdan, very quietly humming a Buddhist *mantra* in the presence of nature. The entire experience was a humbling one. We came back to reality with the fact that even the stout van that we were in, would have sunk to its axles but for its expert driver. On the way back, we were taken up a tributary valley. Down this came a tinkling rivulet. The snow was less thick by the water; trees along its steep bank had little coloured strips of cloth fluttering away as prayers in the breeze. My wife had seen the same thing above the ski lift in Chimgan. Within twenty minutes we were back in the city, a remarkable experience.

The main sights within Almaty with its square roads and formal architecture are few. It is more reputed for its nightclubs, whose bright neon lights we did not penetrate (in Tashkent these spots are tucked away without much advertisement). It has the usual bustling Central Asian markets and an imposing Russian Orthodox Church in the central square and park. Chinese and Korean settlers as well as local Kazakhs dominate the markets. While it was so cold that taking one's gloves off to reach into one's pockets was torture, the profusion of leather and fur, clothing and footwear was interesting. In one market, known as Zhilioni or the Green One, you climb past a vast open space where vegetables and dried fruits are spread out in stalls, to a covered area where a gruesome display of a variety of freshly slaughtered meat will be found. Dangling from hooks on frames are the heads not only of cattle or sheep, but even horses and camels. My wife hurried me away. The crowds clustered here led us to wonder how different we were from the nomadic races who appeared to be obsessed with meat eating. In Tashkent, we had once been presented with a bottle of koumiss, or camel's milk as a favourite delicacy, which we politely declined. Here, koumiss, bottled, vied for space with cow's milk in serried ranks in the shops. The same profusion can be seen of caviar for which the Kazakh Caspian sturgeon is renowned. We did not have a chance to go to the Barakolka, which is said to be the Kazakh version of the Hippodrome in Tashkent, a vast wholesale market area. There was also a region some distance away where the shopping mall was pretty large, and mainly run by Koreans.

The Orthodox Church, with its onion cupolas, is a striking colonial relic. Set amid high trees, it gives an impression of space and calm. The large icons did have worshippers and there was an atmosphere of devotion. Nurgul, accompanying us, had never in her life visited the Church. We were struck by the lack of Kazakh interest even in the architecture. Such have been the massacres, even in Tsarist days, and certainly by the early Bolsheviki, of the tribal population that Christianity and Russian domination are not objects of curiosity to the descendants of the sufferers. They have removed the visual signs of alien religion into a corner of their subconscious. When General Chernaiev rode conquering into Tashkent in 1863, an Orthodox priest rode beside him, holding the Cross aloft before the defeated followers of the crescent in green. A few months after our visit, Pope John Paul made his first visit to Central Asia, where no Pope had ever come, to celebrate Mass in this Church. Christian oecumenism goes hand in hand with the secular economics of market democracy.

Nurgul drove us to the airport. We invited her to come and visit us in Tashkent. She said she would like to, particularly because the only time a few years back, she had tried to see Uzbekistan, she had felt a total lack of welcome. Arriving in the city with her friends in the hope of finding reservations in one of its many hotels, they had been stranded in one, with their passports taken away (a remnant of Soviet custom in all these countries). They were made to wait at the reception for practically a day before being sent up to small cubbyholes. The social rivalry of Uzbeks with their neighbours crept out in this little tale. It is not a threat to peace. It is a pointer to tensions that are the result of competition for primacy in Eurasian consciousness.

THE EURASIAN NODE OF THE 'STRATEGIC TRIANGLE'

We came away from Kazakhstan with a better perception of the Eurasian dimensions of international relations in the context of different pulls and pushes for India. In early 2001, the events of Islamic terrorism against the USA had not been dreamt of. Already it could be understood that emphasis had shifted north and east, from a moribund Central Asia to the Russo-Kazakh-Chinese interface of economy, communication, and technology transfer. This was how it had been in the years after the Second World War, when Russia and China formed part of what may be called the Second World of state socialism, and the Trans-Siberian Railway remained the great link with China. China's assertion of power in its Inner Asian territories from Inner Mongolia through Ningxia and Kansu, and then down through Xinjiang and Tibet to Szechwan, pushed the Soviets out of influence in these peripheries. The Indians too lost assured markets in a Tibet that had had old links with the Gangetic Plains. Both moved into suspicious hostility against China, particularly after the Pakistan-US tilt towards it, and after the Chinese independent nuclear alternative in Lop Nor, close to the Kazakhs and their Soviet nuclear plants. This hostility dominated the Asian aspect of the Cold War until the 1980s, and blew itself out in the Afghan conflagration and Gorbachev and Yeltsin's retreat from Asia.

Contemporaneously with the rise of Jiang Zemin and careful Chinese moderation after a show of strength in Tienanman Square, Russian policies reversed Gorbachev's policy of scuttle and quit in the name of the human face of socialism. Many Central Asians consider that face was harmful to their interests, which were once subordinate to Russia who now appeared a patronizing big brother. The prosperity of Uzbekistan, for instance, had dated back to two decisive upswings—one when Russian industries were shifted from the reach of German attacks on Russia between 1941 and 1945, and the second, after tension with China in the 1960s and the 1970s. Uzbek troops, heavy industries, and cotton surpluses had formed staples of power to be encouraged. Changes after 1990 shifted the balance of power back to the north-east as distinct from Central Asia. This was the material base for the new President of Kazakhstan, Nursultan Nazarbayev, taking the initiative in Gorbachev's vision of Perestroika. Also, oil exploration and the plans of James Baker III and the George Bushes for regulating oil supplies focus are more on the Caspian than further south. The cotton of the Uzbeks is no more white gold, given textile price instabilities in the wake of the synthetics revolution. The shift of tension from Afghanistan to Pakistan's designs on Kashmir, the Karakorums, and perhaps Uighur extremism in Xinjiang south of Kazakhstan has shifted focus from Tashkent to Almaty and Astana.

In the future India's direct connections with Kazakhstan are bound to increase. Kanishka, Sultan Mahmud, Timur, Babur, and later Turani migrants into Hyderabad and Punjab have only romantic value for the Uzbeks, and Nehru's romantic history is now a part of the historiographical archive. For the twenty-first century, India has to participate in the Russia-China-India triangle in a new understanding of strategic partnership, leaving behind the Indo-Chinese rivalry and the Brezhnev-Indira alliance of the 1970s and 1980s. The ground for this is fertile in Kazakhstan. In cultural diplomacy, academic relations are alive and are attracting scholars interested in India rather than Khwarezmian, Ghaznavid, or Baburid myths. In dance and its accompanied music, which the ICCR presents to many countries where it has its centres, Almaty has gone beyond Tashkent. India's dance teacher there, a lady named Ahmaral, whom we did not have the pleasure of meeting as she was on leave, has trained in Adyar in Kalakshetra's tradition, and made a mark among her own Kazakhs with her Bharatnatyam performances.

There is much that is fortuitous in the foreign understanding of Indian culture. All the way from San Francisco and London to Moscow, Almaty, and Tokyo, it is spirituality, whether yogic or Buddhist, meditation and pilgrimage, rather than more secular aspects of culture, that still evoke interest. This came out in a little incident. An Indian official came to know that President Nazarbaev's wife, Sarah—noted for her presence in the elite social scene—was interested in matters transcendental and meditative. He hastened to organize an invitation for her to visit Puttaparthi and receive a special audience from the Sai Baba. There was pleasure all around. Deeper down, however, there is a serious case for greater concentration on studies of Kazakh history in terms of its anthropology and sociology, not too different from our tribal histories; of its industrial obsolescence and restructuring for which many parallels can be found from Ludhiana through Kanpur to Howrah; and of its place as a bridge and buffer between East and West, a role that India too has increasingly begun to play. Such studies could be begun in the now moribund departments of Russian studies in some of our universities, as a diversification towards Eurasia and Mongolia. They should be worked in closer contact (than what used to be practised in the late twentieth century) with Chinese studies in the same universities. In India today, the think tanks have to think of Russia and China as possible co-operators, and not just as prone to conflict over borders. But then, unfortunately, models and paradigms of dialogue and co-operation were less familiar to the hard-nosed strategy experts in Delhi under the BJP-NDA regime than the easier neo-imperialist models of conflict and strife.

OVERBURDENED PUBLIC UTILITIES IN A POST-SOVIET ECONOMY

Snow on the ground had crept over the foothills as the plane in which we returned to Tashkent circled in to land. The snow in the city was nothing to what we had revelled in. The next day, working in the university, a snowstorm came swiftly down in front of the large windows, reminding us that Kazakhstan was not too far away. Back home in the driving snow, I found my wife had, as was usual with her, gone out swaddled in a heavy coat and snow boots, photographing our white environs. She coaxed me out again in the evening, in the eerie light of halogen lamps reflecting on the white ground, in which our boots sank, leaving our footprints deeply embossed as we waded around our quarter. The next morning was Republic Day at the Indian Embassy, when the Ambassador traditionally hoists the tri-colour in front of the Embassy. The ladies singing the national anthem in their best sarees, shivered in the unfamiliarly violent cold. The gathering adjourned to a hall in the recesses of the building for him to read the President's speech, followed by the usual sumptuous repast.

Back home, we settled down at the television set for news, the usual diversion. The BBC was already broadcasting the terrible information about quaking Gujarat. Ahmedabad, it appeared, might be in ruins, Bhuj in Kutch had perhaps been flattened, and quake waves had been felt in Mumbai and Delhi. Panicked about the well-being of a nephew in Ahmedabad, we rang Mumbai. My sister-in-law had just come up to her flat, having left the house because of the ferocity of the shaking. An hour later she rang back that he was safe. People were had been trying to contact Gujarat all day, hunting for news of friends and relatives.

The magnitude of the catastrophe put Gujarat on the mental map of contemporary Uzbeks. Teachers, and even some students, took to stopping me on roads within the campus, and wherever we went in the evenings, people would come up, each to express sympathy with us as Indians. A month later, the bazaar ladies were still asking my wife about the welfare of the Gujaratis. I have never seen the like in India when there has been an earthquake of similar proportion in Georgia or Azerbaijan. In those days of the expression of simple, human solidarity by people who have never seen India, we recalled a French visit on which we asked how people there had reacted to the assassination of Indira Gandhi by her own bodyguards. A very senior academic administrator's reply had been brief. India is too far away. That feeling was impossible in Tashkent. It may have been that their own *zalzala* of mid-1966, after which the city had been rebuilt in large chunks and greatly beautified, was still fresh in their consciousness.

For a week after that, the snow lay heavy on the ground and formed icicles round the bare black twigs and the slanting eaves of the dachas. Uzbeks became nostalgic about Tashkent in their youth. Watching children that year tobogganing on the snowbound roads, they used to recall skating on the streets around their houses by children on hard ice throughout the winter. Most Uzbeks subscribe to the idea that the weather has gone haywire and blame it on nuclear dust, as well as the recent tests in South Asia. But then there is an old Uzbek tendency to ascribe headaches or tummy upsets to the magnetic storms that are supposed to flash around the atmosphere above the city. This preoccupation with weather fluctuations strikes newcomers as weird and superstitious. With the passage of time, I found that on days of overcast skies I would get a sick headache or become breathless climbing the ludicrous monumentally stony stairways of every public building. Friends would tell me to immediately have some freshly brewed tea, black or green, according to my mood. Tea is the Uzbek specific for dealing with atmospheric changes and blood pressure fluctuation: as much as vodka rubbed on the chest is supposed to cure a whole variety of fevers and aches and pains.

Indeed, after the snow had melted, I had a sudden indisposition, which was alarming enough for me to be taken to the International Medical Centre, where Dr. Flewelling of the US embassy was then chief consultant. The treatment, though costly, was friendly and efficient. It allowed me to disregard the propensity of senior Indians to rush back home for check-ups. At that time, Uzbek friends suggested that we could have availed of the excellent facilities in their hospitals and medical centres at half the cost. This advice would be tested in a few weeks.

In February-March, our daughter and grandson came on a brief visit from Florence where they live. Our son-in-law came a week later. We had planned to go to Bukhara and Samarkand, in addition, of course, to the usual sights of Tashkent. Our daughter was expecting her second baby and had left Florence with a straightforward clearance for travel from her doctor there. Two nights before we were due to leave, an emergency medical opinion became necessary. We had to consult a gynaecologist in a reputed hospital in the city centre. The chamber was badly lit, barely furnished, and reeked of dinginess. The gynaecologist commenced examining with a wooden, handheld contraption, to which she put her ear, to listen to the baby's heartbeat. Then she inflicted the regulation injections on our daughter. Queried about her diagnosis, she said a placenta previa was beginning. Asked for clarification, she flared up: 'are you interrogating me? I have been handling such cases for this many years', and prescribed indefinite bed rest and a regular course of injections.

They came back very worried and the night passed in grave concern. In the morning, a friend could contact Dr. Flewelling. He asked us to come over immediately to the medical centre, did a thorough and standard modern check, and gave a clearly reasoned and cheerful diagnosis. On the way home I should stop at the Mir market and buy a few cartons of berry juice. Our daughter needed just that in liberal quantities. People in her condition often had severe dehydration after a long flight, which might have led to her symptoms. She could even travel next day to Samarkand: perhaps Bukhara was too far out: she should be back for the night. That was all. He was sorry people had not given us his mobile number the night before.

We wonder how people cope with the lack of up to date ideas and technology in the public hospitals of countries like Uzbekistan. I am second to none in admiring the democratic access to standard health care and clean treatment in the bulk of the polyclinics that I have visited in Tashkent. The cheapness, which opened these to the common people, cannot, however, be maintained without radical rethinking about the market principles, which run the contemporary economic order in Asia. Saddled with a large defence budget and a breaking down industrial system, based on the armament needs of a non-existent union of republics, and on heavy subsidies from a collapsed planning organization, public utilities such as health or higher education and R and D for them, cannot but get run down. The number of clean and efficient polyclinics, the public spirit of many of the young doctors from whom we have benefited, the cheap costs of elementary medicines available in the apothecaries' shops, all these will diminish as costs rise in the inevitable transition from a protected mass consumer sector to a market, open and fully cash-convertible. What the political fallout will be, is, of course, the question. Iran, which saw such an opening in the Shah's White Revolution of the pre-1980s, had to go through the trauma of Khomeini and his Ayatollahs and then the terrible long haul back to some sanity and moderation. It is still in crisis between reactionaries, moderates, and radicals. Afghanistan with its high rate of modernization in the 1970s after the abdication of the then King Zahir Shah in 1973 went through worse in its twenty-one years of civil war. Its future under the aegis of the eagle, and of Uncle Sam is quite dicey. Turkey, which seemed to be on the road to Westernization, has many hurdles, both political and cultural, as well as of economic transition and religious reaction, to pass through, before it can attain the levels of the Mediterranean lands of Western Europe. The entire Turco-Iranian-Afghan-Pakistani civilization is in a crisis of modernization along the periphery of the CIS.

Another tremendously beneficial public utility, which had grown after the Second World War in the Russian dominated part of the world, was the central supply of electricity, gas, and water, mainly to the 'massifs' or large apartment block complexes, set in their own wooded parks. The common areas inside the buildings (i.e. the staircase wells) have uniformly been in bad repair and grim, but their supply of essentials does create a sense of security for all classes from the middling sort to the working poor. Living three years in such an apartment, gave us a feel for the nitty-gritty of daily life. The electricity fuses blew every now and then, weirdly enough after dinner, leaving us in the dark. On a few occasions the reason was the area lights, switched off arbitrarily to allow road-building repairs to be carried out somewhere else. In most cases we got the help of our good neighbours to get *zecs* (or mechanics) from an office nearby, set up by the *mahalla*, which charged a pittance for rough and ready repairs. But this went on and on. Our neighbour, a Ph.D in geology from Moscow University, who now did business in export and import, and seemed to live quite well, with his younger son in UWED, said the wiring and the central heating pipes had last had a thorough overhaul about thirty years ago, after the great earthquake. There was no money to overhaul them unless the state or private business could generate it.

The situation boiled down to the same as that of the decrepit industrial culture that one lives in, in Calcutta. There are many similarities between Calcutta and Tashkent. Imperial capitals of British India and Russian Turkestan and Semirechiye (the seven rivers of southern Kazakhstan) had broad central thoroughfares and trams already in the nineteenth century, and a tradition of cultural contact with the metropolises of wide world. They rose in the nineteenth century and fell in the twentieth. Calcutta met its doom earlier, first with the shift of the capital in 1912, and then with Bengal becoming involved in the Second World War, and with the rise of communalism and the black market, the 1943 famine, the public slaughter of 1946, and massive refugee influx till 1952. This meant that work culture collapsed half a century ago. Until 1990, this was not the fate of Tashkent. Surely its urban improvements and public utilities made it completely different from what the people of Calcutta have allowed their once proud city to become.

One cannot repeat too often that history does not repeat itself. Tashkent's residual advantages may make redemption possible. Reports have it that the President goes on with ambitious road building programmes: and that a Presidential tax on foreign goods trading briefly shut down the bazaar in Navoi Street and the Hippodrome. We have already seen how quickly parks can come up in an authoritarian society. But there is room to suspect that this is meant as circuses rather than bread. True, road-building programmes are necessary for pump priming when there is no other scope for employment and the poor have to be fed through subsidies. However, if one moves off the great avenues coming up all the way from the airport side towards the South Station to Samarkand, bypassing the city interior, one will still see the poor maintenance of the dachas and doms in which average people live. Heating is often so inadequate during winter that they have to rely on kitchen ovens for that much extra warmth, causing a short supply of centrally piped gas. This was a problem we ourselves faced when the normally abundant gas petered out. These are problems of public economics for which I have no answers. It does still appear that a radical political rethinking of the civil social steps necessary for reformulating socialist principles is incumbent in Asia today.

TALIBAN DESPERATION: THE RISE OF THE SHANGHAI FORUM

Events moved fast forward soon after spring. A variety of sources provide the data; updates on radio and newspaper information about Central Asia that the BBC supplies on the internet, the Delhi publication Public Opinion Trends (POT) with reference to the Pakistan press; and also some indepth handouts of the International Crisis Group (a Brussels based organization run by fairly high profile figures on the international 'track two' scene including neo-liberal intellectual politicians like ex-Congressman Solarz of the USA or ex-Prime Minister I.K. Gujral of India). They all spoke of tensions, economic and political, in the five Republics, and also Afghanistan, now re-oriented in political geography as part of Central Asia.

The Taliban, once touted in the West as wardens of its marches for building oil pipelines from Turkmenistan to the Baluch coast of Pakistan, were going over the edge, maltreating women. Uzbeks were being governed in an excessively authoritarian way by Karimov's clique, which was dragging its feet on the introduction of the two IMF nostrums of capital account convertibility and market liberalization. Other Republics were just about stagnating. There were internal border tensions (about Uzbek-Kazakh cross-border settlement, north and south of Tashkent, about Kyrgyz-Uzbek water sharing between Kyrgyz upper riparian and Ferghana-Uzbek lower riparian feeders into the south bank of Syr Darya and between Turkman-Azerbaijani marine control of Caspian offshore oil prospecting). Central Asia's problems were wholly indigenous, economic and social. Western media managers, however, saw them as matters of the Eurasian security environment, affecting their own affluent capitalist energy reserves. Such a perception was to be paradigmatic of Islamic inversions and hysterical counteraction in the unfolding chain of circumstances. There was a Taliban backlash, peaking with the destruction of the Bamiyan Buddhas. Only after that came the attack on the twin towers of New York.

Three meetings during the year in Tashkent provided pointers. One of the IFEAC seminars had been on the subject of fundamentalism and Islamic revival movements in Central Asia. Speakers included the eminent French historian of Islamic resistance in Afghanistan in the 1980s, Olivier Roy, who later wrote *The Failure of Political Islam*, as well as the principal religious authority in Kyrgyzstan (in whose Batkent boondocks the Hizb-ut-Tahrir was supposed to be spreading fast among the families). This Kyrgyz Muslim cleric was moderate and spoke of Islam as a civilizational force, and not a political one. This had been the standard position of the old USSR before Gorbachev confused the issues. It was not clear to me then how he proposed to deal with Islam-al-Siyasi, i.e. political Islam, unless the state used authoritarianism to control it. Roy, on the other hand, spoke to me personally about his belief that the moment of moderation in Islam as an organized secular and civilizational movement had passed. Even if there had been any prospect of this making its mark after the Mujahid occupation of Kabul, with Najibulla in custody in the UN compound, rifts within the Resistance had made a moderate Islamic state in either Kabul or Kandahar an impossibility. Failure in his lexicon did not just mean lack of success in a particular conjuncture. It meant that the community principle in Islam (for which I use terms like *umma* or Ibn Khaldun's *asabiyya*) had lost meaning and vitality, and now represented forces of decay or reaction.

This gloomy picture had earlier emerged during a chance meeting in the city with Ahmed Rashid, the equally eminent political journalist at the *Far Eastern Economic Review*. He was there to address a high-level national security seminar, sponsored by the Uzbek government. Rashid had written about Islam and the national resurgence in Central Asia from 1991. He was then just about to publish his exhaustive text on the Taliban with all its Pakistani spooky, oil business, ramifications. He gave me a copy of his extremely simple presentation, explicated in the most elementary digits. There was no vitality at all in Mulla Muhammad Omar's state, run from Kandahar. Factionalism rampaged in the two basic groups of the regime. The religious fanatics wanted pristine Koranic purity to spread through their actions. Moderates, although equally religious, wanted to rake in profits by wheeling and dealing with the international community. Pakistan sought to balance the two, but had lost control of the tiger, which it rode. Unless the world took steps to enforce moderation, the situation would explode in its face. How that would happen was not yet clear. He was not optimistic about Uzbekistan either. If moderation was not brought in quickly, Islam ran the danger of further politicization in Central Asia. The drug trade with its criminal forces and links with regional mafias would stir the devil's brew. This general picture, which expressed the feelings of any one of us who had lived some time in the country, did not tally with the public understanding mooted in world capitals, that such problems were those of hole-and-corner fanatics in beards, who could be wished away, as part of the troubles of the periphery of NATO affluence. The needs of countries like Uzbekistan for a middle path played no part in that political rhetoric.

In March, Tashkent had been thick with rumours that the International Monetary Fund was closing down its office, having failed to get the President—or at least his Premier, the low key Utkir Sultanov, who dealt with public policy implementation—to go for strong financial discipline and emphatically helpful measures to open entry for multinational foreign direct investment. The IMF's Resident Representative had spoken to a gathering of the Tashkent Women's International Group, at which my wife had been present, about the economic malaise affecting the country, which was leading European retail outlets like Mothercare to close down due to lack of purchasing power. I got an elaboration of this from him at a tete-a-tete lunch arranged by a common acquaintance. The latter was worried about the financial crisis which he faced due to the regime's embargo on shifting any part of profits in dollars from the country, or in carrying out production operations without political interference from local *hokims* or governors, whose minions angled for cuts and kickbacks. The IMF official, due to return to Washington in a few days, was much less arrogant and far better informed about the state of the land than any expatriate I had so far met. He agreed with me that corruption levels were probably common throughout South Asia and the Middle East. They were less important than antiquated primitive, socialist, policy rigidities, which, as in India to the 1970s, had hampered business fluency. He also agreed that it was not the President himself but the web of interlinked, restrictive business interests that controlled all openings to new enterprise for its bosses and their favourites. In fact, the IMF official, who had had a chance to talk to the President, felt that he appeared to be less dictatorial than what the Western press made him out to be. But the mafia and vested interest kept Karimov and his top layer of officials 'Iron Curtained' from liberalization and convertibility. This web acted as a syndicate—much, as I pointed out to them, as the Old Congress had done in

India in 1960s, and the cronies around Rajiv Gandhi were to do in the 1980s, leading to the Congress collapse in the 1990s. The syndicate ensured that its vested interests would be protected. Little did I understand that directions in the autumn would bring changes—that the Taliban would raise the stakes, that the Uzbek mafia would easily accept the Stars and Stripe's embrace, and that the same multinationals would be setting terms for the return of the IMF to Tashkent.

The BBC increased its pressure on Taliban mismanagement of human rights, as spring turned to summer. In previous years, summer, when the snows melt on the Hindu Kush and the Pamirs, had been the time when international agencies speculate about the condition of the high passes through which the armed emissaries of *jihad* slip into the foothills of Mawar-un-Nahr in the north, and the Kashmir valley in the east, to spread fear and danger in the cities of the plains. In 2001, this was not marked as happenings unfolded within Afghanistan itself. In Kashmir, the post-Kargil situation remained very tense. Radio summaries emphasized that the Taliban were struggling to cope with the tremendous food shortage caused by the lack of normal rain for two years. Religious fanaticism against non-Islam was being stirred up to bolster the faith of the Believers. The cultural agents of Mulla Muhammad began to call for idol breaking, focusing on the priceless treasures of Buddhist art in the Gandhara sections of the Kabul Museum and in the Bamiyan gorge, west of the main route from the capital through the Salang Tunnel to Mazar-i-Sharif in the north. Special targets were Hindu and Sikh remnants, long resident among the Afghans as merchants and shop keepers for centuries past, who were ordered to wear a piece of cloth with a particular colour, generally saffron, as a badge of alienness among the devout majority. The Western mind associated this with the stigma of Jewry in the age of European pogroms. The trends of genocide, which the Christian Serbs and Russians had started against ethnic Muslims in Kosovo or Chechnya, were backfiring into Afghanistan. Some Hindus in Gujarat would reciprocate in what became a triangular contest of fanaticism in the next year.

At that time, there was again a spate of killings of forest guards and militia in the hill villages on the upper reaches of the Charvak Lake in the Chimgan hills. The Mirkasymovs had found it difficult even as residents to drive in and out of the hills, as was their usual practice at this time of the year, because of rigid militia rules for permission of entry. The fruit in their little orchards had begun to grow. As they could not pluck these, poverty-stricken neighbours stripped them bare. This was a common problem with hill dachas—Azad Shamatov had lost his wicket gates in Humsan and bemoaned the need to either travel there or send his son for watch and ward arrangements. I was reminded of the generation after Independence in West Bengal, when plains neglect of the Darjeeling hills led to middle classes with houses in hill resorts like Darjeeling, Takdah and Kalimpong, complaining that local people were stripping absentee landlords of their window frames and household accessories, even burning down untenanted houses in an attempt to grab the land. These signs of dissidence, which sociologists have called the 'weapons of the weak', culminated in the Gorkhaland agitation of the 1980s.[5]

In Chimgan, we were told that joblessness was leading to frustration among the younger generation, to Islamic liberation theology, and to an insurgency funded by wads of dollars, gained from ransoms. Bandits doled out relief to the poor of their neighbourhoods. The more the Uzbek army and militia repressed them, the more the embers of their anger scattered. Many people in the city, whom we quizzed about the problem, were quietly despondent. In a low key, they would murmur, obviously not to be quoted, the boys had no choice, their families had to eat.

We had a chance to see the milieu at closer quarters than even at Chimgan near the actual headwaters of the Charvak. With two other Indian families we were searching for a picnic spot along the banks of the lake. Apart from one place, which is excessively sandy, most of the area is enclosed and guarded for people to pay and enter with their cars. The facilities in each were practically non-existent with primitive sanitation and very little water. I was looking for a village called Brichmulla, where there was said to be a large hotel. I was especially interested in this village way up in the hills since long before the lake was dammed, it was here that the British Indian Political Service spy, Col. F.E. Bailey, sent on a mission to Tashkent in 1918, had fled from the Bolsheviks, and had hidden hunting pigs with the villagers in winter of that year.[6]

As we wound up into the mountains with snow peaks on all sides along a river, we were halted at a check post on the bridge. The militia looked at our diplomatic accreditation cards, but were dubious about letting us through. Phone calls were made in various directions. Perhaps the fact that we were Indians led them to lift the heavy barrier. The village we went through was dark, practically deserted, and totally poverty-stricken. There was no sign of welcome on the faces of the few who gazed at us from the lanes. The hotel, stepped as if like a ziggurat in ancient Babylonia, looked like the model of Gorbachev's palatial dacha in the Crimea, where he had been arrested in the abortive *coup d'état* of 1991. It was closed. Along the paths leading from it to the lake, *aiwans* and terraces were available for picnickers with their own provisions. Village women, traditionally dressed, collected some fees for the use of the grounds. They looked poorer than the others we were to see in hills. Their basic food was chai and lipioski, and perhaps the occasional eggs from domestic chickens, which they offered to sell. The place was beautiful. One could well imagine how pleasant it had been when people came from all over the USSR to these pleasure spots in summer. It was at Brichmulla where army action against cross-border terrorism had brought sorrow into many of the homes in 2000. I came back chastened by the thought of the green meadows of Gulmarg and Anantnag, where the same change must have occurred in recent years.

Through the summer, which was extremely hot—so much so that even in the rooms with one air conditioner on, it was somewhat stifling—the pressure mounted in Afghanistan. It was a drought year that summer, with no rain at all in the knife edged dry *wadis* of the Hindukush and its associated ranges. There had been little rain the previous year as well. Near famine conditions drove the peasantry, already ravaged by Civil War, slaughter and fanaticism, out of the country looking for food and relief. The Central Asian Republics had closed borders, with only Turkmenistan ready to offer a little bit of support. Iran was closed to all but Shias, principally among the Hazara minority in the western hills between Herat and Kandahar, mobilized by the strongly anti-Sunni Taliban, Hizb-i-Wahdat, one of whose principal bases was in the valleys near Bamiyan, where the caves were reputedly a Wahdati stronghold. Only the Pakistan frontier all the way from Hunza, Nagar and Chitral in the north, down to the Helmand was open for a fresh flood of refugees. People sought help at the camps and *madrasas* along the Pakistan side of the border, outposts from which first the mujahideen and then the Taliban had been unleashed to destroy the liberated Afghan state. As the distinction between Afghan and Pakistani became fuzzy among Pakhtuns and Pathans, and as extremist mullahs in Pakistan called for more support to the Kandahar regime, the fanatical element in Kandahar and Kabul began to get the better of the moderate faction, one of whose ministerial leaders died at this time. The community spirit of the Deobandi Sunni mullahs, of Akora Khattak and Binnauri near Karachi from where Imam Bukhari's works were translated into English and circulated in Central Asia, turned to new theological stakes. A short-term gain would divert attention from the drought and the dearth of food, as well as from the refugee outflow. The Bamiyan provocation had captured the gullible Taliban imagination.

The Taliban's cultural wings were involved in a different contest in the cities in the north, Herat, Mazar-i-Sharif, Kunduz, Taloqan. All were rife with locally predominant Shia or Uzbek, as well as Tajik, dissidence and sympathy for Ahmed Shah Masood's Northern Alliance, which was carrying on a guerrilla war for survival in Panjshir. The Taliban mullahs took to invoking their own version of early mediaeval history, not far removed in content from the expansionist fantasies of Uzbekistan and Kazakhstan (about Mangubardi, Timur, Babur, and Mirza Haider Dughlat's exploits in India). The Taliban were explicitly and poisonously anti-idolatrous. They now invoked the ghoulish memory of earlier Afghan Sultans, Mahmud of Ghazni and Muhammad of Ghaur, who had spread rapine and plunder in the Indo-Gangetic plains. They did this in the absurd belief that the exhausted Afghans of the twenty-first century would fight under such reactionary banners.

From Kandahar, *fatwas* were issued: idol breaking must begin. What more striking example could there be than to destroy the highest idol of them all, though one, which had not been worshipped over a millennium, the peaceful Buddha of Bamiyan, slumbering in obscurity since Islam came to the Afghan lands. This was done at a time when the Wahdatis had begun to assert themselves against Taliban garrisons in Hazarajat. Idol breaking, as Muhammad Habib pointed out in his iconoclastic critique of Mahmud of Ghazni more than seventy years ago,[7] has an inner purpose: a secular display of political dominance basic to the religious rhetoric of fanatical purity. Cultural protest began to mount in the affluent northern world. Religious fury now swamped the political sense of Mulla Muhammad's advisers. When the Bamiyan Buddhas were blown up, all that neo-liberalism was complaining about regarding Taliban frenzy against gender rights seemed also justified. This was a once-Western favoured regime. It was a blot on humanity. It was one that could be dispensed with. It should meet the fate that the British African ex-corporal Idi Amin's regime had met with, or the once Western stooge against Iran, Saddam Hussain, had been dealt by the NATO powers.

If Pakistan had not been pulled away from its surrogates in the Pakhtun lands, the Taliban might still have held power, on the principles of basic sovereignty. What changed the situation were the cataclysmic events of September. That brought the Islamic fundamentalist politics centre stage in world affairs. Afghanistan could be treated as a whipping boy, in the name of liberation from fundamentalists, as a site of flagellation and atonement for the attacks on New York and Washington.

Before that happened, the Bamiyan events had a bizarre denouement. Mullah Muhammad, in one of his public statements, was quoted by the BBC Central Asia news abstracts saying, in all sweet reasonableness, that the West was criticizing idol breaking enjoined by the Koran; why was it not sympathizing with the plight of the starving people and providing them with relief. There was a sharply new element of transcendence, the hallmark of the Taliban defiance of modernity and science. There had been no rain for two years, he continued. After the graven images were blown up in the Bamiyan gorge, Allah had sprinkled the blessing of rain on the Afghan people. One of the signs of general alienation is when people seek justification in the irrational. Taliban policy had already entered this phase, buffeted by dearth and by world disapproval.

The policy of 'rallying the moderates' failed in the counsels of those who mould the world media. By summer, the Taliban were targeted as brutes, caning women who dared lift their shrouds above their ankles; as repressive authority, denying women the right to knowledge; as people dragging the world back to mediaevalism. People in Tashkent were ironical. They recalled conversations before the Kosovo War in 1999, when they had pointed out how Milosevic's goons had suddenly gained opprobrium, only after Clinton decided to bomb the Serbs. After all, they said, Chechen gangs led by fundamentalists like Khattab from the Pankisi gorge just south of Russia in Georgia were no better than Juma's men across the Uzbek and Kyrgyz borders in Garm and Karategin valleys, protected by similar gorges from the Tajik forces. Why then was Putin criticized for his assault on the Chechens when CNN and BBC were so obviously preparing the world for a Kosovo repeat on Kabul? This tangle of suspicion and pique about the other's motives has come to mark the tension between different political systems and their ideologies in the contemporary world. It often culminates in catastrophic acts of irrationality.

Beyond this gut reaction against aggressive American foreign policy, instinctive to Russian dominated thought, lay a feeling of complacency about the West, NATO, and the USA coming round to what Uzbeks had been saying about Afghanistan for several years. Uzbek attitudes to the Mujahid-Taliban strife were marked by several factors, some gut social, others depending on ethnic sympathies. Political economic interests conditioned yet others. Deep down in Uzbek consciousness there is a gap between generations. The young, those in their teens in the 1980s conditioned by the corruption, decay, and rising bourgeois expectations of the last days of the USSR, had more sympathy with Islamic conservatism than their parents' generation, which had grown up in the liberalization of the War and post-War years. The young found novelty in a Koran not generally printed before 1989, and its message of the possibility of an alternative public morality, puritan and austere as distinct from the graft, mafia domination and clan nepotism of 'actually existing socialism'. Rather than follow the apparatchiki, they saw no harm in now listening to devout Muslims in the *mahalla*. We know of a young woman who had to travel to Indian provincial cities who was advised by her local guardian's family to wear a *burkha*. She found no contradiction in this. But when she came to the Uzbek Embassy in Delhi, the officials there viewed her with suspicion. She thought it was this which was contradictory, since she had donned the *burkha* in the belief that she was merging herself in what she had been told was Indian Muslim identity. When this was discussed in the presence of her mother, a history teacher, half Tajik and half Russian, the latter was dismayed. Had it come to this, the lady lamented, that her daughter would again wear the *paranja*, which women of the lady's generation had been killed by their elder relatives for throwing away and even burning. Naturally, this elder generation, brought up in a Soviet cliamte against superstition and reaction, found the Taliban repulsive as a force of social reaction, while younger people, less certain about employment, some even involved in dubious business transactions, or drug abuse, and finding a void in public morality, were more confused about how to think.

The situation was complicated by ethnic sympathies, pulling in different directions. Mir Farkhod in Bukhara had his own bitter memories of army brutality. Someone else we had met in Bukhara had a brother who had also fought in an Uzbek regiment between Herat and Kandahar. He had been captured by the Mujahideen in those days, checked whether he could recite the first line of the Koran, and when he did so with devotion, patted on the back and accepted as a fellow Muslim, albeit a misguided one. It was this sort of treatment that created the Juma Nomonghanis. In the case of the soldier we are talking about, he had come back to a country, rejected by the Russians in the collapse of 1991. He would have no great animus against rebels who could have shot him out of hand. There must have many Muslim conscripts out of the army, who shared such neutral sentiments about the civil war, which followed their intervention at Russian orders.

Then there was what was called until 1850 'Little Uzbekistan', across the Amu Darya in the towns from Mazar-i-Sharif through Maimana to Shibarghan. Here Uzbek lineages and landlords had been physically liquidated in the late nineteenth century by Amir Abdur Rahman, himself once detained in Tashkent, and later ruler of Afghanistan, in the process of the consolidation of the Afghan state up to the Amu Darya in what had once been the Uzbek appanage of Balkh. The memory of this may have faded, though it has recently been revived in a tome by a British scholar from British records of the time.[7] Here Uzbek ethnicity was thick on the ground. Mazar was a holy city of Islam, slightly away from the fabled and extensive ruins of the once Bactrian city of Balkh, which the Mongols had destroyed. In Mazar is supposed to be the relic of one of the Prophet's companions. The city was noted for its lack of fanaticism and its support as a bridgehead from Termez and Samarkand across the Amu Darya through its bridge at Khayrattan for Soviet armies, who marched down the Salang tunnel into Kabul during the 1980s. Its commander, the Afghan Uzbek Abdul Rashid Dostum, had trod a very narrow path between faithlessness to his post-Soviet allies and consistency to becoming a once-communist

Uzbek warlord, outside Uzbek state control in the period of troubles from 1991 to 2001. He had been castigated in the *Economist* and the *Far Eastern Economic Review* for being a betrayer many times over, first joining the fanatical Pakhtun, Gulbudin Hekmatyar, to drive the Tajiks and the Shia Wahdatis out of Kabul, and then joining the Tajiks, led by the Panjsheri Masud and ex-President Burhanuddin Rabbani, against Hekmatyar (who retreated to Jalalabad) and then the Taliban when they took Kabul and threatened Mazar-i-Sharif. At that time the Russian airbase at Shibargan had an Indian medical mission helping out. This was evacuated by Indian officials from Tashkent when in 1997, Mazar was captured by Pahalwan, a rival of Dostum. The Taliban took Mazar in 1998, slaughtering Iranian diplomats there, and destroying the cosmopolitan character of this city with its Western dresses and female emancipation. This was after cliques in the Jumbish-i-Milli or national alliance of Dostum had been bought over and then destroyed by Kabul. Only then did Dostum flee. He had spent time looking for help from Turkey, Iran, and Uzbekistan. They had always treated him with a measure of caution, but had always given shelter to Afghans from his region.

A carpet seller we used to visit in Yunusabad in north Tashkent was in the habit of visiting Maimana every year to bring back new carpets from the region for sale in the big city. The Indian Basmati rice we bought in an Afghan-Uzbek shop in Katortal Street was smuggled by trucks from Pakistan through Mazar into Uzbekistan. These supplies would be disrupted only when hostilities flared up between Taliban and the forces of the Northern Alliance, which was struggling to keep together in 2000 and 2001. These hostilities would generally be of short duration during the summer when the passes were open. The trucks would be moving, or the pack animals would carry goods over the hills, when the hostilities halted for winter.

Uzbeks, as much as their government, viewed this cat's-cradle of varied social loyalties with caution. Friends showed no great enthusiasm if I asked them about the presence of ethnic Uzbeks outside their border. In fact, they were not clear about the way in which the Kyrgyz, or the Tajiks, or the Shias in north Afghanistan looked at their presence in neighbouring states. Conflict between Uzbek migrants and local nationalities was a subject they always steered clear of. Part of this was due to the extreme narrowness and close nature of the information base of those taught under the Soviet higher education system, and due to their reading only the simplest texts. Part was also due to a political wariness about Uzbekistan's position, *vis-à-vis* other powers in Asia, *vis-à-vis* the Russian Federation, and *vis-à-vis* the US led NATO bloc. The regime's relation with each was intricate. It formed a gray area of half knowledge in the public mind of UWED, at least in so far as my discussions (admittedly in English and not in Russian or Uzbek) led me to understand. Of course, the Uzbek-US alliance of September 2001 must already have been in the process of preparation.

This gray area, as far as I could follow, takes us back to tensions in the CIS and China's evolving relations with Central Asia, as well as the changes in the Uzbek perspective regarding Asia and Europe. After Karimov in 2000 failed to re-establish interest in New Delhi and with Indian business in Mumbai and Hyderabad regarding direct investment, convertibility and credit lines, the Uzbek vision shifted to East Asia and towards the USA. Some of Karimov's speeches, published in the local press, are pertinent. In 1999, on a trip to China, he had made a speech at the Tashkent airport that Uzbekistan would like to go to Shanghai but in its own interest. This was at a time when with some other Republics, he was putting pressure on Yeltsin in his last days of power to remove the industrialist Berezovsky from the post of Secretary of the CIS, and organize the CIS on a less Russian dominated footing. Particular Uzbek interests were being continually emphasized in foreign policy. Somewhat later, in a conference on matters of regional security in Turkey, where NATO powers were represented, he had declared that he too would like to be European in spirit. The reach of the connectivity of the Uzbek imagination now spanned the lands of the northern hemisphere from the Atlantic to the Pacific across southern Eurasia.

Shanghai is a metropolis which a century ago used to be compared with Calcutta and Melbourne. It has since been transformed by the Peoples' Republic of China from a colonial port of the Yangtze-Kiang hinterland of the China Seas into a thriving trade centre on the Pacific Rim. The five nations on the inner borderlands of China, the Russian Federation, Kazakhstan, Kyrgyzstan and Tajikstan, formed a tentative forum of five nations in northern Asia for cooperation on security as well as economic matters. In 2000, the Shanghai Forum or Shanghai Five as it was known, became a nucleus for broader views of cooperation on both aspects. Uzbekistan staked its claim then to be admitted to the Forum, but specifically in economic matters, while retaining its independence of manoeuvre regarding arms and security. India too had expressed interest in coming closer to the Shanghai Five. It had a long Himalayan border with China, and could not be excluded on the grounds of lack of contiguity. (Uzbekistan, be it noted, was not contiguous. About 150 miles of Kyrgyz territory separated it from Kashgar in Xinjiang.) Pakistan, already linked in strategic partnership, occupation of the Northern Areas, and surrender in 1963 of its Shaksgam valley to China's Xinjiang border north of Siachen, and by the Karakorum Highway from Kashgar to Islamabad, promptly countered India's initiative, claiming that it had real contiguity as much as India. It also applied for membership.

The Five, including Russia, hardly wanted to anger India to Pakistan's benefit. It accepted this checkmate and invited neither. Non-contiguous Uzbekistan, with its trade routes linked to Kashgar and Urumqi was invited, but only as an observer. Another development at that time was the establishment of a focal centre with UN support to monitor drug and arms traffic at Osh, just pass the Uzbek border. All these developments marked the tying together of the northern part of Primakov's idea of Asian international relations triangulation. On a visit to India in 1998, Primakov had proposed a strategic partnership of Russia, China and India, an idea that had been passed over in silence by India and China, which were prepared to think in the future about confidence-building measures, but not about even bilateral strategic partnership. In fact, China had and still has an alliance with Pakistan. Where Primakov had been orthodox in excluding Pakistan from the strategic triangle and according South Asian hegemony to India, contemporary Russian foreign policy came realistically closer to the Chinese and the Central Asians in not demonizing Pakistan, but treating it even as a equal player in the 'new great game' for oil resource regulation and security stabilization.

In summer 2001, the Uzbeks were included as members of the Shanghai Forum. In view of their special position on security and armaments, the character of the Forum, which had increased to Six, was changed and its name was now the 'Economic Cooperation Organization'. This was at a time when Uzbeks could be heard saying that the President was being extra nice to Pakistan's General, who had now had himself declared President. India still had a special role among the common people. In the bazaar for dried fruits in Chorsu, thronged by Tajiks and others, as well as Uzbeks—my wife would often be asked with a note of query 'Hindistanski? Pakistanski?' When she said firmly 'Indiski', the creases on their foreheads would smooth and a smile would appear. However, the idea of British India's Partition is one they still seem to be puzzled by. Their foreign policy experts in particular make a point of not distinguishing in protocol between the two countries, all the more, when they accepted the US version that India was ruled by a Hindu nationalist regime, and not the secularism that their elders had admired, once upon a time, of Nehru and Indira Gandhi. Vajpayee they appeared to like, on the supposed ground that he is really secular, in opportunist Hindutva garb, more anti-communist than Nehru, so all the more acceptable on those grounds. L.K. Advani appeared then to be an unknown quantity to these experts beyond his sponsorship of the Ram *ratha yatra*. Musharraf, whom they had at first been inclined to dismiss as the military ruler of a potentially rogue state, particularly during Kargil and Clinton's stern tone with him then, they began to find more acceptable, after his self legitimation as President. Central Asian Republics, with First Secretaries self-appointed as Presidents, could not afford to be finicky about the democratic niceties. They weighed Prime Ministers and Presidents on the same scale and were least concerned about South Asian internal governance. Only the Taliban threat mattered and Musharraf had access to its mullahs. If the latter could be kept from threatening the Amu Darya borders directly, as they were tending to do in their irascible pronouncements, or if the refugees could be diverted south into Pakistan instead of coming into the Kashka Darya and Surkhan Darya tributaries of the Oxus, it was worth placating the General. India had become too far.

The Islamic Movement of Uzbekistan, led by Juma Nomongani, was claiming to also represent Uighurs across Central and Inner Asian borders. Friends visiting villages on the Andijan-Osh border spoke of the considerable discontent against the government's anti-religious policies, as they were perceived to be, and the arrest of young people in the small towns during the winter. It was reported that a number of women had come out with placards in Andijan, calling on the state to release their young men. This is a form of civil rights protest utterly normal in even as disturbed a part of India as Manipur. It is almost treason even to the post-Soviet mentality. The reports were fairly quickly hushed up but the Uzbek political elite must have realized that its hegemony might soon be challenged and alternative support was necessary.

In Afghanistan, the Northern Alliance had finally got its act together. Ahmed Shah Masud himself had made a well-publicised journey to France, to the European Parliament in Strasbourg, and to Brussels, and drummed up offers of support. His Foreign Minister, Dr. Abdullah Abdullah was making a hit on world television channels. Herat was being challenged in its countryside by Ismael Khan, its old mujahid commandant, who had revolted against Russian invasion in 1980, and had fled from Taliban custody to Iran in 1999, taking his jailor with him. The Hazaras continued to fight around Bamiyan.

American interests in Central Asian security became quite open. Speakers from principal American Universities, such as William Fierman, author of a widely read book on Uzbekistan, came through, giving old-fashioned, conservative presentations criticizing civil rights repression, fundamentalism, and terrorism as evils to be dealt with on an equal basis. The increase of this activity bespoke changes, but of what we could not understand, in the rarefied atmosphere of the Tashkent seminars. A young intern in the US Information Service detailed to interact with me by her Director (after I had presented a view analytically alternative to that of Fierman) to prepare for a future seminar in late September to be held in Samarkand, wondered herself what was wrong; the successors of the KGB, she said, were shadowing American Embassy staffers with a dogged persistence that they had not demonstrated before. It was much later that I could surmise that the SNG were checking which Uzbeks were cosying up to the forthcoming strategic partners, so that tabs could be kept on them.

The USIS sponsored another seminar on a lavish scale in which Uzbek scholars were encouraged to speak of their perceptions of how Central Asia could learn from Chinese experiences of progress to a market economy, and about desert soil ecological conservation. A young Uzbek researcher from the Oriental Institute sought to raise the question of Sino-Indian border rivalry from the point of view of the Indian Embassy. He was sharply hushed by officials from the Institute of Strategic Studies and the Economics University, who were organizing the seminar with the Chinese Charge d' Affaires present in the meeting. The Americans to whom one spoke at this juncture were quite cynical about President Karimov. They described the trial of a group of people charged with the Tashkent bomb blasts of 1999, as 'kangaroo courts', framing people without adequate evidence. Karimov was spoken of as an autocrat, who would be toppled if he did not moderate his attitude to protest.

Ferghana once again began to appear in the news. The raiders were coming, as they had done in September 2000, and the year before. What would have happened to the protesting women of Andijan in such a situation is a matter of conjecture. Indeed what did happen to them, one never knew. Events began to unfold in the second week of September with shocking suddenness.

NOTES

1. Amy Joffe 'Unlocking the Assets: Energy and the Future of Central Asia and the Caucasus', in Omar Noman (ed.), *Central Asia in 2010, Prospects for Human Development* (Regional Bureau for Europe and the CIS, United Nations Development Programme, New York, 1999): 'This is a summary of an energy studies sponsored by the Center for International Political Economy and the James Baker Institute for Public Policy, Rice University, April 1998.'
2. Neal Ascherson, *Black Sea* (Jonathan Cape, London, 1995) in his evocative account of the dispersion of small nationalities in the Ukraine, who were suspected by Stalin of collaborating with Nazis in Hitler's invasion of the Ukraine and the siege of Stalingrad during 1941-4, and who were arbitrarily deported, whole communities of them to Kazakhstan and Uzbekistan, writes that 'like the Crimean Tatars, whose exile they shared, the Pontic Greeks in the Soviet Union did not necessarily sit down and weep by the waters of Babylon. They tried illegally and in secret, to teach Pontian Greek to their children, who at school were being indoctrinated into a monoglot Russian-Soviet culture. In the dusty *kolkhoz* villages of Kazakhstan and Uzbekistan, parents managed to transmit at least fragments of their culture—music and cookery especially. . . . Their sense of identity slowly hardened and changed during the decades in Central Asia . . . into a belief in their own Greek political identity' (pp. 189-90).
3. P. Stobdan (ed.), *Building a Common Future: Indian and Uzbek Perspectives on Security and Economic Issues* (Knowledge World, in

conjunction with Institute of Defence Science and Analysis, New Delhi, 1999) is useful on Indo-Uzbek common positions in the era of the pre-NDA (BJP-led) government in India.

4. Recent accounts of the mass uprooting, sufferings, and survival, in brutal diasporas, of many thousands of ethnic and religious minorities in Eurasia as well as Europe (including German communities sent out by Hitler to colonise Central and Eastern Europe, including the Crimea) can be studied in Ascherson, *Black Sea*, op. cit., and in Mark Mazower, *Dark Continent, Europe's Twentieth Century* (Penguin Books, Harmondsworth, 1998).
5. In 2003, word reached us from Tashkent that the pleasant house of the Mirkasymovs, to which they devoted much personal labour, has been burned down.
6. Lt. Col. F.M. Bailey, *Mission to Tashkent* (Jonathan Cape, London, 1946) is a vivid account by a retired Indian Political Service officer and Himalayan explorer in regions as far distant as Tibet, Yunnan and the Karakorums, as well as Iran of spying in Turkestan and Bukhara in 1918-19 with considerable details about the revolution there and British contacts with the Basmachi rebels, at that time led by Irgash Bey against the Bolsheviks. He makes it clear that from Brichmulla, at the head of the Kok Su River—the Chirchik reservoir had not yet been flooded—a route went up to a bee farm in the hills and then crossed the snow peaks into Ferghana towards what is today western Kyrgyzstan and then Tajikistan. This was the route from Garm towards Tashkent that Juma reactivated in 1999.
7. Muhammad Habib, *Sultan Mahmud of Ghaznin*, reprinted in K.A. Nizami (ed.), in *Politics and Society during the Early Mediaeval Period: Collected Works of Professor Muhammad Habib* (People's Publishing House, Vol. 2, 1981), pp. 36-104.

7

A Diplomatic Revolution and Its Consequences

A CENTRAL ASIAN DIPLOMATIC REVOLUTION: AUTUMN 2001

The usual events on Mustakillik Day, celebrating Independence ten years before, were held with great eclat in Tashkent on 1 September 2001. That year, we accompanied an Indian couple, the husband resident in Tashkent for the last twenty-five years, to the Executive building next to the fountains on Sharaf Rashidov Avenue. On these festival days there are lights on the main roads and crowds stream out through the Metro. They were thronging the avenue when we came up the stairs. We could not get past them to cross the road to the great maidan where dances and variety performances were due to be held in a rapidly constructed stadium of temporary materials. Close to the iron railings we saw the reason. Militia armed with the latest equipment straddled the avenue at the two crossings, and there was not one person who dared to get close to them. They were guarding the guardians of Independence; whose families had special passes to enjoy the public festivities, while the plebeians merely gazed at the troops. Neither question nor dissent was visible in any one's faces; they could have been a crowd out of a mediaeval absolutism. Like an Indian crowd at festival time, they were out on the streets for ice cream and shashlik. We went from there to a park in the neighbourhood of our companions' home. Babur Park as it has been renamed, has the usual lakes, row boats, huge Catherine wheel, merry-go-rounds and eating places, dotted all over the lovely green field.

Our daughter's mother-in-law came on a brief visit. We had returned from a visit with her to the sights of Bukhara (our last trip there) and Samarkand. Early the next morning, driving to the university, Rustom switched on his car radio. 'Masud shot', he said in his laconic style. I was shaken. The Lion of Panjsher had become the icon of Afghan resistance, a liberal and a man of the people who had fought the communists, then Hekmatyar, and then the Taliban, always as a democrat. The Bamiyan cultural atrocity had turned the West against the Taliban, now Ahmed Shah was emerging as the leader of human rights movements and as a focal point of resistance to Islamic fundamentalism and to the Pakistani ISI, pious Muslim as he was. As the news trickled in of the brutal blowing up by North African photographers (or mercenary terrorists) people were dark with foreboding. The Russian news was fuller than the Western media with information, though no one knew that Masud was dead.

The next day my daughter's father-in-law, who was alone in his home in London, rang his wife. 'Take a look at the TV', he said. There it was, people staggering away, as a plane hit the second tower of the World Trade Center. Then came the rest of the horrors of 11 September 2001. What struck me personally at that very time was not so much the actual ghastliness of the twin tower collapse, as the attack on the Pentagon and the possibility of the White House also being hit. Living in the academic dreariness of UWED, one relied too much on the anodynes of Clancy blockbusters. There was an air of Islamic post-modernism as the spy thrillers caricature it, in the *déjà vu* of the episode. What was then more frightening was the prospect of the US military machine being hit to the point of immediate retaliation by the establishment that had perpetrated Desert Storm eleven years before. The crash of one of the planes on the Pennsylvania hillside did not remove the tension. It merely created black doubts among the young people with whom we talked, whether it had been shot down, as one Russian news indeed said, and whether there were more to follow. It seemed that the Taliban were acting out the role of the horsemen of the Apocalypse.

The next day, news came that Masud was dead, perhaps killed by the initial explosion. The Northern Alliance was apparently in tatters, with no charismatic figure to hold it together. The US was in a state of shock, told that Osama bin Laden had masterminded the attack from Afghanistan. Had radical political Islam then risen from the ashes and brought a stalemate against the great Satan, as Khomeini had once called the USA? From being just one of the peripheries of the oil interests of the Western world, Central Asia had moved fast forward into becoming a theatre of global strife. From being on the fringes of the problems of drugs and terror, President Bush junior, emerging from the hidey hole where he was said to have been hustled by his security guards, had brought it centre stage as the battleground of what the CNN would later headline as 'The War Against Terror', and what Indian newspapers would be found avidly repeating.

This sudden shift of focus was best visualized in the changing sketch maps of BBC and CNN. For the previous three years, we had been tantalized by their weather maps, where you could find out the temperature of the Asian rimlands, Turkey, Iran, South Asia, South-East Asia, the Far East, but no further north, excluding the entire heartland Asian segment of the CIS. We were left in the Anglophone vacuum about the weather in Tashkent, high up in the cloud haze in the map, except once in the week after the bomb blasts of February 1999. Then BBC gave the information, presumably in the interest of multinationals, preparing to evacuate whenever the order came. Now Uzbekistan, pointing down at the route towards Kabul, began to feature prominently in the sketches and weather map, though we never rose to the rating of knowing our maximum and minimum temperatures in the Latin script. That was left to the Cyrillic script of the Russian news.

One expected the Russians to make the most of these circumstances to gain a position in Uzbek minds. President Putin had made a few trips before, to confer with Karimov. Russia's interest was then to firm up its relations with China, newly laid in the Shanghai Forum. While the world agonized over Bamiyan, the northern axis of the Asian triangle was undergoing a shift of tectonic plates, with Jiang Zemin's strategic partnership declaration with the Russian Federation. Kazakhstan was very much a part of this. So was Tajikistan, a Russian satellite, one of the original members of the Shanghai Five. The Uzbeks and the Turkmen were isolated and the Russian news remained cautious about their reactions. Terrorism was something the people in the CIS, like the average Uzbek in the street, had been crying themselves hoarse about. The CIS, or rather Georgia, Uzbekistan, and Russia had been coping with terrorism long before CNN screamed its headlines of 'America Under Attack'. So had India. Now, all of them waited, as presumably did the Chinese, for the emasculation of political Islam at the cost of and by the agency of the revenging Americans.

Below this pragmatic level, the mood of the young people among the Uzbeks with whom we spoke was one of black cynicism. Not one believed that such a complex operation, as four plane hijacks from four different points of penetration past airport entries, could be co-ordinated in such a way as to demolish the World Trade Center and part of the Pentagon, and come close to knocking out the White House itself. They premised the standard thriller twist. Much more powerful forces than ex-CIA agents from Southern Arabia or mullah-trained Non-Resident Asians and Africans in West Germany and USA, our Uzbek friends said, must have co-ordinated a counterfeit terror. The purpose must have been to unleash war against Iraq, which was being called the instigator of revenge for the havoc of the Gulf War by Bush's father. This was an angle that I mistakenly ignored as I puzzled out the future outcomes. On the face of it public opinion in Uzbekistan seemed to be way out and far-fetched. What I missed at that time was its closeness to middle-of-the-road US public opinion, which linked Iraq with the radical aspect of Osama's Islam. Both had been the stooges of the USA, who had turned as subalterns against former secret sponsors. Both were now seen as snakes in the grass to be crushed. This was the feeling behind the Uzbek alliance with the USA, which was secretly maturing. The energy interests in the USA, represented by Condoleeza Rice, no less than James Baker III, had worked its way into the Uzbek strategic consciousness. An immediate result would be that the Uzbeks flipped their airbases over to the USA. But in the long run, it would be Iraq that would be targeted, after Central Asia and Afghanistan had been turned over into the American camp.

The US President's own mawkish cowboy language, and image of a blustering Texan oil tycoon, did nothing to help the acceptability of US state pronouncements. It is perhaps not an exaggeration to say that I had heard far more sympathy for the victims of the Gujarat earthquake than for the people slaughtered in the Twin Towers. But then they may have been equally politely expressing sympathy to the US citizens whom they met. Certain it is that there was no change in the pace of life in Tashkent in September and early October, contrary to what everyone thought. The only difference was the typical knee-jerk reaction to any threat to security in the neighbourhood of the country. This was the quick appearance of a larger number of militia on the avenues, of heightened tension about where to drive, and perhaps—though how is one to vouch for this—in the speed with which the President's cavalcade zipped down the roads. At our own average citizens' level, our driver was once about to take a completely legitimate turning out of our residential quarter, and was stopped by a militiaman. Asked the reason for being stopped, the guard gripped his gun, and said, if you don't make a U-turn now, you are going to get shot. This was said while my wife was sitting in the back of the car.

This happened on the day Bush announced the carpet-bombing of Afghanistan. Much water had flowed down the Amu Darya before that. The changes were imperceptible. Perhaps my reconstruction of them is based on hindsight. First of all, helicopters would rattle over our house early in the morning, while we were still asleep. It was as if people were keeping guard in the skies, or it could have been troop movements southwards from Chirchik military airbase between the city and the Chimgan range, a base, which used to figure as backup strategy for Soviet troop movements across the Amu Darya during the Afghan War. Stories on a very popular radio channel were beamed from Russia that Uzbekistan had indicated its interest in being an airbase for the US in its war against terrorism. This was at a time when Russia, China, and Iran, none of whom had any sympathy with the Taliban, had given no inkling of their inclinations in response to the frantic appeals for help and support that Bush, Powell and Rumsfeld, were making. In fact one state that had shown an eagerness to supply airbases for action against the Afghans, was the BJP-led NDA Central Government of our own country, India. Its eagerness had been turned down, since that would have meant over-flying Pakistan, and thus driving its General further into the embraces of the mullahs who had trained the Taliban themselves. India was by no means a major player in the game for Central Asia. It had no contiguous frontiers. They had gone to Pakistan in 1947 after Partition, and the occupation of the Northern Areas. Even those like us, denied access to the goings on in US-Uzbek diplomacy, should have realized at this point that Uzbekistan had begun to think of abandoning its isolation in heartland Asia for its own benefit.

First Pakistan tilted away from its Islamic allies across the Durand Line, which to all intents and purposes, the North West Frontier Province *madrasa* students had negated with their connection between Quetta in Baluchistan and the new Afghan capital of Kandahar, just across the Bolan Pass border. Musharaff performed the first of his about turns, going public with his plea for enlightened self-interest and recognition of realities by the unabashed forsaking of old allies of the Inter Services Intelligence of his army, as well as of Pakistan's own creature, the Taliban. He balanced the act by calling upon Indians in his barracks Urdu to 'lay off' (this delivered in English)—presumably from their aid to the Northern Alliance in the shape of medical aid, etc., but perhaps also to warn them not to cozy up to the Americans with malice towards his state. The rhetoric of a 'new Ataturk', favourable to Western interests, was beginning to reemerge. After a round of display on TV of violent demonstrations, mainly on the frontier led by mullahs against him, to establish that he was indeed in dire political straits, it became clear that the US were closing in from the east of Afghanistan, while their fleet moved up to the Baluchistan coast from where sea-based rocketry could hit the Afghan south. All that remained was to put a leash on the north, since in the west, Shia Iran, hostile to Sunni fanaticism in Herat, held the ring round the doomed country.

Things were still quiet in Tashkent, though by the end of September, rumours were coming thick and fast that American planes were beginning to land at Chirchik itself. The official version was bland. Uzbekistan was as usual opposed to cross-border terrorism and was guarding its frontiers on the Amu Darya against Juma infiltration. These were Nomonghani's last days. No one knew what to believe. Meanwhile, even the Taliban were heard of less than the mysterious organization about whom US officials now began to talk, but without impartial data, the al Qaida, which we were told meant 'the base', from which the unseen Osama spun his spider's web. The world was being forged into an alliance to break this shadow. Trust in action for revenge of hurt superpower pride were more important than academic calls for hard data about who, or what exactly, would be targets for revenge.

The mood of the times surfaced in a seminar sponsored by the US Embassy and the Uzbek Security Studies Institute, in which a American political attaché gave an ideological call for support to the war against terror. A rather hippy-looking US Visiting Professor brought from Kyrgyzstan for the seminar, was allowed to uphold democratic values of freedom by violently ranting against his country's imperialist foreign policy, and distributing photocopies of Arundhati Roy's condemnation of it. The Uzbek scholars cautiously and urbanely distanced themselves from both. They reiterated their feelings of sorrow at the New York deaths, their critique of religious fundamentalism, and above all the suspicion of the Afghan regime that every post-Soviet state felt. The tension was finally released—may one say, almost with a macabre sense of relief—when one evening, the TV displayed crackling red and orange flashes along dry hills. Bush was bombing Afghanistan. Osama, one was expected to feel reassured, would soon be brought 'dead or alive' as had been promised.

The first version of the attack on Afghanistan that we heard was that, like Clinton's rockets targeting Osama in Khost near the Pakistan frontier some years before, the attacks were coming from the sea. Public opinion in Tashkent was still not clear if the war was going to be anything more than the pounding of Iraq in 1990. But there was still no open sign of an Uzbek understanding with the USA on the military plane, only vague talk of humanitarian aid for victims in northern Afghanistan, for which the US was supposed to be negotiating air bases in the country. At this time, the Russian language *Pravda Vostoka* carried a big cartoon on the front page. The US President in his cowboy hat, with his trademark grin, was peering through a magnifying glass at a map of Asia. 'He is looking for Uzbekistan', said the caption. It was clear to the Russians that a swing was coming. They seemed quite placid about Uzbekistan—once their bridge to South Asia—now becoming a bridge to the USA.

In UWED, people were not talking of NATO any more. The links with the USA were becoming more emphatic. In fact, a colleague gave me an effusion to read. It described the great freedom that the people of the United States had permitted its air travellers to use when they taxied from one city to another, but advised them to be more security conscious, and to learn to live with terror as Central Asians had learned, since their own Afghan debacle a decade before. A common fraternity and sorority of national security began to bond the Uzbek elite with the victims of 11 September. Advertisements appeared in the Uzbek press of the CIA, asking for job applications as Uzbek teachers and translators for American intelligence. One of our friends would leave after a month, suddenly successful in efforts, diligently pursued through the year, to follow her classmates in a job as a translator in a Pacific seaboard university. She is now happily located with a Ph.D. fellowship.

That the USA's interest in Uzbek public opinion was on a scale remarkably higher than that of the previous year must have been clear to any watcher of the seminar scene more perceptive than myself. Madeleine Albright, in her last months as Secretary of State, had paid a visit in 2000 to UWED to administer a bromide about the need for Uzbek co-operation in US-led efforts to monitor terrorism in Central Asia. Only a select group of the University staff and students, vetted by the internal security, were invited to listen to her in the main hall. Many of my colleagues told me that they were put off by her hectoring tone, as if talking down to school children being taught the ABC of political clientage. This was dismissed as the personal style of a democrat egghead. However, very soon after the US Supreme Court's dicey appointment of the arch conservative Bush in place of the neo-liberal Gore (for whom I heard no Uzbek express sympathy), US interest obviously developed in specifically Uzbek affairs, as distinct from the drug monitoring from Osh. A colleague was invited to a Christian NGO's breakfast meeting in Washington to meet the new President as early as February. The World Bank, previously concerned only with the oil-rich eastern Caucasus and Kazakhstan, i.e. with the Caspian basin, had officials stopping off in Tashkent. One of them, a Turkish lady, more stiff upper-lipped than Albright herself, got her contacts to take her to the best artists in town, who laid out their finest wares in the hope of lucrative purchases. She had come to organize a project evaluating rural development in the Amu Darya basin, for which, her contacts complained, foreigners would be paid at rates double that of which they as local consultants hoped to do the slog work: they did not get the contract.

The uprisings gained ground. Abdullah Abdullah, the Foreign Minister in the Government of the Panjsheri resistance, toured Europe drumming up support, and evoked sighs of admiration from the expatriate ladies of Tashkent. His fluent English, heavily accented, and his sweet reasonableness crested the growing swell of sympathy for what, only a year before, the same people had called a defeated washout—the prospects of Mujahid revival. The big powers had decided that the Taliban were dispensable. Ahmed Rashid's strategy of rallying the moderates had begun to prevail. Perhaps, as one had heard, he did have clout with the Republican security establishment and not just with the *Far Eastern Economic Review* as a journalist. But in the context of toppling the Taliban, 'the 'moderates' were such warlords as the once vilified Judas of Mazar-i-Sharif, General Dostum with his Uzbek connections, Ismael Khan, the veteran Tajik mujahid, back from Iran, raising the country around Herat with his son, and Karim Khalili and other assorted members of Hazara tribes, oppressed by Tajiks and Pushtuns alike, in the mountains between Herat and Bamiyan, whose fierce resistance to the Taliban had swayed round the villages of the region all summer. The Afghan north-west was all that mattered in Tashkent.

As the war mounted in cities like Mazar, Taloqan and Kunduz, Hazara intellectuals could be met through common contacts. One of them, later to become important in the new establishment, one day engaged me in a conversation about the prospects of federalism in Afghanistan. The country had never seriously thought of any political solution other than the ethnic majoritarian domination of the Pushtun dynastic monarchy, based on Kandahar and the south, he said. In that context, conflict over a share in power had been held down among Tajiks, Uzbeks, and Hazaras, by the stern, apparently benevolent, Muhammadzais. But Zahir Shah could never be king after twenty-nine years absence. It was high time the Hazaras, the most oppressed minority of the state, came up with proposals for equitable federalism. What was the literature available on the subject? As a historian, with no practical knowledge of contemporary political science, I pleaded ignorance, beyond talking about how a friend in Bangladesh in 1973 had gone back to his teacher, Sir Kenneth Wheare, in Oxford to draft its first constitution. I wondered who would draft Afghanistan's new constitution and how long that would last: the one in Bangladesh had not. These shadowy machinations for power sharing in a new coalition structure were accompanied by a more open influx of first television-camera teams, and then more established journalists presenting war to the global evening news audience. They brought some liveliness to the sedate newslessness of the city.

The first media people who came were a couple from Saeed Naqvi's programme, which gives commentaries on world affairs to India's Doordarshan on Sunday mornings. This is an interesting and committed programme. A friend who liaised with media persons from home passed on to me the two young people who had come, one to interview and the other to wield the cameras, for introductions to city academics. A Doordarshan senior correspondent based in the Emirates, who was more conversant with Arab affairs than with Central Asia, followed them. Like people of my generation, he equated this area with the periphery of Brezhnev and Chernenko's Soviet Asia. The Afghan problem to him was still seen through spectacles tinted by the long deceased Najibullah and his friendship for India. Then came a clutch of correspondents. They were either trying to go to the Panjsher valley south of the Tajik border on the Amu Darya, where Muhammad Fahim was grouping the forces of Masud to join Dostum. Or, some had got there from Delhi via Dushanbe. They were now coming out to take the flight back via Tashkent, which was an easier journey.

The stories which they told had none of the old style individualism that one used to associate with the reportage of the early days of the Mujahideen, when single correspondents like Sandy Gall went in with only cameras and a sharp eye for the news about Masud, or when Olivier Roy was constructing his theoretical understanding of a new type of Islamic resistance, and later of the dead end reached by Political Islam in the fanaticism and tribal warfare into which the former had degenerated. Till the 1980s, the political reportage of 'little wars' waged in Africa and Asia, such as by the Kurds (covered in the 1920s by Rosita Forbes), or the Abyssinians (covered in the 1930s by Evelyn Waugh), had been written in the style of a parody of the early Georgian, Boys Own Paper version of high adventure among coloured people, that lies at the base, for instance, of the magnificent prose of *Seven Pillars of Wisdom*. Since the collapse of Yugoslavia and the Chechen Wars of the 1990s, reportage of this nature had been affected by changes in media technology and by changes in the nature of the warfare itself. From the time of the Gulf War, the 'strikes' first by air, then by raising insurgent groups on the fringes of the targeted nations, and then finally by a big push before the targets climbed down, had been co-ordinated with the aid of satellite telephones, TV imagery, and accompanying newsbytes acting as complementary news formative agency. Personalization of information would be imparted by some big names like Christiane Amanpour or Simpson being seen in various trouble spots, such as Kosovo or Kabul, giving on-the-spot commentaries about current affairs. Around them would be lesser fry from various nations, each forming small teams, the correspondent, herself or himself, a cameraman, and if the agency was flush with funds, others wielding the expensive satellite phoning systems. Carnage reporting had become highly capital intensive, a change from its individual freelance reporting days.

We heard many tales of these elements of enterprise and management connected with news from the front, as Indians came through Tashkent. For instance, movement across the Tajik border, even with certification by Northern Alliance authorities, was an opportunity for profit by the dismally poor people in the vicinity. The hire of broken-down cars for the journey from the river into the hills was a matter of bargaining capacity. Americans and Germans lavish with hard currency had ruined the market for the less well-endowed Indians teams, who were paying anything like three times the standard rates and were quite cash strapped by the time they came back to the north.

Easy liquidity bred bizarre aberrations. As the dry knife-edge hills loomed up on the way into the Hindukush, where the actual fighting was going on, correspondents from NATO countries, eager to get their pictures into circulation and their reports filed before others, had even hired young boys, fitted them out with guns, and set them up close to the Taliban lines, for a 'realistic' photo opportunity of uprising against the wicked men sheltering al Qaida. These novices, shelled by the Taliban levies, fell back, leaving one dead and others wounded. This was photographed as a war scene and dispatched for global distribution.

Moving further to the Mujahideen encampments, the observers were struck by the harshness of the terrain, the lack of food beyond bread and dried fruits, and the extremely unsanitary nature of living conditions. It was not as if this was the product of devastation by war, just a tradition of complete underdevelopment in a part of Afghanistan, where civilization whether purveyed by imperialism or by communism had never had a chance. The only change the new interest of the world had brought was that the local economy, such as it was, had gone haywire. Exchange of commodities for cash was now in dollars, that too on the basis of the evaluation of the buyers' capacity to hold out against the whim of the vendor. The notional rate of exchange of the dollar was calculated in thousands and even hundred of thousands of Afghanis.

Some Indian journalists went even further, walking over the

ranges into the gorges where the Panjsheris faced Kabul's fanatics. They came back with pictures which must rank among the first to have been recently taken by Indians, covering contemporary warfare outside South Asia. Most spoke with envy about the more advanced technology at the disposal of the Western journalists. I was reminded of my own frustration in trying to wheedle funds out of the Human Resource Development Ministry in Delhi in the mid-1990s to build up a good library on Central Asia in Calcutta, when such libraries, stocked with the latest materials, were sprouting all over the nations on either side of the Atlantic and the Pacific.

While journalists who came out from Delhi were enthusiastic, acute, and eager for news about the stalemate which existed between the carpet bombing of the Afghan villages by US planes and the attack on Mazar-i-Sharif, heralding the fall of the north, they had very little access to hard information from the Uzbek side. One of them, the political correspondent of a leading Delhi daily, was accredited to the US information First Secretary's briefings, conducted several times in the week. Even he had no real information about the nature of discussions that were going on between the US Secretary of Defence, Donald Rumsfeld, and the Uzbek Minister for Defense, Gulyamov (son of one of the greatest modern Uzbek poets and friend of India, Gafur Gulom). The Indian Embassy's links with the Northern Alliance people, which had been strong till 1998 had dried up. This was reflected in the lumpiness of information that our correspondents got from their own Embassy in these days when the city was a cauldron of rumours about the changing times. Indian diplomats proper had become dependant on the Uzbek establishment itself. The result was that our country had little presence in the tilt towards the US angle and US perception, except complaisance to it. There never was any independent view from the south, except with regard to the Hazaras and Dostum. The Pakistanis in Tashkent represented by a Major General, reputed to be from ISI with experience in 'drug control', were utterly low key.

It may not have been the Embassy as such, but the foreign policy of the Bharatiya Janata Party that was responsible for downscaling the missions in Muslim Central Asia. They focused on the affluent countries of the north, as on Russia and US interests. Pragmatists to the core, the Indian Right wing might have decided by then that competitive influence in the old southern territories in the Soviet Union, cultural contacts with whom my generation had set so much store, basing ourselves on old Kushan-Mughal links, was a matter of the past. All the cards in the pack were with the US oil barons.

By the end of October, it was clear that the US was firmly, and indeed literally, entrenched in Uzbek soil. The military aerodrome of Khanabad lies 6 miles to the east of the old town of Karshi, between the Samarkand-Bukhara road and the Amu Darya. Built by the Soviets for total cover from the air, the runways are said to go down into a broad tunnel extending underground through a warren of installations, including, one is told, hangars, giving exit for planes on the other side. It is said that there is another such airport, south of the Amu, in Turkmenstan, near the city of Mary (the old historical Merv, up to which the Russians had come in the 1880s in the Old Great Game). Along with a third airport at Shiberghan in Afghanistan, between Herat and Mazar-i-Sharif, these formed a triangle of Soviet forward bases in the Russian thrusts towards the warm waters of the Arabian Sea. Now, the Uzbeks permitted, for humanitarian flights, it was sanctimoniously said, the US air force to land planes, staff, and a thousand guards at Khanabad. The whole area was sealed off, so that local people and correspondents alike were stopped on the road to it outside Karshi. Food packets for the starving peasants were indeed dropped, with pamphlets explaining the purposes of the bombing, and calling on people to hand over Osama and Mullah Omar. Other planes simply bombed habitations and people. Medical aid did go in to boost the Russian and Indian presence in the Panjsher, on a greatly competitive scale. Rumour, however, had it that as the war hotted up in the north, strafing missions were also taking off from Khanabad. This increased the US military presence far more than the naval rocketry from the south of Pakistan. The Uzbek-Pakistani strategic vice of the USA's military presence in south Central Asia had closed its jaws on Afghanistan. The CIA Director of the 1980s, William Casey, had had the vision described by the ISI Brigadier, Muhammad Yousuf and Captain Adkin, *The Bear Trap*, of hitting the soft underbelly of Soviet Central Asia in the Amu Darya bend, with mujahid agency. This vision had come full circle through the agency of the successors of the mujahids. The Taliban and the old CIA contact, Osama bin Laden had proved to be *deus ex machina*, for a people whom Russia, the Soviet successor-state had already given up for lost.

Uzbekistan itself took this diplomatic revolution in its usual taciturn style. It was indeed a diplomatic revolution with the country acting as a bridge between Putin and the Shanghai association, and the USA's outreach into South Asia through Pakistan and the renewed Pakistani clientage of General Musharraf. A junior colleague in the university at that point of time was looking forward to participating in a World Bank project, and joked about the people in his native town of Karshi, when he found me scanning a large-scale map of Central Asia in our Department in which two Khanabads are shown, one of them north of Taloqan. The Karshi shopkeepers, he said, were looking forward to the two thousand Americans in the airport purchasing fresh food and other goods with lovely greenbacks for a long time in the future. One was reminded of the way petty capitalists of early British India had welcomed the early Sahibs with open arms. But even that relationship was not to be. The same scholar was still jocular but also rueful in mid-November. Not only had the World Bank project gone to some other institution, the shopkeepers had found that the Yanks were flying in their fresh produce every day from the USA or Europe and leading totally insulated lives as if they were in a separate time capsule. There was no question of mingling with the natives.

Every thing remained hush-hush, but stories grew that even the Pushtuns were rising, not for the long-fled King Zahir Shah, but for refugee leaders in Pakistan close to the royal clan. One of them was betrayed by a rival group, after being airdropped in his native mountains, and was executed by the Taliban. Another was found who had lost his father to assassins. The Indian news assessments of Hamid Karzai were puerile. Karzai, it appeared, had taken a degree from Himachal Pradesh University, but left Shimla after that to join his family's hotel\restaurant chain in the USA. Before he had time to really rouse long dead anti-extremist sentiment, the northern pincers had closed from Hazarajat in the west and Panjsher in the east on the two cities of Mazar and Kabul. The Taliban were hemmed in on either side. Fighting grew in the heights to the south of Mazar and in the relatively fertile Shomali plain, north of Kabul, and then there was a sudden BBC TV picture: a hearty Englishman, who had run quite a competently innovative series of group interviews of trouble spots from Kosovo to Kabul, called Simpson's World, was seen walking with a group of tribal people along a road of bombed out houses. 'Here we are, walking into Kabul', he announced expansively. Whether he thought he was Stanley greating Dr. Livingstone, I presume, in darkest East Africa, or whether he thought he was the bagpiper playing 'the Campbells are coming, oho, oho' as the Army relieved the British Residency in Lucknow in 1858 we will never know. We admired his verve.

THE AFTERMATH OF A LITTLE WAR

The events of 11 September had set a kaleidoscope whirling. Much has since been written about the way the world changed, or conversely remained on the same track, as a result. Central Asia certainly changed. The change was very soon evident. It was not just the public advertisements that have been mentioned, asking for Uzbek interns to bolster up the CIA. There was an air of secularist relief in general that fundamentalism had retreated.

People were talking about the news that Jumaboy Khojiev, who had called himself Nomonghani, and whose men had moved at will in the villages of Ferghana, spreading the Koran, dollars, and terror had died in the siege of one of the towns where the Taliban had been holed up in the last Northern encirclements.[1] The relief was an elite sentiment; we had no way of knowing what the common people thought. There was no feeling that the real Islam had been defeated. There was rejoicing that moderate Muslims had been helped to eradicate fanaticism.

An Indologist once high in the councils of the old Uzbek communist establishment told me about this time that Muslim fanatics had been dealt with in Afghanistan, with US help, in the way the Chinese had dealt with fanatics among the Uighurs in Xinjiang through the years. Where lay the similarity? I enquired. Well, he said, what had to be done by force this year, the Chinese had been doing by sending in large numbers of peasants, who intermarried into the Uighur population and changed their stock, so that the Muslim propensity for going back to the Koran was diluted. Genocide or eugenics, the result was the same. He was brazen. If national interest demanded it, sores in the body politic had to be burned out. After all racial intermingling meant the diffusion of cultural diversity, did it not? There was hardly any point in pushing the conversation any further. I was to hear enough of it from Hindus critical of what they called 'pseudo-secularism' in middle-class India, after the Gujarat riots, following the Godhra atrocity the next year.

Neither was radical Islamic sentiment destroyed by the retaliation for 11 September. There is no evidence that the ostensible targets of the bombing raids are dead. In Mullah Omar's case, the shadowy Amir-ul-Mumineen has just been forgotten. We had heard an old CIA official speaking on CNN at the height of the bombing. He had been asked what would happen if the two wanted Taliban and al Qaida leaders were captured, not dead but alive. He recalled the time when a religious opponent of US imperialism in mid-twentieth century Lebanon had been captured. To try him and execute him would turn him into an Islamic martyr. It would be remembered that he had fought imperialism. So, he had been flown out over the Eastern Mediterranean with stones tied to his feet and just pushed off into the sea. The gentleman suggested that this would be the best treatment for Omar or Osama.

The Taliban may well have shifted back across the borders, not necessarily Wazaristan across the border from Khost this time into the northern areas of Pakistan, Hunza, Nagar, Gilgit, and Skardu, along the Karakorum borders, not only of Kargil and Ladakh, but also of Yarkand and Kashgar in south Xinjiang, with its old tradition of Muslim identity and nineteenth century revolts by Yakub Beg against China. It is quite possible that the puritanism of Hizb-ut-Tahrir extends in a belt from Termez in Uzbekistan, north of Khorog in Tajikistan, past the Pamirs, up to Kashgar and the southern oases of Niya and Keriya in Xinjiang. One would not be so foolish as to argue that there will not be a new set of rebel fanatics. It is now necessary to look at the new prospects of Muslim identity in Central Asia, a different thing from Gorbachev and his advisors' red herring, worldwide Muslim fundamentalism, which the US found useful to propagate. Before one goes into that question and its ramification for the future, let us see how the country looked in the last two months that we were there.

The fall of Kabul in November led to a brief euphoria. The road to Mazar, which had fallen to Dostum's Uzbek Sunni Jumbish, and not to Khalili's Hazara Shia Wahadat, remained blocked. It passes from Termez, the ancient nodal point of many Soghdian, Bactrian and Kushan sites, over the Amu at a point called Khairattan or

Hayrattan by a bridge made famous by the last Soviet army commander in Afghanistan, crossing it on foot with his dog, behind his retreating troops in 1989. When Tohir Yuldashev and Juma had revived fears of the Islamic movements of Uzbekistan, surging across the river, the approaches to the bridge had been land mined and heavily guarded against any Taliban attacks, the last of which had been made around the time that the Bamiyan statues were blown up. Now, it was a question of when the de-mining operation would begin. People did not know. One told me the story that the Defence Ministry was searching for the plans of the laid mines. The files had been mislaid and no one dared go in and test the ground! This was very probably the sort of black joke against the establishment that flourishes in all late communist and subsequent societies! It was believed that nothing would be done till the jittery Uzbek establishment was assured of total stability in the neighbouring state. No matter, others said, the Americans were working at it, and the road would soon be sorted out.

It was life as usual again in Tashkent. Embassy acquaintances were thinning out. The Indian Cultural Centre had lost the vitality of the early days, when it had been a pleasant refuge, even when we sat reading books in the library or ten-day old Indian newspapers and the weeklies in the hall. A Yoga group had now increased its presence. One of the last new local people whom we met there was a gentleman who has specialized in heritage buildings in Tsarist Tashkent.

He cherished stories and photographs about buildings and gardens, a hundred years old, and also of Indian merchants, in the city of those days, who had been described in the late nineteenth-century St. Petersburg Press. Since we had come to the city three years ago, many changes were evident in the rather brash villas coming up in open plots on the fringes of the city centre. What friends, proud of the old ambience, found disturbing was that the quaint, one-storied, stucco bungalows, often with a semi-circular corner frontage on two roads, were being pulled down to be replaced by garish large blocks. Mr. Golender (whose surname we were told meant Hollander) was worried that the history of an age in Tashkent when the young Kerensky (who had been Prime Minister of Russia between the March and the October Revolutions of 1917) had fished in the central canal, or workers had listened to Social Democrat speeches in the last days of the Tsar, would be forgotten, with the demolition of the small town surroundings where such events had taken place. The talk he gave on the subject in the Cultural Centre was the last I attended. What was notable was the audience, civilized ladies and gentlemen of the intelligentsia, whom I had not seen before, and who waxed passionate on points of detail of urban history. They moved me to hold forth on the heritage building conservation movement in Calcutta. I pleaded that they take a lead in starting such a movement, if they wished to be active about retaining a sense of history, the loss of which they so obviously regretted, and which was so close to their times—as distinct from Amir Timur or Babur. There was the usual silence. Later at tea, I gathered that any suggestions that they should be activist about—let alone against—matters that obviously had state sanction, such as building demolition and promotion, were not looked on with favour. All expression of opinion that could roll into protest, however small, was feared. The culture of introversion and complaisance, with its roots in fear of poking a finger into a hornet's nest, which we had sensed when we came to the city, remained like a pall as we were about to leave.

We had strongly mixed feelings about leaving Tashkent for home. It is a lovely city, Elysian in its leafiness and its sense of space with clear unpolluted air. Its people were uniformly courteous. We do not remember a rude word, ever uttered. If they know you are Indian, you invariably get an extra dollop of warmth. Sometimes that can be embarrassing. On the last trip we went to Samarkand in October, at the height of the bombing of Afghanistan, I had accompanied our companion on that occasion to the shrine of Shah-i-Zinda, while my wife rested at the foot of the steep ramp of steps. In a trice, there were a group of young mendicants—common to such spots—around her. When she waved away the trinkets and beads, their real interest in her was explicated. As an Indian getting on in years, she must have seen Raj Kapoor and Nargis, they said. They knew that these veterans of the screen had passed away. But what could the *khanim* tell them about Shah Rukh and Jimmy. Shah Rukh she had seen on the screen, my wife said, but Jimmy, they persisted, what about Jimmy. When she looked baffled, they proceeded to jig and sway, in a manner distinctly reminiscent of Mithun Chakrabarty in his younger and more athletic days. When she asked whether they were talking of him, they were overjoyed—'da, da, Mithoon, we are so fond of him'. Changing times, but the continuities are clear. Indian cinema of the popular variety is still the way to the Uzbek heart, as it is now being seen it still remains the way to liberated popular Afghan sympathy. We recalled how the history scholar who had come all the way from Samarkand to escort us to the Babur seminar in 2000, had explained why he thought his generation of the 1960s and 1970s admired 'Raj' so much. It was because, he said, their parents' generation felt that the values and attitudes that Raj Kapoor stood for in films were those around which they could build their morality. As we came away from the Timurid precincts, we wondered as we had done in Humsan in our first months in Uzbekistan, whether present-day Hindi commercials were giving them even such values.

An air of lassitude permeated Tashkent, despite its broad, clean avenues, with the lovely shop fronts and stores stocked with all the goods that one was used to in the West, window-shopping which we so much enjoyed. UWED's library of English books I had exhausted. Every colleague said that the Russian literature there was text books and reference encyclopaedias. The main Tashkent library had developed cracks in the bomb blast of February 1999, and there was little talk about its opening. The Regional and Strategic Studies Institute had some English books, but was going through one of the interminable Uzbek rituals of kicking one Director up to a less important post and bringing in a more recent political favourite. I never did get the permission to read in the library: my application had been lost in their files, I was told, would I please apply again. I gave up after the third time. If one is interested in the details of Uzbek events, or in the narratives of just Central Asia's mediaeval past, or its ancient sculpture and script, there may be incentives for going back to the place. The longer you stay, the more you will be cut off from the pulsating world of, even the Asian rim countries, with their freer news media, their participation in public life not dominated by one boss and his delegates. In China, however authoritarian it may be, there is at least its throbbing economic energy and social utility. Lacking these, one succumbs to a sense of ennui.

THE PAINTERS OF SAILGOKH

In these last days we began to frequent Broadway—our familiar Sailgokh—once again, to chaffer with its painters and picture vendors. Since we had discovered the pleasures of walking this broad, leafy precinct in the centre of the city, my wife had been attracted by the paintings, which the local artists sold on the pavements, through their relatives and assistants. Many of them were unremarkable, average copies of imaginary Turkestan scenery, with a domed edifice, or ruined archways, and people in carts or camels passing by. They could also be depictions of still life, flowers or fruits: or of ships at sea, unfamiliar for a landlocked country. These oils on canvas were imitations of what Russian painters in Tashkent in Soviet, in earlier Tsarist days, used to paint for a colonial middle class clientele. Specimens cluttered the walls of the picture gallery rooms on the upper floors of the Tashkent Museum of Art, jumbled with old style chests of drawers and other furniture, or Bukhara carpets, horse trappings, and fine examples of needle-point embroidery. They were as undistinguished as the similar, relatively inferior, paintings on the cobbled paving around the Place du Tertre on the Heights of Montmartre in Paris, of which Sailgokh is perhaps an eccentric miniature.

Over the years, the cultural difference became more marked from an average European city square for regular festivity, which gives Tashkent's Broadway its Eurasian ambience. The emphasis was gradually shifting from copies of the standard European styles with a distinct Russian flavour, to more oriental themes. More and more street scenes were painted of the sloping roofed, hutment fronts of bye-lanes in *mahallas*, done in delicate tints. Then little miniatures on paper began to appear, mounted on cardboard and framed, of old Uzbek figures, in the quaint bent style of the late mediaeval illustrations that are copies of the old Turki masters of the era of Mirza Kamoluddin Bihzad. We had earlier seen them hawked in the heritage spots of Samarkand and Bukhara. They were becoming commonly available: by the end of 2000, old *madrasas* on the edges of the old city which were being restored as heritage buildings had their study cells on the ground floors put to use as secular ateliers where craftsmen plied their trade for inflated prices, in dollars. On Sailgokh, however, where the local people far outnumbered the few tourists, one could bargain for them in soum. Also, what became more common were portraits of women, languorously spread over low couches, in the style of the post-Ingres variety to be seen in the Louvre. My wife asked one of the painters about the source of his design. He said the model was his wife at home.

The taste for paintings was obviously changing. The new nomenklatura of the turn of the century had tired of the moralistic pastoral ruins and copies from Russian painters, drawing for ethnographic albums about Bukhara or Khiva (or for that matter, Jaipur in India) at the turn of the last century, such as Verestchagin. They were now interested, not so much in modern art, but in a slightly later nineteenth and early twentieth-century style of painting, which relied on European Orientalism, depicting eastern women at ease or at work, or large portraits of men, generally with lined faces, marked by strong character and Oriental headgear, so that a non-European identity was established. Identity—not in the religious Islamic sense, but in a secular Central Asian way of expression of broad national features separate from Europe—was showed in the novelty of the forms of painting. The changes could be discerned, only if one kept going back to the pavements off and on, and were not very marked. The same landscapes copied from Russian paintings, of mountains and streams, continued to feature since tourist spots remained. So did the sea, reminding one of the Caspian, not too far away, or cascading water, prized for its rarity in the Central Asian wastes (which is why perhaps its two-dimensional perpendicular channels are so marked in the Mughal gardens, which Babur brought to north India for his dynasty to Indianize). By 2001, striking copies of Romantic Orientalism, probably taken from Western catalogues, were increasingly available—full scale paintings.

Our interest led us to a few studios. Some of the artists have been well known for the last few decades and have exhibited in the Russian cities, in eastern Europe, and even West and India. Their themes and treatment compare well with the general markets. They are priced at that level, which was beyond our means. Other artists, living on the margins of indigence, were prepared to make large-scale copies of any painting given to them, whether Matisse or Ravi Verma. Most of them, even the less well to do, had large apartments, perhaps in the attics of the massive buildings. They were able to display their wares with a fair degree of space. The old Soviet system had always specially patronized arts and culture, however shackled it was by thought control and regulatory practices.

Artistic creativity is quite active among Uzbek craftspeople and painters. While no development is visible to transform the fine and intricate miniature styles of pictorial depiction and tiled decoration into new forms of creative design, still there is encouragement from the regime itself to recover, retain, and carry on old traditional styles. One has only to go to the innermost part of the shrine, just above the legendary well, of Shah-i-Zinda, or to the ground level sanctum of the domed chamber of Gur Emir, or to the *madrasa* cloisters in central Tashkent, to see how the restoration and renewed training of the old crafts of design are being developed. The most remarkable example of this is two edged. The complex of Imam Bukhari around the little *makbara* of the nineteenth century legist, who compiled the *Sahih*, or verified sayings attributed to the Prophet's companions and generation, near Samarkand, has come up as the post-communist state's endeavour to ally itself with moderate and established Sunni theology. As a result, there has been considerable interest on artisan skills of decoration, which bid fair to compete with the scale of the sixteenth and seventeenth-century investment in the decoration and frontage of the Registan itself. However, an exhibition to which we were taken in the central exhibition hall on Uzbekistan Avenue, opposite GUM, of the present condition of Khwarezm art, appeared to be repetitive and non-innovative in its concepts. If further transformation is not taking place throughout Central Asia, this is due to the lack of innovations and risk, which as in industry, tends to turn all post-Soviet productivity into Jurassic Parks.

CHECKING OUT

Preparing to pack up a household after a stay of three years brought one close to bureaucratic realities and the dead hand of state regulation. Among the articles for decorating our apartment were some paintings, and three metal samovars of different styles, which we had bought at the open street markets of Tizikovka and Sailgokh. At the time when we bought them government rules for taking objects of even domestic use such as pianos and paintings were subject to inspection by the Ministry of Culture, and a small charge for the requisite license of transportation. But even these rules did not apply to samovars. Samovars are the traditional large urns with a tap near the base and a built-in chimney for a small wood fire to keep the water boiling through the day. This used to be the Russian procedure for regular availability of hot water for the tea. This method is still used, but recent day samovars are far more utilitarian, and lack the old-world charm of the brass ones made in Tsarist days. When we reached Tashkent, the latter type were available only second-hand. There was no question of exports being forbidden. Suddenly, in 2001, such a rule was dreamed up in some obscure ministry. So, we made enquiries about the inspection procedure and fees. The mandarins in charge were adamant. No samovar with a mark of manufactured date, fifty years before, could go out. They were antiques and we had to leave them behind. In the case of paintings, the small inspection fee had been hiked by the same officials, greedy for dollars, to very large amounts, which were 'negotiated' between the mandatory forwarding agents and the petty functionaries of the ministry. A lady in a multinational who had brought into the country her paintings left for the next posting of her husband and was charged those exorbitant rates for taking back her own painted work, because she was not able to produce the itemized inventory receipts issued three years before to prove that she herself had painted the canvases. In our case, ordinary frames, strengthened by printed cardboard backing, were charged at the same rates as the few paintings we had bought.

The Uzbek government, strapped for foreign exchange, might have the logic that their sovereignty permits imposition of new rules from time to time for public profit, and by these new rules their officials were behaving legitimately. But the forwarding agents pleaded that they had to negotiate bribes for custom clearance. The fact was—as in every country that degenerates into corrupt practices—that it was the officials and the con men, who operate as agents for the new private enterprise, for instance of commodity transfer, whose private interest triumphs over public gain. The rules created, not only in this, but also in practically all operations for transfer of commodities, networking of opportunities for 'speed money' or evasion of inspection, proliferating out of the mire of corruption, for which the Uzbek regime and its systems of administration is known in the entire region.

Looking back over the previous three years, we saw that this system was indeed inherent in 'actually existing socialism' since the growth of communist totalitarianism. As early as 1999, the general manager of a pharmaceutical enterprise from India, with a set of branches in different parts of the world, whom I had asked about the truth of charges made by Americans and British managers about pervasive corruption, had been dismissive. Why call it corruption, he said, it was the rules of the game. He was not the sort to be aware of the irony in his choice of words—the Great Game, whether old or new, Russian or British, had always worked through corruption of the semi-feudal variety. He was correct about the systemic relevance of corruption in broken-down economies, shifting gear from the command system of authoritarian socialism to the mixed economies of the new democracy, adjusting to uncertain market practices. Either the economy was given full convertibility and thus greater privileges for multinational capital transfer on a global scale. This had the cost of making the benefits of world consumer goods available to a restricted, managerial elite, with a high level of hardship and immiserization for the working masses, or, the Uzbek, and partly Turkmen or Tajik, method could be taken. Foreign investments could be soaked of their profits, earned within the states' sovereignty to build up the dollar reserves by means of a labyrinthine network of permits and licenses. The result would be that the state retained the power to expend on subsidies for social benefits, provided since the communist days, such as cheap central heating, water, domestic electricity and gas in practically in every home, rich or poor.

This structure of tranquilization of the masses kept the regime stable. It did not preclude the greed of the middle-level functionaries in all sectors of the economy, who used the permit-license network for their private profits, making corruption institutional, and in that sense 'the rules of the game', through rules revised from those of the previous communist regime. Corruption had become endemic, whether to pass students in college, or to move through airport customs with declared extra luggage, or with suddenly embargoed carpets, or on more lucrative scales for all concerned to set up and maintain foreign enterprise, without which the country could not get dollars or know-how.

These were the dilemmas that remained in Uzbekistan as the open alliance with the USA clarified and the bombing of Afghanistan ended. The average citizen was quite happy. Juma Nomongani was reported killed in Kunduz. The Taliban had vanished as spookily as they had appeared, back to the refugee camps of Pakistan. American and British troops held the Hindukush, facing the Russians in Tajikistan, and were combing the Tora Bora hills of the Sulaiman ranges for Osama. The new mood was one of good riddance to the instabilities of South Asia. There Pakistan and India were again hostile as terrorist fundamentalism stepped up its activities in Kashmir against India, and in Pakistan itself against Americans and local Christians. The average Uzbek was now decisively looking to the West. In Chorsu bazaar, where my wife had gone to help our driver select a new camera, the stalls were full of American, Japanese, and European models. 'Don't you have any from our part of Asia', she had asked. 'No, I have good European ones; I want to be a European', was the answer. We had never heard such a definitive statement before.

Leaving Tashkent was of course a wrench, particularly its friendly people and the general ambience. But we feared the boredom in the intellectual atmosphere, based as it was on obsolete text books and trumped-up chauvinism, subservience to the West, and above all the collusive silences bred out of the fear of retribution or denial of rewards by the state. Uzbekistan seemed less on the verge of change in the twenty-first century than it had been poised for in the late twentieth century.

The moment of transition appeared to have passed. The Karimov regime, and the vested interests that maintained it, were, if anything, more secure. It had bought US protective cover by handing over its Khanabad airbase, which is as close to China as it is to Pakistan. A new era of geopolitics was dawning—with the omens pointing at the inner borders of China. Uzbekistan would perhaps play little part in it. The stakes on the board had shifted south and east—towards the approaches to the Karakorums, the Kuen Lun, and Lop Nor as well as Tibet. There was little prospect for Uzbek development, except as a US satellite, twinned with Afghanistan, for checkmating the growing solidarity of the Shanghai Forum.

NOTE

1. Ahmed Rashid's book, *Jihad* was rushed to the press by October, so it does not mention the news of Juma's death.

8

Towards a Dialogue of Civilization

EURASIAN TECTONICS: THE SHIFT TOWARDS THE WEST

Two types of transitions have marked Uzbekistan in recent years. The first is a transition in geopolitical space. The second is a transition in historical time. The manifold dimensions of the intertwining of these essentially social happenings impart a very strong element of complexity, even uncertainty, to any attempt to look at processes of transition in the country as a whole.

Geopolitical dimensions have radically changed since the days when Tashkent was the headquarters of the Tsar's Governor-General of Turkestan and Semirechiye (the seven rivers of Kyrgyzstan and Southern Kazakhstan); or even from the days when it was a wartime backup industrial reserve, far south of embattled Stalingrad. Through the second half of the twentieth century, Tashkent remained the largest commercial and industrial node of the southern lobe of the Late Soviet heartland. Road, rail and air routes converged on it. Other republics, including the Kazakh republic and the other four nationals round Uzbekistan, did defer to its old plains culture and its traditions of settled political authority and statehood, more developed than the tribalism of its surrounding Republics. Its economic position flourished since the 1940s because of Moscow's subsidy, in return for investment in cotton cultivation, on the one hand, and textile manufacture, armaments, and heavy industrial production on the other. By the early 1980s, observers from the West, such as Edward Allworth, Michael Rywkin, Gregory Gleason, and William Fierman were talking about a new wave of assertive Uzbek nationalism.

This was best expressed by the First Secretary of the Uzbek Communist Party, Sharaf Rashidov, an apparatchik from Dzizhak north of Samarkand, whose 'clan' affinities built up a clique who were brokers of Brezhnev's power in Moscow, similar to Kunayev in Alma Ata or Nabiev in Dushanbe. This southern satrap admired the Nehruvian politics of non-alignment and elitist democracy, precariously poised in the later period over state politics of graft and patronage, practised in independent India. He was no enemy of Pakistan's position in the Indus basin, or of the last Muhammadzai dynasty rulers in Afghanistan. He represented that aspect of Soviet international relations which sought trade access for the landlocked southern parts of the USSR to the Indian Ocean. Within a decade of his fall, Uzbekistan's southern perspectives also lay in ruins, and it was back to its double-borders landlocking.

The reason lies in the character of Soviet trade and geopolitics in the era of the 'second' Cold War. The Soviets after Khruschev went through a period of expansion of influence in the Middle East and Africa, in South Asia in Vietnam, as well as in its north Pacific Rim beyond Japan. In reaction, Kissinger's tilt via Pakistan towards China, US recovery of prestige after the Vietnam muddle, the recession of democracy all over South Asia and the Middle East as well as in Africa, with attendant acceleration of violence and the spread of wars and famine, and above all 'mature' capitalism's recouping of its innovative capacity for research and development, all led the USA under Reagan and the senior Bush to flex its muscles. The consequent tension and the growth of 'Baroque Arsenals' as Mary Kaldor called them in the 1980s, not only developed proliferated armaments systems of the super powers, and the competitiveness of regional powers, such as Britain, France, and China. It also led to the growth of the proxy war in Afghanistan, of which the Khalq-Parcham local communists, and the various Harkats and Hizbs of mujahidin were fronts: these also had a weird effect as safety valves for the mounting trend towards a third world war.

The USSR, with its top-heavy industrialization, withdrew first in the war of nerves with the West. This was a struggle in which Asia, including communist China, stood by, either helpless or aloof, preparing for capitalist liberalization. New urbanization, growing trends of bourgeois aspiration among a nascent industrial middle class, and the lure of North Atlantic cultural and affluent values, all added up to the incapacity of Gorbachev and his advisors to contain the implosion within socialist morale. Nascent nationalism in Uzbekistan coincided with nuclear disarmament movements in

Kazakhstan, dissidence by Central Asian intellectuals, the Chernobyl pollution catastrophe in the Ukraine, religious and ethnic protest in the Baltic Republics, small nationality linguistic and religious dissent against Georgian and Russian majoritarianism in the Caucasus[1] and the spillover of Afghan insurgency against Tajikistan. Ethnic riots followed among exiled Caucasian and Volga-Don nationalities deported during the war to Central Asia. There was a brief burst of religious fundamentalism among the Uzbeks. It was fuelled from across the Amu Darya from about 1987 to 1993. There was also anger against the Russians for the brutalities of the procuratorial 'Gdlyan gang' of Armenians against the paternalist structure of vested interest that had been built in Rashidov's time. All this finally meant the coming of what a British analyst, Jonathan Grant, contrasting events with the changes in the British Commonwealth from 1945 to 1950, in the 1994 issue of *Central Asian Survey,* called 'decolonization by default'.

Boris Yeltsin and his neo-liberal advisors believed that the USA would shore up Russia's privatization plans and would bail out the crony capitalism from which the mafia hankered to profit. That speculative bubble burst by the early 1990s. It led to deep financial crisis. Civil War broke out on the peripheries of the Black Sea, the Caspian, and the Pamirs, i.e. in Moldova, Abkhazia, Chechnya, Azerbaijan, and Tajikistan. Ex-communists with strong authoritarian tendencies like the Afghan war veteran, General Anatoli Lebed, the Georgian ex-Foreign Minister of the USSR, Eduard Shevardnadze, and the Tajik kolkhoz operator from rural Kulyob, Emomali Rachmanov, were in demand. It was expected that they would stop the tottering peripheral economies from going over the brink into anarchy.

Uzbekistan tried to steer between the extremes of neo-liberalism and disorder. In those days of inverted terminologies, what the older democracies of Europe and Afro-Asia called the Right—belief in free enterprise and the reassertion of religious values, considered backward by secularists—was called the Left in the new Commonwealth of Independent States. What was considered in the democracies to be the Left—communism, socialism and the defence of the public sector—was called the Right. In Uzbekistan, post-Soviet neo-liberals of their Left stood for a relaxation of the Party's control over non-central regions such as Khwarezm in the west and Ferghana in the east. Others called for a greater degree of

Islamic Puritanism, particularly control of feminine aspirations for freedom of dress and morality, and for the spread of Koranic and early Islamic values.

It would be wrong to emphasize only Ferghana as a hotbed of Islamic revival and *jihadi* mentality, diffused from Tajikistan in the south. That it might have been. But Haji Akbar Turajonzode and Saiyid Abdullo Nuri represented the Islamic Revival Party's thrust for religious autonomy among the Tajiks: the Khwarezm leader, Muhammad Salih stood for the post of President against Karimov. Salih took 13 per cent of the national vote. Most of this came from Khwarezm and the region affected by the desertification of the Aral region in the interests of upper riparian prosperity. It should also not be forgotten that, by 1995, these problems seemed to be tapering off.

Western analysts (particularly neo-liberals committed to ultra-democratic versions of individual human rights in advanced capitalist state) lumped together the plight of Salih and his one-time liberal collaborators, the intellectual brothers Abdur Rakhmon and Abdumanob Pulatov, who popularized information about their physical harrassment by goons, who presumably worked for the government. They sought refuge in the USA. As it happens, Salih and Erk drifted towards terrorism, though whether he was hand-in-glove with Tohir and Juma from Ferghana, as the President alleged, is not proven. The Birlik Party of the Pulatovs has now been permitted to hold meetings again in Uzbekistan presumably with US mediation, as a result of the Uzbek tilt towards the USA and the World Bank.

Within Uzbekistan itself, people who came to Tashkent in the early 1990s spoke of the once clean pavements, strewn with masses of Indian goods from the Punjab and Delhi, of Bangladesh youth, educated in Russia, travelling to Singapore to buy containers full of word processors to be flogged at four times their price in Uzbekistan, of cell phones being hawked to passers-by in the Metro, and of the general atmosphere of 'spend as much as you can' as well as 'get rich quick'. Those were the days of fly-by-night partnerships between Pakistani or Indian operators and Uzbeks, on the basis of sharp practice. By the middle of the decade, however, partnerships in retail trade with South Asia had failed.

This situation was not unlike the uncertainties of violence in other republics. New norms of post-communist authoritarianism prevailed. It was not Karimov who grabbed power, it was the exigencies of retaining power that led the old elite to vest their interest in the figure of Karimov, and invest him and his family with supreme oligarchic authority. This elite of professional families, the old guard of the Rashidov era, such as the latter's son-in-law Komilov (who became Foreign Minister) or Gafurov (the Defence Minister and son of the national poet Gofur Gulom) and the then new young Finance Minister, Rustom Azimov, retained the real power.

A third stage in this transition came with Uzbekistan's inevitable turn to the West, following perhaps its Russian mentors, but seeking to do so on its own, negotiating with countries such as Germany, Austria, to a lesser degree Britain, and above all the USA. This was related to friction within the Commonwealth of Independent States and the leeway permitted to new industrial barons, such as the erstwhile Prime Minister of Russia, Chernomyrdin, and the CIS Secretary General, Berezovsky, in their economic and political deals with neighbouring Republics. In this context of internal Central Asian contradictions, friction grew with Uzbekistan's larger northern neighbour, Kazakhstan. President Nazarbaev had ranked much higher in the last days of the communist hierarchy and had established good working relationships with Gorbachev and Yeltsin. His new activities gave him a leading position in the CIS, equal to that of Leonid Kuchma in the economically powerful and European Republic of Ukraine.

In the late 1990s Karimov was consolidating his internal position in the Uzbek regime, intent on subordinating all opposition or even competition from his peers, a most powerful one of whom, Djurabekov he temporarily banished, albeit to a villa in Nice, for his indecent display of wealth (flinging dollars and not mere soum to the dancers at a wedding, as rumour had it). It was in these years that Karimov really became the supremo that he appears to be in the version that is nowadays current. There was a difference, which Western journalists and those who base their judgements on such opinion, have consistently ignored since 1991, between the insecure ex-First Secretary (with very little experience of democracy or even top rank power in a period of political chaos) arm-twisting equally inexperienced democratic competitors outside his own tottering Party, and the more assured President consolidating his newly gained power. Karimov was not then, nor is he today, a dictator. He only represents sterile aspects of post-communist authoritarianism. This will survive only so long as the people are not prepared for democracy, or have had it crushed for too long by the permeation of 'partiinost', i.e. 'Partyist', discipline—for which another term is Stalinism—in all social matters.

In geopolitical terms, i.e. in terms of what I have called the second transition, the transition in the dimension of space, the Uzbek regime has sought to be the eastern node of the CIS southern tier. We have seen how, already at the end of the twentieth century, the embryonic economic association of TRACECA and the nascent political and strategic partnership of GUUAM brought the Partnership for Peace, and behind it NATO, from the Ukraine and Moldova down to the Caucasus and Central Asia. This bloc spanned the land and water routes of the Aral, Caspian, and Black Seas. It linked Eurasia with the new Middle Europe, which is represented by Austria and Germany.

Uzbeks found their way to the lumpenproletariat of Hamburg, to University Departments in Koln, to elite seminars in Salzburg. An exodus began in the mid 1990s. Members of wealthy families, the middle class, workers (who could find labour contractors) too, went west in search of better incomes, job satisfaction, and easier lives. This was much in the same way as in East Germany in 1989 or in our own city of Calcutta. This followed market principles. Amenities, opportunities, even books for scholars trying to gain access to long established knowledge, all of which had developed many years before in the Atlantic civilization, are desired lifestyles or commodities, all over Asia and Africa. Uzbekistan was only becoming subsumed in globalizing trends. This meant the sundering of its recent links with India, which also, in this period (though on a different trajectory) was making its own US tilt.

South to north, and east to west, Uzbekistan had shifted by the end of the twentieth century into an explicitly Eurasian position. It was no more a buffer between Europe and Asia, but had become a Eurasian periphery. Many times in these years, I recalled two US foreign policy experts who had visited Calcutta in the early 1990s.

Just before the Soviet Union collapsed, one of Calcutta's Russian teachers started a Centre for Soviet Studies to undertake projects on Indo-USSR relations. In its preparatory stages, the United States Information Service sent a senior US professor, experienced in study of the 'northern tier' countries, Afghanistan, Iran and Turkey, and the USSR's relations with them, Alvin Rubinstein, to interact with that Centre. His first query was—and this was perhaps in 1993—why the term 'Soviet' was still being used, when even the Russians had given it up. The founder informed him that the entity had been created by the Soviets and should be remembered. The American was dismissive about such historical sentimentality. The State Department, he said, had renamed its Soviet desk as the desk for Eurasia.

On another occasion, some of us in area study fields in the early 1990s were invited by the USIS to meet Clinton's Ambassador in India, Frank Wisner, who, after retiring from the post, has represented US business interests on a global scale. Told that I was organizing research in Calcutta on Central Asia, Wisner spoke enthusiastically of the Turkish model of modernization, then popular. Iran was also showing interest in the Tajik regions of Samarkand, Karshi, and Bukhara, where the language was similar to Persian, I said. His retort was definite. The Persians only exported Shi'ite fundamentalism and represented an unstable force in Asian affairs, Turks stood betwixt and between Europe and Asia and could be Uzbekistan's bridge to world markets and political stability. He was unfazed by the riposte that Turkey as well as the Rabita-i-Alam (based on Saudi Arab sponsorship) also exported Korans. Even so, he repeated, the Saudis were stable, and the Turks modernist. India would do well to align with Turkey and Saudi Arabia, not Iran.

What the US Ambassador did not say was that the Turks and the Saudis had been allies of the USA in the Gulf War. The Iranians had consistently steered clear of any affinity with the USA. Iran then was moving towards a détente with the Russian Federation and with China, reviving the prospects of 'neither war nor peace' with NATO. (These prospects would last till Osama bin Laden's attack on the US changed the dimensions.)

To return. Uzbekistan was seen as a subordinate subject in international relations, not an active player with diplomatic initiatives on its own. Yet it was Karimov's initiative in the late 1990s that gave his state a definite Eurasian position. This position was quite different from the Kazakh pro-Russian stance.

Changes began in 1998-9. Yeltsin had defeated both the Communist challenge and General Lebed's Bonapartist ambitions. The moderate ex-KGB chief and previous head of the Moscow Oriental

Institute, Primakov, who had harboured hopes of becoming President himself, had been inducted as Yeltsin's Prime Minister. The Iraq crisis of winter 1998-9 and Primakov's talk of a triangular strategic partnership between Russia, China and India were overshadowed by the USA's intervention in the Yugoslav attempts to 'cleanse' Bosnia and Kosovo. The Kosovo war played its part in increasing Islamic tensions against Western hegemony, already irritated—for instance in the case of the ex-agent for CIA funds during the Afghan War, Osama bin Laden, an Arab meddler in Pan Islamic affairs, whom the Taliban had sheltered—by US military presence in Wahhabite Saudi Arabia during the Gulf War. These events, in their turn, were eclipsed by the course of political events in the CIS. In late 1999, Karimov who had left his old Party, the People's Democratic Party (a cloak for the Uzbek Communists) and founded a new Party committed only to his own power, called Fidokarlar, or 'Faithfuls'. He held elections, followed in the next year by a 're-election' of himself as President. About the same time, Vladimir Putin became Yeltsin's successor as President of Russia.

The elections were obvious travesties, in which *mahalla* bosses struck deals with locality residents, bargaining for better water, energy supplies, or road repairs, or jobs for children, and then collected votes from their homes, to be cast in batches in the booths. This caricature is possible only if the elections are judged by the yardsticks of Western democracy. These have taken at least three hundred years to develop even in England. In a country with a long history of Tsarist absolutism followed by seventy years of communist rule, it might have been reasonable for such politics to be a way of training the lowest levels of voters to wheel and deal with locality managers, so that they could negotiate the principles of decentralized decision-making. But then, of course, training for guided democracy will always be a failure, as has been the case in royal, feudal Nepal, if the trainers insist on remaining authoritarian.

In the Uzbek case, the elections could be condemned out of court by the way in which, in January 2000, Karimov won the Presidential election with 92 per cent of the vote. This mandate might have carried more weight, had not the only alternative candidate, Abdul Hafiz Jalalov acknowledged that he himself had voted for Karimov in the interest of 'stability, peace, our nation's independence, and the development of Uzbekistan'. Uzbekistan, even less than Russia, had no democratic tradition. Karimov's advisors and intellectuals seeking to maintain stability through the gradual injection of guided democracy from the top were speaking at this time, for instance in the Political Science Department of UWED, about the need to create an appearance of democracy in order to familiarize people, accustomed since birth to authoritarianism, with the practices of a completely new concept. This included the abandonment of a party tarnished by the failure of communism, and the creation of what was to all intents and purposes, a faction of 'President's friends'. Jalalov, who became the new Chairman of the old PDP, only to merge his Party later with the Fidokarlar, was not at all the buffoon that his statement might lead us to believe. Professor of Philosophy in an important research institute, he represented the sort of intellectual that the Soviet Communists had produced—concerned with their privileged status as elites, speaking for the masses, but cut off from their ways of life, intelligent and keen witted, but prepared to shift with every turn in the political wind. They may have been expendable, but very many people in their country did follow their social standards.

Academician Primakov came from the same class and had the same attributes. A competent Prime Minister, he was perhaps too old, or too set in the late communist ways, to satisfy the new vested interests in a Russia which had outgrown even Yeltsin. When Putin came as Prime Minister, following a feeble replacement for Primakov, a Tashkent lady interpreter who was born of Russian Army stock from Kyrgyzstan told me that Putin had the brains of Primakov, but the stamina of a young KGB agent. She said this with great admiration, overjoyed when he replaced Yeltsin as President.

Primakov and Jalalov represented the social order of the last days of the Soviet Union, a high intelligentsia, which had been coddled by the state for the use of its analytical skills, with access to facilities for easy living and creature comforts that were closed to the masses. This order collapsed with the onset of mafia vested interests, as well as with the rise of radical Islam. The latter challenged the feeble morality of complaisance and fear of the security services. The first dominated this morality; radical Islam took refuge in violence or total withdrawal for alternatives.

The sharp polarization of the 1990s between the party of order and the party of dissent and revolt, all over the peripheries of the CIS, had a by-product. This was a sharp distinction between secularist pro-Westernism (which the mullahs in the Arab world, Iran, Afghanistan and Pakistan equated with Christianity) and radical Islamic piety (which popular journalist and politicians nowadays equate with terrorism). It led to the party of order being controlled by strong men who could repress the forces of Islamic dissent. In this context, men like Putin and Karimov were the forces who ran the new regimes—pragmatists, ruthless and opportunist in their shifting alliances with the USA and China, but determined to suppress and indeed bury political Islam, whether in Chechnya and Daghestan, in Ferghana or in Khwarezm.

CULTURAL ISLAM *vs.* NEO-RELIGIOUS FUNDAMENTALISM

The northern hemisphere's global development far outpaced the South in the twentieth century. A sudden, almost revolutionary, set of changes took place. The early capitalist forces of the mid-twentieth century and the challenge to them by socialist idealism had both become obsolete. Central Asian regimes needed to put brakes on the speed with which they rolled into the uncertainties of market freedom. When *perestroika* was at its height but the dissolution of the Soviet Union not even predicted, a newspaper article in Calcutta had spoken of the feeling among conservatives that a catastrophic breakdown might take place in the executive order of the state, if *perestroika*, that is to say, a change of gears, was not accompanied by *uzhkareniya* or application of the brakes. Such a feeling must have gained ground when the first post-communist Presidents saw order slipping away from their control in the first half of the 1990s.

The new leaders exercised varying degrees of repression. They may be communist remnants. But it is difficult to see whether the populations of their republics, underdeveloped by internal colonialism of the economic and social arena, increasing trends of migration westwards, and the consequent loss of technical and professional skills and talent, and by the greed and corruption of those who remained in power, could have done anything else than accept this order, or choose anarchy, in the first ten years of independence. A new consensus of constructive discussion as well as non-violent protest, what Gandhi called *Satyagraha*, is what Central Asia lacks.

The violence in which fundamentalist Islam, whether Mujahideen or Taliban or its allies, the Islamic Movement of Uzbekistan, the Arab-Afghans, and other fighters from Algeria to Chechnya, indulged since the 1980s, rising to a crescendo in the 1990s, proved that 'Political Islam' of the most recent variety has been a failure in building a new civil society. Only new ideas of social orders, neither corrupted late communist, nor capitalism without ethics that represents the market today, can provide the moral base for civil society. World opinion has sought to impress on President Bush and his hard-line advisors that fundamentalism is not all there is to religion and spirituality, whether in Christianity or in Islam. Nor is spirituality subordinate to fundamentalism. Spirituality is a personal matter, much broader than religion that is its organized and inevitably sectarian form.

The aggressive element in Christian triumphalism that led to the subjugation of Hindu, Confucian, and ultimately Islamic, ideas, peaked in the nineteenth century with the spread of bourgeois conquest of the globe. It then went into a trough under the influence of rationalism, whose scientistic form of secularism sought to curb the excesses of religious fanaticism and the conflict of creeds against each other, with attendant brutalities and massacres, of Europeans and Turks, and the genocide of indigenous races. The indigenous spiritual practices of the Americas and Australasia were practically exterminated by Christian white settler colonists. By the second half of the twentieth century, communism too—embattled against Islam as well as Christianity—had, in its actually existing aspects, undergone a transition. It generated new sets of texts or dogmas of varying 'sanctity'. Dusty controversies obscured whatever was said to be against the Party line. By the 1960s, there was almost a 'religiosity' in the acceptance of communism. Spirituality and inspiration were replaced by a somewhat cynical materialism, or at best arid trust in science and logic. Neither death, nor natural disaster such as happened at Chernobyl or Bhopal met with any consolation, or genuine transcendence from this element in the degeneration of the secularist outlook.

Dissidence with both capitalist and socialist materialism and communism led to new forms of protest, not all of which were fundamentalist or violent. Only Mid-Western Christian fundamentalists in the USA, such as Billy Graham or Barry Goldwater, and some fanatical mullahs of Egypt, Iran, and Syria, whom Americans compared with Christian 'fundamentalists' got media coverage. There were many others, attacking the materialist and consumerist core of capitalism, as well as of socialism. They were to be found in Green, conservationist, and communal self-help movements.

Such movements came late to the Soviet Union, but were important in the 1980s. Nationalist Christianity raised the banner of recently lost independence in the Baltic Republics that the USSR had swallowed in collusion with the Nazis in 1940. The Orthodox Church, as well as the Armenian patriarchy, played their part in the collapse of communism in the Caucasus. There was the counterforce of Islam, Sunni as well as Shia in Azerbaijan and the mountains to its north. A novelist like Chingis Aitmatov in Kyrgyzstan, Olzhas Soleyman with his anti-nuclear pollution movement in Kazakhstan, and the cinematographer Davlat Khudonazarov, who stood for President against the post-communists in Tajikistan, by their creative work in fiction and film stirred not just the Central Asian, but also the entire Eurasian spirit. These are intellectual movements, changing the outlook of late communism, which have not been adequately described, perhaps obscured by journalistic sensationalism about desertification, oil politics and Taliban brutality.

All this meant a certain growth of the traditional identity that had been swamped by communist secularism in Central Asia and Kazakhstan. The Pakistani analyst, Ahmed Rashid, following Bennigsen and Wimbush, called this submerged sense of traditional identity an 'underground Islam'. Anyone who spoke not just to religious fanatics but also to average women or men and scholars during the four years from 1997 to 2001, would have realized that this was more a endogenous civilizational need to fill a gap created by the discredit of the old Russian and Communist ideology. Merely importing American and European language and life styles could not fill the void. This has been shown by the atrophy of Kemalism in Turkey and the collapse in Iran of the Shah's stooges in Iran. The Ayatollahs the new Islamic revival movements in Turkey, and the Taliban backlash among Pathans particularly the Waziris of the North West Frontier Province as well as in Baluchistan, in

Pakistan are all factors that Uzbekistan and Tajikistan must be concerned about. They do have an anti-imperialist and radical flavour, however Right wing and reactionary they may be.

The Arab social scientist Anouar Abdel Malek in the 1980s used to refer to the distinction between Islam-al-Hadari 'civilizational Islam' and Islam-al-Siyasi or 'political Islam'. A social scientist speaking frankly to me said while she did not practice religious tenets in any way, she felt every bit a part of Muslim culture and had no problems with its practices, provided she wished to participate in them. Thus, fasting during Ramzan did not concern her, but she found peace in all the social practices of Islam after the demise of a much beloved mother. On the other hand, there were women who observed the Ramzan fast scrupulously, some because they had always believed in it, others because it was a new way to diet and keep the figure trim, and yet others because influential people in the *mahalla* had taken to it. And then there was the sheer novelty of a generation discovering the roots of its identification outside Samarkand, Bukhara, and Turkestan.

The change in these three years has clarified the Uzbek place in what has been referred to as civilizational Islam. Muslim identity lost its fear of cultural assertion. Here independence had its most positive impact. The early confusion about the power of the sort of fundamentalism that Juma and Tohir Yuldashev propagated, first in Nomongan and then from Tajik valleys in Garm and Karategin did not catch on. The Hizb-ut-Tahrir did make some impact on the private morality of domestic groups who knew Arabic, studied in madrasas, and felt alienated from the state power, particularly in Ferghana and regions close to it. It was not clearly evident elsewhere as a danger, either in society or in the state, beyond the propaganda which it received about repression by the state. The defeat of the Islamic Movement of Uzbekistan's guerrillas, fighting with the Taliban against the Northern Alliance and its US backers in autumn 2001, and the reported death of its one real hero, the Soviet soldier turned mujahid, Juma, in the siege of Kunduz, was a major blow to the prospect of actually challenging Uzbek state power. The latter was now shored up by the US alliance. Ahmed Rashid's dire prognostications about the dangers of Juma's charisma were put at rest by the gory end of the Taliban challenge. Whether a new Juma will arise, or in his absence, be invented, is anybody's guess.

The forces of dissent do not always repeat themselves. Shorn of military backing, Tohir may go the same way as the Pulatov brothers and their liberal Birlik Party of the early 1990s, or Muhammad Salih and his Erk faction. Tohir will hardly get sanctuary in the USA or in Turkey in an age of 'war against terror' as his predecessors got with the backing of human rights activists. In any case, the American military presence has now come to Karimov's aid and the moderate aspect of Birlik has been legimated under US aegis. The clarification of Muslim identity in Central Asia has a national perspective, and is not necessarily dominated by Islamic fundamentalism and Pan-Islamic political extremism.

The forces that create Islamic anger, for instance in Sumatra, Bali, or among the Chechens, seem to be less potent in twenty-first century Central Asia. The rise of the Taliban in Afghanistan, their retrogressive social practices, and the publicity given to them by NATO public opinion and Hindu nationalists alike, arose from particularly specific conditions of immature and oligarchic modernization. This was the product of Sovietization from above. All this was further complicated by the CIA/ISI twin machinations of the first Afghan Civil War in the 1980s. This created a general feeling that fundamentalists are rife in the Uzbek population. Three years of living among them gave us the feeling that this is a wrong perception. What does exist in Uzbekistan is a sense of belonging more to the western Asiatic or even the European Islamist conservative world. There is also a contradiction between statist authoritarian secularism and new assertions of Muslim practice, more in the realm of morality than of religion.

Such a contradiction is common to the entire northern tier of Western Asia, in countries like Turkey, Iran and Afghanistan, where occurred movements after 1918: Kemalism in Turkey, the Pahlavi 'white revolution' in Iran under the Shah, Khatami's recent moderation of Shi'ite excesses in Iran, and the conflict between secularist modernism and mullah-led Deobandi religious fanaticism, which goes back to the times of Amir Amanullah and his opponent, the bandit Bacha-i-Saqao (the brat of a water carrier) in the 1920s in Afghanistan. This contradiction is very much in the forefront in the polyglot countries of the Turko-Iranian civilization, as distinct from the more homogeneous Arab-Sunni civilization.

From Istanbul to Andijan, and from Tashkent to Bandar Abbas, from the Bosphorus to the Syr Darya and from Tien Shan to the Persian Gulf, a new zone of political culture has emerged since the collapse of the USSR. In this extensive region the struggle for secularism is as vital as it is in the North African countries from Egypt to the Maghreb. Certainly, secular culture is challenged by fanaticism and terrorism. Most definitely, the underpinning of army rule in Turkey not to speak of the political authoritarianism of consumerist, middle-class elites, weakens the democratic base of movements for secularism. However, the struggle for secularism has by no means been lost in the zone where Turko-Iranian civilization prevails; any more than it has been lost due to the rise of Hindu nationalism, whether demagogic in India or monarchical in Nepal, or of Pakistani or Bangladeshi mullah ideology. The struggle goes on: indeed secularism scored a significant victory in the Indian election of 2004.

This struggle to maintain the heritage of Ataturk, or Iranian civility as distinct from Ayatollah fanaticism, or of Amanullah's reform in Afghanistan, or the tradition of Soviet control of the mullahs of Turkistan in the face of Islamic revivalism in the 1980s and the 1990s, is what gave dimension to Central Asia's significance for the countries to its south. Central Asia did lose out to the revival of primitive Islam that the Hizb-ut-Tahrir's preachers or the Islamic Movement of Uzbekistan's guerrilla fighters sought to establish at the turn of the millennium. Islamic radicals in the Middle East did grow, whether Sunni Taliban in Afghanistan, Shia Hizbullahs in Iran, or assorted fundamentalists in Turkey. But Taliban excesses before the attack on the US seaboard in 2001 self-destructed its moral authority. Islamic radicalism was turned into a bogey for the US and its client Eurasian governments to frighten other Asians.

Secularism has not gained legitimacy in Central Asia any more than it has in Afghanistan. The people, by and large, are happy with a Eurasian security system, an outgrowth of the turn-of-century Partnership for Peace with the NATO. They are pleased with the fact that the old Russian hegemony is over. This has strengthened local ethnic sentiments and a generally cultural Muslim identity. The mood is conservative and culturally revivalist. Fundamentalists have been repressed into a low-key mode. There does not seem to be any real development of freedom of thought or consumer choices or the other elements that make up even elementary democracy.

INDIAN CULTURAL DIPLOMACY AND THE CENTRAL ASIAN RELATIONSHIP

Its distinction from South Asia marks the relevance of Central Asia for the South, a decade after Central Asian independence. When the USSR crumbled in 1992 and 1993 South Asia was as interested in the newly independent republics as was the rest of the world. Pakistanis immediately emphasized their close cultural affinities with Central Asia in language, diet and eating practices, social norms and ceremonial, and political traditions of warrior dominance and Islam. This made geostrategists from Peshawar and Islamabad colour the map from the Syr Darya to the Sutlej in green. Benazir Bhutto, as Prime Minister sponsored the Taliban at the frontier *madrasas*, as a link to guard the short-distance oil pipeline routes that were expected to suck in dollars for the region's prosperity.

Indians were further off: they were connected with the republics through lucrative contracts for airplanes made in Tashkent, other business deals there, and space research and steel deals with Kazakhstan. Indian diplomats saw in Central Asia continuities of the development of new markets for its consumer goods, based on the old experience of the Indo-Soviet Treaty, and the old favourable rupee-ruble rate of exchange, as well as arrangements for student exchange programmes, particularly in the field of medicine availed by students from Kashmir, Punjab, and Uttar Pradesh. Considerable sums were expended in the five new embassies that were set up with ancillary business, cultural and academic support systems, with Tashkent as the node. Delhi's South Block hoped that a new arc of support for secular India would arise in the far north-west, sandwiching Pakistan and Afghanistan between it and the Indian land mass. Thus, the USSR's collapse would be counter-balanced. Even in Bangladesh in those days, leading international lawyers versed in the intricacies of oil negotiations, and managers and accountants capable of working for multi-nationals in Muslim countries, or just people wishing to make pilgrimage to the holy shrines of early Islam in Samarkand and Bukhara, or to hop from there on cheap flights to Mecca and Medina, or to Muslim shrines in Jerusalem, all expected benefits from Central Asian independence. This was boom time for Central Asia in the South Asian consciousness in the 1990s. But the bubble of interest soon burst, at least in India, where a period of liberalization had began. An economy of obsolescence, and that too just north of Pakistan and Afghanistan (with which India's relations suddenly slumped in the Taliban years and in the recurrence of Kashmir insurgency) was not a factor to invest in.

Cultural relations can grow fruitfully in international diplomacy only on a firm base, compatible with economic interests. India may be a vast country, but this is not an indicator of flexibility of choice in making capital and credit lines available or for rebuilding the post-colonial positions which were previously bolstered by massive central subsidies. India's own skewed development in the period, in which the public sector grew at the expense of private capitalist initiatives, led it to focus on strengthening economic relations with captive areas of international trade. Apart from Kazakhstan with its steel, nuclear and space research strengths, the rest of Central Asia was economically unknown to Indian industry, except for the Tashkent aircraft industry.

Karimov's policy, on the other hand, has been one of getting something for nothing. His trips to India were conducted on the same premise as his wooing of the Far East. The Korean multinational Daewoo had been lured to its Ferghana concession at Asaka, with the prospect of monopolizing the Uzbek car sales industry. So was UzBAT, first in Tashkent and then in Samarkand, with the prospect of keeping out Philip Morris, which had been lured under similar premises to Kazakhstan. In return for this growth of employment and disposable income, the Uzbek government, hidebound by a multitude of restrictive practices relating to capital transfer that go back to Soviet practices of the 1920s, was quite incapable of finding ways and means to give the new multinational foreign capital 'full convertibility' of profits and surplus, into dollars. The Uzbeks were the most restrictive of all Central Asian states, presumably because they had the largest population with a decent standard of living to provide for—in areas of public services and social utilities that had been high in the previous generation. Their establishment chose the social concomitants of national security, rather than satisfaction of multinational interests. It also chose the rhetoric of democracy and human rights, which the media associated with the multinationals were quick to hurl at Karimov and the vested interests around him. One should not condemn him alone for this choice. The new sovereign republic's path was as authoritarian, as tough and gritty as the one taken by Indira Gandhi in India between 1966 and 1977. The result certainly was as hard for dissidents, whether democratic like the Pulatov brothers of the Birlik Party, Muhammad Salih of Erk, and the Adolat leaders of Ferghana, or militants and terrorists all the way from underground sympathizers of the Islamic Movement of Uzbekistan, as it had been in India for the Naxalites in 1968 to 1971, or for railway workers in 1974, or for protestors in the Jayaprakash Narayan-led movement against the Indian declaration of a national Emergency in 1975-7.

In the circumstances of the 1990s, the little Indian investment that did take place, principally in the pharmaceutical industry and in healthcare, was incompatible with Uzbek greed for foreign capital without commensurate returns. It is significant that a delegation which travelled in the mid-1990s under Confederation of Indian Industries sponsorship to explore the development of Indian tea marketing from Karshi (proximate also to Turkmenistan and Tajikistan) failed to get off the ground. Indian capital and its CII lobby in Tashkent suffered from the same bureaucratic hurdles as all expatriate capital did—greed for kickbacks and lack of convertibility. No wonder that diplomats in a mission once known for its contribution to Indo-Uzbek friendship lost interest in economic relations, and took to advising CII functionaries to not bother too much with promotion of enterprise, against the grain of Uzbek Ministerial indifference. The State Bank of India and then the CII outpost languished and closed down by the end of the century. Nothing came to my notice till the end of 2001 to indicate any upswing in economic relations.

After the Uzbek involvement (since 2000) across their border with their kin led by Dostum in Mazar-i-Sharif, there was some talk in the Embassy of a consulate being opened in Mazar. Statements had emanated in New Delhi at the end of 2001 that India's presence in Afghanistan would be increased to three consulates outside Kabul, two in their old locations in Kandahar and Jalalabad, and now one to signal the Tashkent Embassy's outreach. Such grandiose ideas were not fulfilled. A newspaper article on 16 December 2002 by a well-informed foreign affairs correspondent says 'India opened two more consulates at Kandahar and Jalalabad in Afghanistan, making it clear that Delhi is in no mood to go slow in what till recently was considered to Islamabad's backyard . . . however, India will only be an observer at the forthcoming meeting of the six foreign ministers of . . . Pakistan, China, Iran, Turkmenistan, Tajikistan and Uzbekistan—the six countries that have common border with Afghanistan—[who] will sign a pact of non-interference in the internal affairs of Afghanistan'.[2] A natural function of all this appeared to be official indifference to any but the most routine cultural relations with the Uzbeks whom the Ministry of External Affairs appeared to see as within the US sphere of influence.

The verve with which Indian classical dance and musical accompaniment were being propagated and had been beginning to gain popularity in Uzbekistan (not only in Tashkent but in many towns outside where its practitioners use to be invited) was suddenly forsaken and stopped in mid-2001 by the Embassy. The tabla-instructor's contract was not renewed. On the other hand, an excessively populist mode of movie-style entertainments, laced with Ram Vandana, was encouraged. A picture of Mahatma Gandhi leaning on his staff had graced the main performance hall. It was taken down and replaced by a picture of Swami Vivekananda in saffron robes. It was left to the Uzbeks, who knew little about him, to admire the picture of a 'Hindu monk'. Such was the apathy to the secular aspects of Indian culture that Uzbek audiences and their petty government functionaries, invited from time to time to these entertainments, found the strong Hindu flavour quite normal, while they themselves increased repression against Islamic fundamentalism. To be fair, one should also note that the Indian Council of Cultural Relations at last in 2002 posted a Foreign Service diplomat, instead of the earlier Soviet-trained academics, in the Cultural Centre, and the tabla teachers' post was again filled.

By 2001, Uzbekistan's Eurasianism had moved westwards. Its interest in India is now one of fantasy and spiritualist antiquarianism. This was indicated by an Uzbek friend who had visited one of the officers of the Embassy in my company. There is a picture by an Uzbek painter on a wall there, of the early sixteenth century Babur (he could be any figure with a pointed little beard) gazing by a riverbank at the mid-seventeenth century Taj Mahal (which could be any domed structure with minarets). Wondering at the caption, I had in the three previous years, pointed out the grotesque anachronism to my Indian colleagues. They paid little heed to historical accuracy. No one bothered to have it taken down. When I mentioned this to my friend, she was surprised by my reaction, and not by theirs. It is so symbolic, she said, it expresses the imaginative connection of our national hero with your national symbol! No matter, was the implication, that Babur was shown looking at what his great-great grandson built. Uzbek and Indian alike are complicit in mutual indifference, however dressed it may be in personal friendship. This entire memoir has stressed that personal friendships, if one cares to cultivate them, are deep and genuine, both in the national spirit and also when one can establish them individually. But they should not be confused with the lack of economic viability, or of current political compatibility, or cultural co-operation between two countries dissimilar in size, different in historical culture (however comparable the circumstances of neo-colonialism or present-day reliance on US shields for authoritarianism) and with present world-views, which are quite differently attuned to Westernization and ghost-hunting.

The understanding of Uzbekistan cannot any more be based on fantasies of historical cross-fertilization, whatever the legends about Zoroaster, Kushanas, Khwarezm, Baburids, migrant Uzbek soldiery or south Punjab merchants. The circumstances of those older relationships were relevant in the past. In the present, Central Asia is under super-power hegemony. The Russian-Chinese strategic partnership and the Shanghai Organization make Central Asia a ground of contention between the West and the East for control of energy resources, and for strategic bases for which the US is greedy, or for the rebuilding of trade links. In this context many regional powers of the North, such as China, Russia, Japan, Germany and France or the multinationals have their part to play. In that set of evolving relations, India with its sights fixed elsewhere in the rimlands and lobes of the great peninsula of Asia, the Middle East, and to South-East Asia, Australasia and the archipelagoes of the Pacific Rim, will have minimal concern in Central Asia; beyond specific commodities and industries, such as aircraft production (where trade partnership has already been established in the Indo-Soviet Treaty of 1972, a partnership still active in 2003).

Kabul is back to being India's listening post on Central and Inner Asia. Even the British in the bad old colonial days used Kashgar (now Kashi) in southwest Xinjiang as a listening post for all Turkestan, as a series of travel books from the days of Robert Shaw and Younghusband, through Mrs. Macartney, C.P. Skrine, and the Hopkirks, will testify.[3] Kashgar's Consulate was closed down in the early 1950s: Chini Bagh, as it used to be known, became a youth hostel. Since Indo-Chinese relations across the Karakoram frontier will take many years to heal, there is no reason why cultural goodwill in Tashkent for India's secular values and democratic traditions, should be cut down by any diversion of interest or funds. Uzbekistan and the rest of Central Asia certainly do have common concerns relating to Muslim identity, but this should by no means be equated with pan-Islam or Pakistan. It also relates to contra-terrorist and drug control security *vis-à-vis* Pakistan and Jammu & Kashmir. Trade contacts with north and west India will certainly remain. There can be no question of downgrading this region of the world in Indian cultural and economic diplomacy.

The Pakistan-sponsored return of the mujahids to Kabul and Kandahar divested Tashkent of its potential for a deep strategic relationship with South Asia. The approaches to the problem of Asia are quite dissimilar in Uzbekistan and India. The differences between a westward looking Eurasian state, and the urges of India to become by 2025 a great Asian rimland market node facing the Indian Ocean, are real. This includes investment in the knowledge industry, such as information technology, translation, and English language teaching. The demand for the latter in Uzbekistan at the end of the 1990s was sadly neglected. Indo-Uzbek relations should build on those cultural strengths, in what many Asian powers following the lead of the UNESCO for the last decade called 'the dialogue of civilizations'.

TOWARDS NEW ASIAN INTERNATIONAL RELATIONS

The dialogue of civilizations was an idea popularized by states and leaders of the late 1990s who were firmly opposed to Western capitalist morality, such as Khatami of Iran and Jiang Zemin of China. It seeks to make diplomacy conscious of the search for new and alternatively harmonious as well as pluralist approaches to international culture as a base for global co-existence.

The concept grew out of the churning of world-views that used to be based on the old stability during the 'short twentieth century' from the First World War of 1914-18 to the 'second Cold War' of the 1980s. Gorbachev's *perestroika* began the breakdown of the Soviet arsenal. The Afghan debacle, natural disasters and genocide in Afro-Asia, 'low intensity warfare' and other concepts developed during the 'long peace' (as American strategists saw it after their leaders dropped atom bombs on Asiatic Japan in 1945) all added up to a revival of Hobbes' ideas about the brutality of the state of nature in international affairs. An attempt was made to rationalize this by the concept of the 'conflict of civilizations' developed by a US theorist of strategic globalization, Samuel P. Huntington.

This idea grouped blocs of states according to the unifying force of religious identity into religious communities of state. These communities, called Christianity, Islam, Confucianism, Hinduism, Buddhism, etc., were then treated as synonyms for individual civilizations. The focus was shifted from material interest to a vaguely communitarian spiritual ideology, seen as the new world trend of the future. In the uncertainties of international paradigm shift between 1989 and 1992, this idea gained Messianic force among young Right wing intellectuals and bureaucrats seeking to make sense of the new world, who found no clarity in the esoteric revision of Marxism or liberalism.

New thinking identified Islam as the main power alternative to the dominant Christian ecumenical international relations paradigm. In 1990, men like Pope John Paul II (previously Cardinal Wojtyla, Poland's challenge to 'actually existing socialism') or George Bush senior (earlier Director of the CIA) were icons of the people—they had defeated communism. Islam on the other hand was seen in the image of radical militants, with Osama bin Laden, once a CIA subaltern, as its brand image, with Saddam Hussain in Iraq, no mujahid or Taliban at all, lurking in the background, defeated but unvanquished. Secular as well as militantly religious Islam was treated as the principal contradiction in the brand of unipolar world politics that US strategy espoused in the 1990s. In this calculation, other non-Christian faiths such as Hinduism, also politically resurgent at this time, came to be treated as secondary to the main conflict. By the end of the twentieth century, Hindu political activism in India and among Indians abroad had swung overwhelmingly into a mode, subordinate to the US logic described above.

This set of socio-political simplifications practised by ruling powers, which included neutral forces such as Putin in Russia, began to be challenged at the beginning of this new century by China, Germany, France, Iran, and even Turkey. As, first the Clinton administration, blundering into the Serbian imbroglio in Kosovo, and then the Bush administration switching into 'war against terror' mode in 2001, with reference to its military presence in Pakistan and Uzbekistan and its attempts to encircle Iraq, increased the tension in Asia, moderate forces in Western Europe, Iran, and China began to distance themselves from US ideologies and NATO politics. This also meant distancing from the radical extremism of non-conformist Islam, and from the marginal people in the backward parts of Afro-Asia, who cherished beliefs in a millennial *Amirat ul Mumineen* or 'universal Caliphate'. The new moderate international relations approach, in which forces for the Right such as Chirac in France or more centrist forces such as Schroder in Germany have come closer, and in which even Russia and China are involved (despite their local problems in Chechnya or Xinjiang), has again brought to the forefront the need for harmonious and moderate socio cultural alternatives.

'Dialogue of civilization' is an idea of bilateral and multilateral understanding between intermediate regime states. These are not only intermediate between capitalism and the regulated economies of the Chinese varieties, but are today intermediate between super power and mini-powers rather than being mixed economy regimes, in the way the Polish economist Michael Kalecki defined them in the 1960s and 1970s. They are median, seeking to resist over-weening force, but also to assert themselves, not necessarily by giving up self-interest, certainly to foster peaceful development of commerce and social intercourse on a global scale. These powers are not superpower aspirants, nor are they the clients or satellites of such powers. Somewhat like the premises of the Non-Aligned Movement in the mid-nineteenth century, they desire balance in maintaining careful, principled distance from overweening force and struggles for international hegemony. If these ideas could gain authority in the UN Security Council, this would mean the restriction of war and aggression to a regional and not global scale. The idea is of course not the same as the over-idealistic abstractions of the pacifist contra-power-bloc theory of NAM, by which leaders of the mid-twentieth century like Nehru, Nasser, Sukarno and Tito had sought to establish an equidistant autonomy from the First and Second Worlds of capitalism and communism, which failed to build a neutral Third World power bloc.

Traditional and changing material interests form a web of pragmatic considerations, making up the conception of national interest of each state. Such generalized abstractions as 'The Concert of Europe' or 'The League of Nations' or 'Non-Alignment' could not give positive force to the life of such coalitions beyond the brief periods of charisma of particular leaders, or the capacities, long-lasting or ephemeral, of purposive manipulation by diplomats associated with them. In the case of NAM, multiple and divergent national interest pulled in different direction, some towards the West, some seeking aid from both the West and the opposed Soviet and Warsaw Pact powers, some towards the alternative model of Chinese foreign policy, which grouped smaller nations like Pakistan, Burma (later Myanmar) or Tanzania into security arrangements against stronger or more aggressive neighbours in the same sub-continental area or against super power patronage. All these led to NAM lacking efficiency to build strong bonds. When the poles from which NAM claimed equidistance changed magnetism, new terms of discourse emerged at the end of the century. Their guiding idea was to initiate new processes of dialogue, which would create more flexible relationships, with greater elasticity to tensions and conflicts that had warped the previous generation of so called 'long peace' punctuated by low intensity warfare and international terrorism.

A nation, which espoused this new idea, was Iran. It had emerged from racking conflicts of the 1980s with the USA on the one hand, and USA's Frankenstein, Iraq, on the other, with a distinctly neutralist position. It has now begun to stir against its praetorian authoritarianism, which goes back past the Ayatollahs and the Shahs to the breakdown of Qajar tyranny in the early twentieth century, and the restructuring within this, of the absolutist Reza Shah dynasty. It has succeeded in maintaining national control over its part of the Gulf and the Caspian oil resources, combined with a strategic straddle between South Asia and Central Asia. Its search for oil and natural gas pipelines from Central Asia to India and under the sea to South-East Asia makes Iran a natural competitor in US designs for a new great game in Central Asia, Iraq and Pakistan. Also, its Shia conscience-keepers, including the *wilayat-i-fakih*, himself, Khomeni's successor, Ali Khamenei, are as suspicious of the Sunni inveteracy of the Deobandi theologian mullahs of Pakistan, as they are to Christian human rights charges from the USA. Iran's new friendliness with the Russian Federation and its amity with India through Shia connection with Oudh, as much as with common oil interests and industrial liaisons, has not prevented it from coming closer to China. Till he stepped up, and away from, the day-to-day reins of top administrator of the People's Republic of China, Jiang Zemin's measures represented China's outreach towards Central Asia, by means of the Shanghai Organization as a support system for its entente with Russia in the Putin-Jiang accords of 2001. His friendliness with Khatami was couched in the specific language of 'dialogue of civilizations'.

India and China have placed their border differences on the back burner for some time. In 2002, at the height of India-Pakistan tension, following terrorist attacks on the State Legislature in Srinagar and Parliament in New Delhi, China seems to have played a mediatory role along with Russia. Following this, India discussed its problems with China and Russia separately in Almaty. This was while the Shanghai Organization deliberations were going on there. Tension lessened considerably. While 'the strategic triangle' idea has not been revived, a dialogue seems to be opening up bilaterally between the three large powers of Asia. China's friendship with Pakistan is perhaps nowadays an insurance of Asian security, rather than a threat to it. China has much greater interest in tapping the great Indian market. In January 2003, Prime Minister Khatami visited both Pakistan and India and showed an even-handed approach to the locally bilateral South Asian resolution of Kashmir problems. He was the annual guest of honour at India's Republic Day parade. His speeches mentioned the 'dialogue of civilizations' on a general basis. All these events bespeak a cautious networking across Asia from the east and north to the south and west for more harmony and less confrontation. Atal Behari Vajpayee's visit to China and the limited understanding on Tibet-Sikim trade through the Nathula Pass in the Eastern Himalayas in the last year of the BJP-led NDA governemnt must be seen in this context. There is now a general feeling in Asia that dialogue and not conflict should be the agenda for the future.

2003 saw an alarming revival of nineteenth-century style imperialist assault on Asia. The US attack on Iraq, which Uzbeks were predicting in the autumn of 2001, came, as if inevitably, two years later. Has the diplomatic revolution that we witnessed in 2001 led Uzbekistan away from its natural alliance with the Shanghai Association? It may not have. Turkey, a natural ally of the USA in Asia, has been guarded in its acceptance of Bush's crusade. However, Turkey has a direct interest in the Kurdish problem. Uzbekistan, for its part, looks north and east towards the Caspian and Black Seas, and towards China. It has much less interest in Western Asia. It also has close financial links with the Germans and cultural links with the French, both of whom were even firmer than Turkey in differentiating themselves from the US-British aggression. Uzbekistan's position *vis-à-vis* the Partnership for Peace on the west and the Shanghai Association on the east are as important as its links with the USA. US air power has been able to poise itself in an arc through Bishkek, Khanabad and the Pakistan Frontier. At the very least, this menaces Chinese Xinjiang. The Uzbek perception of this tricky geo-strategy of neo-imperialism remains to be clarified.

Uzbekistan is no more the copula of Russian-Indian understanding. Nor is the way of the 1990s relevant, when India had sought specific trade affinities with each Central Asian Republic on the basis of the temporary economic bubble. Since then the Taliban upthrust and the US counteraction of it, positioning US–British control over airbases over Central Asia and Pakistan, and a subordinate semi-liberal regime in Afghanistan with tacit support from India and Iran, has affected strategy and cultural orientation in Uzbekistan. Stray accounts do surface of religious strife in the Helmand salient of Afghanistan between Pakistani Baluchistan and eastern Iran and also perhaps in the subterranean public opinion of Ferghana, Kashka Darya and Surkhan Darya. This is nowhere as politically significant at present, as it briefly became during the Taliban upthrust. Uzbekistan's coming significance lies in being like Georgia in the Caucasus, a peripherally competitive lower median power within the CIS. It is not pro Russian. It relies on the fringes of the NATO security system. The westward direction taken by President Shevardnadze and President Karimov were in this respect different from the more northern or southern blocs cemented from China through Kazakhstan to Russia, and from India towards

Iran and Egypt on the one hand, and towards Myanmar and Indonesia on the other. Uzbekistan at present seems to be the tip of the West's spear poised at militant Islam in Asia.

India's policies are less expansively friendly with regard to it than they were ten years ago. Other than the traditional nexus of aircraft industrial and spares connections, and a very small presence of the pharmaceutical industry, business connection has become low. Even in the rapidly expanding IT presence of Indians abroad, Uzbekistan's capacity to absorb Indian professionals is minimal. While it seeks contacts with the West, it retains a strong position about not opening its markets for employment to any but utterly necessary multinationals. Significant collaboration has been made with the French and the Japanese in archaeological exploration, and with the Germans in language and technical studies, and above all with the US in academic exchange programmes. India's role became far more low profile than it was at the end of the Soviet Union.

It is still possible, without any trace of idealism or naivete and keeping material interests in view, to posit a greater concern for the cultural understanding of present-day economic and political forces in civil society and democracy, and not to rely on the more recently familiar trends of Indian spiritualism, mysticism and fantasy, to create an interest in Central Asian and Indian mutual understanding. On the secular level, India, Central Asia, as well as the rest of the CIS are in the throes of a difficult political transition, of economic transformation from command statism to economic liberalization, and from nationalist isolation to the more potentially dangerous socio-economic tensions of cultural globalization.

It was just our luck to reach Tashkent, the hub from where changes used to be defused, and to watch the new developments at the turn of the century. This book has recorded a phase in which India took a back seat in the dialogue of civilization in the Commonwealth of Independent States, and particularly so in Uzbekistan as it passed from the Bear Hug to the cries of the Screaming Eagle. Is it too much to hope that India is again beginning to live up to the responsibilities of secular cultural outreach for which the opportunities have still not closed?

NOTES

1. Neal Ascherson, *Black Sea* (Jonathan Cape, London, 1995), is the most evocative account we have of the social uprooting of Crimeans, sent by Stalin to Turkestan, trying to flee back after the ethnic riots during the early 1990s.
2. Pranay Sharma, 'Consulate boost to Kabul ties', *The Telegraph*, Kolkata, 17 December 2002.
3. See Kathleen Hopkirk, *Central Asia: A Traveller's Companion* (John Murray, London, 1993), pp. 94-122, particularly p. 115.

9

Postscript

These pages were written in 2002-3, when the experience was still fresh of living in Uzbekistan at the turn of the twentieth into the twenty-first century. It is now 2004 and the country has become accustomed to moving out of the post-Soviet aegis into the extended family of the US political economic periphery. What we sensed between 1998 and 2001 seems to have clarified.

President Karimov, who even before the September 2001 attack on the Twin Towers of New York, took pride in informing his nation that in the UN he had spoken just after the US representative—fortuitously because alphabetically Uzbekistan follows USA—still remains President, though reports persist of his increasing ill health as well as of there being no alternative to him as the leader. Rustom Azimov's plans for making Uzbekistan a prime location for European—as well as US—multinational investment by welcoming the European Union to conferences in the capital do not seem to have borne results, beyond the elementary building boom of peripheral highways around the southern part of Tashkent, bypassing it from Ferghana to Samarkand. There are no reports of a revival or of diversification in the sick industries in the chicken's neck of the Republic, south of Tashkent in the Kokand region between Tajikistan and Kazakhstan, where once cotton textile mills had flourished. Other Ministers have changed: Utkir Sultanov, an old apparatchik, has been removed from Prime Minister, the President's favourite Sodyk Safayev is now Foreign Minister and is presumed to be as close to the US as Azimov is to the World Bank. These changes in the top layer of the political elite are very little relevant for any new look in the society and the economy.

The country briefly returned to the media frontline when the USA prevailed on Pakistan to put pressure on Taliban refugees, who had fled across the Afghan border from the Tora Bora hills into the almost ungoverned hill fastnesses of southern Waziristan in the Wana Agency of the North-West Frontier, just to the north of Baluchistan. This pressure is part of the new policy, subsequent to the Afghan War of 2001, by which President Musharraf turned his country round at Bush's behest from support of Islamic fundamentalism in Afghanistan and Kashmir to a more limited and moderate stance in the Pakistan heartland of the Indus Basin. Several bomb outrages, some directed against him, even by his own Air Force personnel, trained by al Qaida, led to a concerted attacks by Pakistani troops and tribesmen in their pay on Taliban whom the Waziris had sheltered. In the course of this, several of the latter were reported killed or wounded. One name resurrected from oblivion was Tohir Yuldashev the spiritual mentor, from Nomongan of 1992, of Juma Khojaev, who had been reported killed in a north Afghan city in November 2001. Tohir obviously had a large following of Uzbek fighters of the anti-secularist fundamentalist resistance with Hizb-ut-Tahrir backing in the lands of the Uzbeks, Kyrgyz and Uighurs. He is reported to be severely wounded, but not captured. These reports were followed in the early part of this year by a series of bomb blasts, with severe casualties once again (after February 1999) in Tashkent, and also this time in Bukhara, where there had earlier been no reports of fundamentalism or violent extremism. In Tashkent the area affected, seem to be in the southern suburbs, newly built up from slums rather than in the center of the city, as before. Other reports allude to a spurt in crime and violence against domestic individuals and of private feuds and murder, as well as of police raids flushing out terrorism in poverty stricken areas.

One argument, by students of the international security scene in Eurasia, would have it that Russia has given up its interest in Central Asia directly south of the Caspian and is more focused on its friendly relationship with Kazakhstan, reaching out to China: and that the Caucasus has been given up to US oil interests all the way from Ukraine and the Black Sea towards Azerbaijan. This view is bolstered by the 'rose revolution' early this year, which led to the flight from Georgia of Eduard Shevardnadze and the installation of the pro-US Saakashvili as the new Georgian President. Accordingly also, the logic runs, Central Asian oil, natural gas and other resources are within the ambit of US influences, which has now stretched from the latitudes of Turkey to Kyrgyzstan, south into Iraq, so that in effect West and Central Asia—with the significant exceptions of Syria and Iran—all the way from the Caspian and the Aegean Seas up to the Arabian Sea are under US domination. This is an interpretation of the fall-out of the autumn 2001 diplomatic revolution that has been described, which relegates the Uzbeks into a position of subordination and even irrelevance as independent diplomatic actors in the Asian international scene.

The interpretation is one that might appeal to hard-nosed, power pragmatists of Indian foreign policy. Their sights are fixed on the more immediate concerns of the Indus basin and Pakistani threats to national security, whose missile forms can be resurrected from time to time, now that the parallel forms to Pakistani fundamentalism in Hindu politics have taken a back seat in the Indian national scene. From this angle, Pakistan and Uzbekistan are different aspects of an ultimately US strategy, and perhaps the best line from this angle would be to deal directly with Russia and China for Asian counterpoises.

External policy is not merely power pragmatism of the simple Machiavellian variety. Paucity of satisfying employment and job satisfaction may be driving many Asians, including Indians as much as Central Asians, with the benefit of Westernized education in which their countries themselves excel towards ever greener pastures in the West itself. All the same the fund of intra-Asian good will, the *bhai-bhai* spirit that has existed since 1947 and Jawaharlal Nehru's Asian Relation Conference does remain at the people to people level in most of the Asian countries, whether in post-Soviet Central Asia, or in Iran or in many parts of the Middle East. Strong cultural relations can be built on them, not least in Uzbekistan and this remains the agenda for the immediate future.

References Cited in the Text

Allworth, Edward (ed.) with Helene Carrere d'Encausse, Ian Murray Matley, Karl H. Menges, Johanna Spector, Arthur Sprague, *Central Asia: A Century of Russian Rule* (Columbia University Press, New York and London, 1967).

Ascherson, Neal, *Black Sea* (Jonathan Cape, London, 1995).

Bailey, Lt. Col. F.M., *Mission to Tashkent* (Jonathan Cape, London, 1946).

Beveridge, Annette Susannah, translated from the original Turki text, *Baburnama* (*Memoirs of Babur*) (Low Price Publishers reprint edition, Delhi, 1997).

Biswas, Dilip Kumar, 'Acharya Prabodh Chandra Bagchi Shatabarsher Shraddhanjali' (in Bengali), in *Bangadarshan*, New Series, No. 3, November 2001 (Bankim Bhavan Gaveshana Kendra, Kantalpara, Naihati, West Bengal).

Council for Foreign Relations Ferghana Valley Working Report, *Calming the Ferghana Valley: Development and Dialogue in the Heart of Central Asia* (Century Foundation Press, New York, 1999).

Cordovez, Diego, Selig S. Harrison, *Out of Afghanistan: The Inside Story of the Soviet Withdrawal* (Oxford University Press, New York, 1995).

Dale, Stephen Frederick, *Indian Merchants and Eurasian Trade, 1600-1750* (Cambridge University Press, 1994).

De, Barun, 'Geopolitics and Regional Identity: South Asia's Northwest Frontiers', *Economic and Political Weekly*, XXXVII, 14 September 2002, pp. 3812-17.

Dixit, J.N., *My South Block Years: Memoirs of a Foreign Secretary* (UBS Publishers, New Delhi, 1996).

Eaton, Richard M., *The Rise of Islam and the Bengal Frontier, 1204-1760* (Oxford University Press, New Delhi, 1994).

Elias, N. (ed. with Commentary, Notes and Map) and E. Denison Ross (translation), *The Tarikh-i-Rashidi of Mirza Muhammad Haider Dughlat: A History of the Mughals of Central Asia* (Academia Asiatica, Patna, 1973).

Habib, Muhammad (ed. by K.A. Nizami), *Politics and Society during the Early Mediaeval Period: Collected Works of Professor Muhammad Habib* (People's Publishing House, New Delhi, Vol. 2, 1981).

Habib, Muhammad and Khaliq Ahmed Nizami, *A Comprehensive History of India*, Vol. 5, *The Delhi Sultanat, AD 1206-1526* (Indian History Congress and People's Publishing House, New Delhi, 1982).

Hauner, Milan, *What is Asia to US ? Russia's Asian Heartland, Yesterday, Today* (Unwin, London, 1990).

Hiro, Dilip, *Between Marx and Muhammad: The Changing Face of Central Asia* (Harper Collins, London, 1994).

Hodgson, Marshall, *The Venture of Islam: Conscience and History in a World of Civilization*, 3 vols. (Chicago University Press, 1974).

Hopkirk, Kathleen, *Central Asia, A Travellers' Companion* (John Murray, London, 1993).

Hopkirk, Peter, *Foreign Devils on the Silk Road* (OUP, 1980).

———, *Setting the East Ablaze* (OUP, 1984).

———, *The Great Game* (OUP, 1990).

Joffe, Amy, 'Unlocking the Assets; Energy and the Future of Central Asia and the Caucasus', in Omar Noman (ed.), *Central Asia 2010, Prospects for Human Development* (Regional Bureau for Europe and the CIS, United Nations Development Programme, New York, 1999).

Kosambi, D.D., *Myth and Reality: Studies in the Formation of Indian Culture* (Popular Prakashan, Bombay, 1994 edition).

Lake, Anthony, *Six Nightmares: Real Threats in a Dangerous World and How America Meets Them* (Boston, Little, Brown, 2000).

Mazower, Mark, *Dark Continent: Europe's Twentieth Century* (Penguin Books, Harmondsworth, 1998).

Pandey, Gyanendra, 'The Civilized and the "Barbarian": The New Politics of Late Twentieth Century India and the World', in Gyanendra Pandey (ed.), *Hindus and Others: The Question of Identity in India Today* (Viking, New Delhi, 1993).

Puri, Madanmohan, 'Central Asian Geopolitics: the Indian View', *Central Asian Survey*, Vol. 9, No. 1, 1994, pp. 45-56.

Racine, Jean-Luc, 'Le cercle de Samarcande: geopolitique de l'Asie centrale', in *Le Cercle de Samarcande*, 2e trimestre, 1997, *Herodote*, Revue de geographie et de geopolitique, No. 84 (Paris).

Rashid, Ahmed, *Jihad: The Rise of Militant Islam in Central Asia* (Yale University Press and Orient Longman, India, 2002).

Sharma, Pranay, 'Consulate boost to Kabul ties', *The Telegraph*, Kolkata, 17 December 2002.

Stobdan, P. (ed.), *Building a Common Future: Indian and Uzbek Perspectives on Security and Economic Issues* (New Delhi, 1999).

Trofimov, Dmitri A., 'Islam in the Political Culture of the Former Soviet Union: Central Asia and Azerbaijan', in *Hamburger Beitrage zur Friedensforschung und Sicherheitspolitik* (Hamburg University, Falkenstein 1, Hamburg, 22587, n.d.).

Vambery, Arminius, *Travels in Central Asia: Being an Account of a Journey from Teheran Across the Turkoman Desert to Khiva, Bukhara and Samarkand* (1st published 1864; Bhavana Books and Prints, New Delhi, 1996).

Warikoo, K., *Central Asia and Kashmir: A Study in the Context of Anglo-Russian Rivalry* (Gian Publishers, New Delhi, 1989).

Yusuf, Brig. Muhammad and Mark Adkin, *The Bear Trap* (Lahore, 1991).

Index